Acclaim for Debra J. Dickerson's

AN AMERICAN STORY

"[Dickerson's] memoir is indeed *An American Story*—not only because it chronicles a variation on our national myth of upward mobility but because, like the essays of Emerson . . . it embodies the solitude often borne by American free thinkers."

—*The Washington Post Book World*

"You may not like her opinions or the way she expresses them, but it's hard not to admire Dickerson's determination and her relentless passion for teasing ideas apart and then putting them back together in her own, atypical way."

—*Salon*

"A landmark. . . . *An American Story* is at once a brilliant account of a singular human being and of her participation in her cultural, social, and racial context."

—Henry Louis Gates, Jr.

"A remarkable document that illuminates brightly features of American society that many people would just as soon ignore, if not hide. Her honesty will get her into trouble. Her insight will win her a broad audience."

—Randall Kennedy

"Dickerson . . . has finally told the American story that we have needed to hear. And what a scorching story it is—a remarkable journey to consciousness."

—*Ms.*

"No matter your cultural or class origins, or political persuasion, you will be challenged by the iconoclasm of [Dickerson's] views about change and social justice in America. An accomplished writer, she portrays a remarkable journey to self-acceptance in the face of constant social signifiers of contempt."

—*Black Issues Book Review*

Debra J. Dickerson

AN AMERICAN STORY

Debra J. Dickerson holds a J.D. from Harvard Law School, an M.A. from St. Mary's University, and a B.A. from the University of Maryland. She is a Senior Fellow at the New America Foundation, where she writes about poverty and race. She has been both a senior and a contributing editor for *U.S. News & World Report,* and her writings have appeared in, among other publications, *The Washington Post, The New York Times Magazine, The New Republic, The Nation, Slate, The Village Voice,* and *Essence.* She lives in Washington, D.C.

AN AMERICAN STORY

Debra J. Dickerson

ANCHOR BOOKS
A DIVISION OF RANDOM HOUSE, INC.
NEW YORK

FIRST ANCHOR BOOKS EDITION, SEPTEMBER 2001

 Published in the United States by Anchor Books, a division of Random House, Inc., New York, and simultaneously in Canada by Random House of Canada Limited, Toronto. Originally published in hardcover in the United States by Pantheon Books, a division of Random House, Inc., New York, in 2000.

The Library of Congress has cataloged the Pantheon edition as follows:
Dickerson, Debra J., 1959–
An American story / Debra J. Dickerson.
p. cm.
ISBN 0-375-42069-X
1. Dickerson, Debra J., 1959– 2. Journalists—United States—Biography. 3. Afro-American journalists—United States—Biography. I. Title.
PN4874.D435 A3 2000
070′.92—dc21 [B] 00-029862

Anchor ISBN: 0-385-72028-9

Book design by Fearn Cutler de Vicq

www.anchorbooks.com

Printed in the United States of America
10 9 8 7 6 5 4 3 2 1

CONTENTS

For my hero, my heart. My mother
For the father I wished I'd known
For the United States Air Force—it aimed me high and let me go

INTRODUCTION

It was 1983, I was twenty-four years old and all alone in the world. I had five siblings, a mother, more relatives than a Kennedy, and was a member of the United States Air Force. But I was alone, though I did not yet know it.

I "knew" some other things, however. I knew that people were poor by choice. I knew that the civil rights movement had ended racism and inequality. I knew that hard work was all that was required for a successful, stable life. Those blacks who came of age after the 1964 Civil Rights Act (which I knew had ended discrimination) but who were still marginalized were losers for whom I need feel neither compassion nor a sense of connection. I was not "black"; I was a "human being" who was looking forward to voting for Ronald Reagan in the next election. I had no use for the alcoholics, the unwed mothers, the high school dropouts of my black working-class childhood and, after a youth spent in self-effacing, Southern Baptist misogynist silence, had become a woman with the courage to say all of that and oh so much more.

By my third of what would be five and a half years enlisted in the Air Force, coming home was a torment. Black north St. Louis was a city frozen in time, a bad time. Back home, I bought gas for my rental car from wary-eyed attendants huddled behind four inches of bulletproof glass and chicken wire. They were barely audible through the tiny, skinnier-than-shotgun-barrel-sized slot allotted for communication that I had to bend over double to yell through. I ate rib tip sandwiches at ghetto greasy spoons with ripped, thrift-store furniture.

Their names were usually a homespun combination of initials like E&J's Bar B Q or T&P's Deluxe, their restaurant inspection stickers likely gray market. At night, my sisters and I went to cheesy clubs with carpet tacked to the walls and overflowing toilets in bathrooms filled with dope smoke and women so overdressed they might have been attending a potentate's diamond jubilee. There would be one tough waitress for every fifty patrons; she'd rather curse you out than take your order because she knew that black people didn't tip. We used to sneak into those same clubs when we were teenagers, where unsmiling men wearing black shades at midnight would snarl "Open yo purse!" at the door so they could check for guns. Even so, we often had to duck for cover behind overturned tables when the shooting began. It seemed an adventure back then in the bell-bottomed seventies, when no one aimed to kill.

But in the parallel universe of my posting in Monterey, California, I was seeing my first ocean, tasting my first bagel, discovering room service and skycaps. I was living in a world where the oddballs were those who *wouldn't* live by the rules and I was falling in love with a man whose white skin and New England twang were a comfort to me. I looked at that skin and saw safety, dignity, progress. My white boyfriend could not believe discrimination and failure really existed, and when I was with him, neither could I. But back in St. Louis, no matter when I visited, everyone always seemed to be swirling powerlessly through a never-ending cycle of layoffs, plant closings, Section 8 waiting lists, and child support that never came; same struggles, different day. It all seemed so willfully pointless.

Wasn't it obvious that education was the way out of all this? It had been for me. My two and a half years of college had recruiters hounding me and earned me two stripes upon enlisting—the rank, responsibilities, and pay of an E-3 airman first class rather than the E-1 airman mere high school graduates were awarded. Those credits put me two years ahead of the game in the highly competitive U.S. Air Force and made me stand out from the first day of basic training. After only three years, I'd added forty or so college credits to my previous total, was earning a salary few of them could ever hope for, and was en route to becoming an Air Force officer with a master's degree, a triple A credit rating, and the approval of a grateful nation. It still wasn't too late for them to improve themselves through education, but most of my homies did little besides graduate from their substandard high schools and prove repeatedly how fertile they were without being able to sustain a healthy, long-term relationship. Wasn't it clear that hard work, savings, health, home, and auto insurance were the answers? Babies postwedlock rather than in the doomed, antediluvian hope that they will cause wedlock? Their willfully poor judgment was a source of endless exasperation to me. My eyes would narrow evilly when I spied new microwaves, new floor-model TVs and VCRs in every room of a household teetering on the brink of eviction (and which also owed me money). I wouldn't own any of those appliances until after 1986 when I was an officer and, finally, middle class; my money went for my education and to bail family members out of the disaster du jour. I took self-righteous comfort in the eyeball-rolling that commenced every time I passed on half-price Gucci bags hot from a "trunk sale." I knew they thought me a spoilsport who wouldn't know a good time if it gave me a free Gucci bag. But I also knew the irony of pulling WIC paperwork from a designer bag was utterly lost on them.

I could never relax when home from the service because I was always anticipating the next awkward moment. I would answer folks' phones in an attempt to be helpful: how was I to know they were screening for bill collectors? What a strain it was not to roll my eyes when an answering machine identified the household as "United Office Support Systems" or some such nonsense. I'd have to hightail it to the bathroom while a homegirl returned the call in her best fake "white" voice and verified the employment of her ne'er-do-well "husband." I finally learned not to answer the phone, that all calls are screened in such households. Papering over iffy work histories in this manner seemed much more difficult to me than simply working diligently. And, of course, working diligently was all that was required for getting ahead in life.

I held my tongue but my disapproval was unmistakable. I would sneer inwardly at the latest on-the-job "back injury" lawsuit being waged by the neighbor who still managed to be the last man off the dance floor. I would struggle not to suck my teeth at someone's pregnant granddaughter waddling by to rejoin the jobless boyfriend she was cohabiting with in the basement, always biting my lip to keep from screaming from the depths of my soul, "Girl, why are you pregnant again?"

When you open the refrigerator in many black working-class homes, you see everything in twos and threes—multiple OJ cartons, four different brands of beer, three kinds of luncheon meat—each truculently labeled with the name of some grown person come back to sponge off hardworking parents or grandparents but too selfish to share. When you eat in one, you may get sandwiches made with meat kept refrigerated outside on winter windowsills in homes without electricity. Perhaps you'll take a 'ho bath in sinks with water heated in electric woks in homes without gas. You can ride around downtown St. Louis at 11:37 P.M. jetlagged from an international flight while a grim-faced sibling hand-delivers utility payments just minutes short of cutoff. Then, you can endure a ride home elongated by half an hour because of all the unincorporated, vicious little municipalities that target blacks and that she and her expired license plates must take the long way around.

One Christmas, as I visited with a friend and her in-laws, I watched as her two grown sisters-in-law, both of whom had managed to supply themselves with illegitimate children but no homes of their own, entertained their babies' different gift-bearing fathers seriatim. A "father" would appear bearing something useless for the child he'd barely seen all year, the appropriate child would be peeled from its half siblings (all with Venusian names) and duly presented for an awkward moment of head-patting from the father, incomprehension and tears from the child, and fuming around the edges from the long-discarded mother. One of these dads had so many kids around town (four named "Jr."), I imagined he earned Frequent Father Miles on all the major holidays. It took all I had not to switch Shontay for Kiwansha to see if "Dad" could tell the difference.

Being back home gave me a headache, as if I were squinting at life there through microscope glasses. So, when home from the Air Force in the 1980s, I did the same thing I'd done growing up there in the 1970s. I parked myself on the couch at either my mother's or one of my sisters' and stayed there until it was time to return to the airport. Except for having to trade insults with my useless brother, I mostly managed to avoid north St. Louis in all its downtrodden entirety. I might as well have been visiting a stranger's hometown.

The Air Force was the only place where I was comfortable. Six months here, eighteen there, a whole planet to choose from in the amorphous maw of the gargantuan American military. I wasn't black anymore, I was blue, Air Force blue, and my name was "Airman," just like the thousands of folks surrounding me. In the Air Force there was order, there were rules, there was a yellow brick road to advancement and any number of people not only willing to show me the way but inextricably bound to my personal and professional development. It takes a whole lot of folks pulling together to launch just one F-15; no one can fall by the wayside. And in the military, it's "up or out"; if you don't progress, you have to leave. But it's not easy to fail to progress; if you can't handle one career field, there's no stigma attached to choosing another more suited to your talents. All military jobs need doing, and a staff sergeant who sprays for bugs is treated no differently than a multilingual one who translates documents from foreign governments.

The military let me reinvent myself every time I changed stations. When I enlisted on March 10, 1980, just shy of my twenty-first birthday, I was a clinically depressed, college dropout, binge-eating insomniac who literally wished she were dead. When I graduated from basic training six weeks later, I was a swaggering little Pattonette. What I'd wanted most in life was not to be me: black, working class, female, and therefore a social weakling destined for a life of pointless drudgery while tormented by vague yearnings I was too browbeaten to give full volume to. The Air Force had let me escape both my social fate and my self-imposed limitations. With every move over the twelve years I spent in the military (six and a half as an officer), I'd become a new and improved Debra Dickerson: I went from wallflower to butch hard-partier and jock, to glamorous vamp and quiet college girl, to radical, driven social reformer, to budding artist.

But I didn't know any of that was going to happen when I joined. I didn't know that from day one I would be pushed, cajoled, praised, and punished into high achievement. Enlisting had been my way of giving up. I was accepting my pink collar and place at the end of the line. Bitterly, I'd thought, If I'm going to type, might as well do it in another time zone. At the same time, though, some tiny, desperate part of me was daring the Air Force to make something of me.

Joining up wasn't my first lurch toward a better future, though; the first would have been attending community college, which I did for a year and a half after graduating from high school. Having gone to a gifted grade school, I was thrown back into a regular high school in 1973. There was no public gifted one; families of means paid for their progeny to attend Country Day or Mary Institute, the all-boy and all-girl (and nearly all-white) private high schools of choice. My parents, on the other hand, were too busy struggling to keep the family afloat to give much thought to the relative merits of different high schools, and too poor to pay tuition when there was free schooling to be had. Unsophisticated and overburdened, they had to settle for that which the government provided.

My parents were manual laborers, neither of whom had gone to high school, neither of whom assumed my lot would much surpass theirs. It was enough for them that I accomplish that, a high school diploma, and maybe learn to type as an added bonus so I could have a "sit-down" job and keep my hands clean. Sharecroppers weaned in the Depression and recently migrated from Mississippi and Tennessee, they had no conception that the American Dream could be mine. Even though I grew up in a period of great political and social upheaval, little of it filtered through to us. I wasn't raised to fight the power. I was raised to wait patiently for my reward in the Great By-and-by, that great gettin up mornin when the dead in Christ gon rise, when the lion gon lie down with the lamb and when Jesus gon call His faithful servants home. Well done, good an faithful servant, He gon say. Well done.

Between that day and this one, stoicism, the occasional backyard barbecue, and the Old Testament were supposed to tide me over. My love of books was tolerated in our no-nonsense household, but not encouraged. Much more emphasis was placed on the five Dickerson girls learning the womanly, God-fearing arts of housekeeping and child-rearing. The manual labor jobs I was destined for would no doubt be self-explanatory.

No one could have foretold the havoc that the inherent contradictions between the way of life my parents brought with them from the South and the way of life open to us up North would wreak on our family. I've spent my whole life trying to avail myself of what's good about one way without closing the door on the other. After forty years, I've just about got it figured out. All that's best and worst about me derives from the fact that I'm a daughter of the Great Migration.

The Great Migration: 5 million African-Americans over thirty years fleeing northward, the greatest mass migration in American history. Modern-day chattel, taxed but unrepresented, jailed as a matter of public policy, raped but loving their offspring no less, saying "No, thank you, Mistah Charlie" to grim reality and "Now! goddammit it" to a wild-eyed dream, even when it cost them their lives. The people famous for making a way out of no way.

Eyes on the future, scared to hope but terrified to stand still. Unsure and often self-hating, but maddeningly prodded by the intuition that maybe, just maybe, there's more to life than either the plantation, the Black Belt, the inner city, the welfare rolls, or the cellblock. Escape route learned by heart and secreted there, but feisty and loudmouthed in spite of themselves. Like Harriet Tubman, who, on the day she planned to escape, looked her master in the eye and saucily sang: "Good-bye, I'm goin fer to leave you." Anchored in and strengthened by the past and by family, but firmly enough so as to use it as a dependable, two-way springboard: out into the wider world in search of material progress but back again each evening into the bosom of generations.

As is the case with all migrants, the future held for us mixed blessings and the "in it but not of it" that all those who have challenged their destinies experience, but we've always known there was no going back. And as we alternated between losing hard and winning big up North, we've always known what happens when you get what you pray for.

But I'm getting ahead of myself.

With her family, my mother migrated north from the Mississippi Delta during World War II. After the war ended and my father mustered out of the Marines, he made his way north, too, from Covington, Tennessee. Both from sharecropping families, neither had much schooling when they met, married, and produced six children with me the fourth. Settled in black north St. Louis, they overlaid their backcountry ways on the big, godless city. Given the strict enforcement of the color line back then, everyone I knew was just like me: recently arrived from and still firmly tied to the Deep South. In short, I come from a long line of folks well used to surviving against the odds so that, come Sunday, they could sing with bitter defiance, "Wunt take nothin for my journey now, Lord." Had we not excelled at figuring work-arounds and making do, we would never have made it.

It wasn't only the lack of material wealth that we'd had to overcome. My adolescent mother had once cowered with her seven siblings under a bed while angry white men ringed their cabin and my grandfather emptied his shotgun through the front door (knowing my grandfather, he'd had it coming). Her maternal great-grandmother was an illegitimate, full-blooded white woman given away to the slaves to raise, her paternal great-grandmother a full-blooded African slave sold away and lost forever to her family. The lost one's husband was full-blooded Cherokee. Her mother, my grandmother, made my grandfather wait an entire year to consummate the marriage; given her childbed death, eight stair-step children and several miscarriages later, maybe there was more than modesty behind her refusal. My father's struggles as a Depression-era TB orphan raised by an abusive grandfather were so painful he barely spoke of them. Facing each day of my formative years with all this in the back of my mind, I couldn't help noticing that modern-day racism and deprivation couldn't hold a candle to what we'd left behind.

My parents should have been radicalized by their circumstances, but like most of their kind, they focused on work and family. They were largely apolitical except for voting straight-line Democrat; I recall almost no political discussion in our house. They shielded us from all adult affairs; we were banished from any room where a relative wouldn't be shushed from speaking of a divorce, a pregnancy, or the like. Even so, my first awareness of politics and ideology came when I was very young, maybe seven or eight. I was watching television with my mother while she ironed. I can still vaguely recall lots of white people standing on a stage with, I believe, Hubert Humphrey. I asked her what these "Demcrats" and "Publicans" everybody kept talking about were. Her words made a lasting impression on me.

"Democrat is what you are. Democrats'll let the little man have somethin. Caint have much as the white man, naturally, but they will let us ordinary folk get somewhere." She sprinkled water on my father's work shirt and set it sizzling under the hot iron. "Republicans don't want nobody else to have nothin."

Thirty years, a J.D., and two political science degrees later, I still find Mama's explanation useful.

In my working-class family of migrated sharecroppers, we were all unthinking Democrats. In content, though, our politics were conservative. When I was a child in the 1960s, my father called civil rights protesters "knuckleheads" who "should take their fists out the air and get jobs." My mother opposed busing because "chiren should stay in they own neighborhoods. What y'all look like passin one school jes to get to the next un?" Fundamentalist Christians, they opposed abortion, supported capital (and corporal) punishment, kept hunting guns, disapproved of welfare recipients, unwed mothers, and those who didn't work. Raised to strict obedience, I didn't understand that there were alternatives (or problematics) to those positions, so until I was about twenty-four, I had no conscious politics. As close as I came was to know this: that rich white men ran the world and that I was going to have to work like a dog, like my parents, for survival. I had no plans to fight them, merely to outlast them and give no offense. I didn't register to vote when I turned eighteen in 1977 and gave no thought at all to politics until about 1983 or 1984. By then, I had become consciously, vehemently conservative and wanted the whole world to know it.

In 1983, newly back from two years on active duty in Korea, I was focused like a death ray on finishing my B.A. so I could become an officer in the United States Air Force. I wanted nothing else in life. Flushed with the support and external validation I'd never had before, I had all the answers to the pressing questions of the day—welfare, abortion, unemployment, education—and the answer was always the same: every man for himself. No one owes anybody else anything, and anybody who tells you differently is a whining loser who wants a handout.

My success in the military had gone directly to my head. It would be years before I'd realize that my travels from the inner city to places like Korea, Turkey, and the Pentagon were not the real journey. The real odyssey was the pilgrimage from Debbie to Debra, from self-hating to sane, from mental ghetto to mental freedom.

PART I

THE PERSONAL

CHAPTER ONE

FAMILY HISTORY

MAMA

It wasn't just the social and historical contexts into which I was born that made me gnaw at the corners of my place in the scheme of things; there were also the specifics of my large and close-knit family. My mother's side, my closest side, is full of vinegary characters who, out of pure cussedness, loved to fight whatever power was closest to hand. (Usually, this fight was verbal rather than legal or physical; in my family, a cutting wit is the weapon of choice. Since the little guy couldn't actually change his situation, we believe, he might as well make fun of it.) Despite their many years sharecropping in the Mississippi Delta, they rarely expended much of their hell-raising energy railing against whites.

My maternal grandfather, John Bishop "Paw Paw" Gooch, was not exactly a Norman Rockwell figure. His stories, and he had lots of them, were always either profane, sacrilegious, or X-rated, but blacks were almost always the main players. "White folks don bother me," he used to say, "you know in the fust fi minutes where you stands wid any particular one of em. 'S niggers that cause all my problems." He cackled about having been too young to fight in World War I and too old for World War II. He cheated his great-grandchildren at board games and blew smoke in their faces if they complained. He once tossed a crumpled dollar bill at a preteen collecting for football uniforms on the street and sneered, "Now quit beggin." He pinched my teenage girlfriends' behinds at holiday gatherings and convinced his cronies that I was his wife. I was eleven.

When the Gooches got together, laughter and liquor flowed and everybody yelled at once, jockeying for the floor in a wonderful cacophony. Their stories, by and large, all had punch lines rather than the indictments one might have expected. They were intended to entertain, to capture the spirit of the times and the personalities of their friends and neighbors. While there were, of course, stand-alone stories of white brutality and the like, those were rare. Jim Crow was the backdrop to all their lives, but they seemed to regard it with the same spirit of inventiveness and perspicacity as they did the weather: something to be circumvented and outfoxed, or, failing that, to be borne. Rarely was the degradation the point of a story; it was merely the framework. Their stories were of people, not politics.

Born in 1927, my mother, Johnnie Florence Gooch, was her mother's right hand, just as I am to her. Paw Paw had fourteen siblings, my grandmother Ouida six; my mother was the third of their eight children. The surrounding area teemed with Gooch relations as her family farmed for the man who owned nearly everything and everyone for miles. When her mother died trying to give birth for the ninth time, fifteen-year-old Johnnie took on the role that still defines her: mother. Though life was hard, with so many relatives able to hunt, fish, and farm, the family managed.

My grandmother's side of the family was highly prized for its looks—meaning, of course, their light skin and "good" hair. These traits come from ancestors like my great-great-grandmother. Belle was white, the illegitimate child of the master's daughter and a white stable hand. When his daughter got pregnant, the master hid her away and forced her to give birth in secret to my great-great-grandmother. Then, my entirely white ancestor was torn from her mother and given to the slaves to raise. Granma Belle, now "black," married Henry, a Mohawk Indian, and had six children. Looking white was one of the few assets the Williams line possessed; they knew it had value. When my mother's oldest sibling was born, my white-looking grandmother wept because she was dark, like my grandfather. "Y'all married dark," she'd wailed to two of her sisters, "but yo babies aint black." At gatherings, my mother's aunts inspected the child for signs of lightening as she stood helplessly under their disapproving gaze. While my mother is a medium brown, her long, wavy Indian-black hair and Lena Horne looks spared her this indignity.

On my grandfather's side, another ancestor's master freed him on his deathbed; he resold himself into slavery for a fancy pair of boots. One of their children married an Indian and gave birth to my great-grandmother. Paw Paw's grandmother, an African-born slave, also married an Indian. She had nine children before being sold away and lost to the family forever. Grandpa George, her Cherokee husband, was shot and killed in an argument over who was going to call at a square dance.

With this pedigree, there was no way this family could take itself too seriously. So they sang, they danced, they drank on the holidays and didn't think about work or white folks except when dealing with either directly. And they had lots of kids: I have thirty first cousins.

To think of sharecropping, Depression-era Mississippi is to think of oppression and deprivation. But in the Mississippi I heard about at home, there were usually only little stories; not lynchings but church lunches. Not rape but revival meetings. Like the local man with two wives—one for planting-time and one for harvest-time. One was so mean, with a wife so timid, that he kept her home just by sprinkling a ring of soot around the house and forbidding her to cross it. But another mean wife-beater wasn't quite so good at his job. His wife, the one he thought he'd cowed, used heavy twine to sew him up in their thick muslin sheets as he slept and beat him half to death with a poker. I heard about the several white families near the Gooches who were so poor my grandmother would take them in during cold spells so they wouldn't freeze to death. All the kids, black and white, slept together like a brood of snuggling puppies. The next day, my grandmother would delouse her children with lye; everybody knew that poor white trash had lice.

Dire though their circumstances were, I'm hard pressed to come up with many Gooch stories about the particular evil of Mississippi whites.

Hard pressed but not incapable.

There was the time the rich white landowner took a driving tour through his feudal holdings, spied my great-great-aunt's lush garden, kicked open their door, and demanded half: "What grows on my land belongs to me!" He made clear his intention to claim half in perpetuity, so they plowed the garden under that night. And then there were all the times the overlord sent for his vassals to perform some menial labor in his baronial mansion, like furniture-moving or trash-hauling.

They made a habit of showing up drunk, so that custom withered away as heirloom china shattered on the polished oak floors of de Big House.

Degradation was a daily occurrence for them, yet I have to comb through my memory for stories like that. I don't believe I could come up with many more. Except, of course, for the worst one, the one I'll never forgive that Southern system of apartheid for.

Though for years my mother moved me to tears with the sad story of her mother's childbed death, I was nearly grown before she added the details many others would have put first. A white doctor had managed to stabilize my grandmother, though her condition remained grave. He left firm instructions that she was to be left alone, that only he would attend her. White interns, eager to practice their newfound surgical arts, operated on her for practice anyway. Drastically weakened, infected from the botched job, and afraid of what else they might do to her, my grandmother hid the pills they gave her in the masses of her curly black hair and died. It's not clear that the pills would have saved her, or even exactly what they were for, but none of the family ever doubted the wisdom of her refusing further treatment. Having heard about the forced surgery, the Gooches were coming to take her home to safety. But they were too late.

To my mother, that story is only about inevitability and loss. It's about hearing those tiny little pills click-clack against the floor tiles when they came to claim the body, watching them skitter heedlessly, impotently buffeted by forces so much stronger than they. This was not—as it was for me, when I tried to radicalize her later—a story about white perfidy and the valuelessness of black existence. To accept that version, she would have had to have been a different person, a person who could hate.

She rarely told a story the point of which was anything other than simple entertainment. She kept up with the yearly (pre-VCR) showings of *Cinderella, The Wizard of Oz,* and *Peter Pan;* she clapped as hard as we did to keep Tinkerbell alive. She made the simplest tasks and events seem fabulous, which is not to suggest that she wasn't a stern taskmaster; no drill sergeant set higher standards than did she. For her, there were only two ways to do anything: "my way and the wrong way." The wrong way got you whipped, so we stepped lively. Take hanging out the wash.

After manhandling it through our wringer washer (a big improvement over the scrub board and big iron tub that used to turn Mama's knuckles to sausage, but still hard work), our job had just begun. It had to be hung in a particular order (men's shirts, men's pants, all underwear—in their proper, gendered order—obscured in the middle for decency's sake); in a particular manner (right side out, right side up, front facing the house if out back, the basement stairs if inside); and with a specified number of pins (five per sheet, two per shirt unless it's a baby's, in which case . . .); pinned in a prescribed fashion (shirts: one at each shoulder . . .). An overuse of clothespins was wasteful, an underuse was trifling, slovenly. Any deviation was "jes doin things any ol' kinda way."

Worse than her whippings was her wit. If I daydreamed while a pot of water hissed and bubbled unnoticed, Mama would quip, "What you want that pot to do 'sides boil?" If some lazybones replaced an empty box in the pantry, she'd ask innocently, "When you colleck enough, you get a prize?" But when the housework was done, she let her hair down.

Everything arouses wonder and curiosity in Johnnie Florence. She doesn't hate whites or the rich or the bosses, merely the unkind. When I asked her how it felt to live under Jim Crow, she said guilelessly, "I guess I just dint wan go nowhere the white folks dint want me going ner do nothing they dint want me doin." This kind of talk infuriated my father because, you see, my daddy was a person who could hate.

DADDY

Born in 1924 in Covington, Tennessee, Eddie Mack Dickerson's family was very small and soon to become even smaller. Both his parents (Robert and Landora) were dead of tuberculosis by the time he was six. He didn't even remember his mother; she was dead by his second birthday, another grandmother I would never know. Mary, his only sibling, would succumb to that same killer in a few years. He was shunted from one ever more distant relative to another as TB devastated his entire region along with his family.

Orphaned and no doubt traumatized, my father and my aunt, who would soon leave him, first landed with their grandparents, Eddie and

Mariah. Eddie drank and used his fists. So much so, his own daughters married at the onset of menses to escape him. His wife, lacking such an alternative, rarely roused herself to take note of her surroundings. My father, the little boy, eventually cowed his bestial grandfather into drunken submission and provided a safe haven for his fading sister and grandmother. "Safety," in such circumstances, however, was a relative term.

Though they were no longer beaten, my great-grandfather continued to drink. No longer free to physically maul and maim, he made their miserable shotgun cabin a place haunted by a living, malevolent ghost. His drinking made him incapable of bringing in the crop: this task fell to my eleven-year-old father. So, the prepubescent Eddie Mack spent those years hat in hand, begging the white folks for more time, more credit, more daylight so he could get it all done.

All in all, my father had a loveless, most un-Gooch-like childhood and he rarely discussed it with his children.

What he did discuss was white people and their evil. Most of his stories revolved around one basic theme: the fortitude required of blacks living in a white man's world. Whites made his grandfather a drunk, whites made him farm land he could never own, whites killed his family with overwork and inhumane conditions. Whites set him adrift in the world, a peasant chained to a country they never let him forget wasn't his. He lived his life at a slow boil, always on the verge of an eruption. His anger at life's unfairness (a.k.a. "the white man") was a seething socket deep within him that he plugged into for energy and drive.

Daddy was confused about whites, though. He must have been, because when World War II began, he voluntarily enlisted. Why fight for a country of which you consider yourself a noncitizen, a country you consider to be profoundly evil and incapable of change? But in the end, his service was the thing he was most proud of in life. In the United States Marine Corps he found the family he desperately longed to have. The Marines made him part of something larger than himself, that had a glorious history, and that ensnared him in bonds of familiarity and joint effort. No more loneliness, no more adolescence and fear. Just as the Air Force would for me forty years later, the Marines set his fighting spirit alight; that light never went out again, not for the rest of his life. It put the finishing touches on the stoicism and grit he'd honed as a child and young man and gave it direction. Eddie Mack Dickerson was a United States marine until the day he died.

Unfortunately, once the war was over, there was little call for trained killers.

Mustered out, he joined some distant cousins in St. Louis and married my mother. He'd fought on Okinawa with her cousin Smitty, whom she pen-palled through the war. Daddy bartered his precious cigarettes for her photo as they steamed toward Okinawa. He vowed to marry the beauty in the picture he carried for the rest of the war when he got home, and that's exactly what he did.

Daddy did his best to train us to follow in his gritty footsteps. He taught us the proper way to bayonet an enemy (which was much simpler with the scrawny Japanese than when he'd practiced in boot camp at Parris Island), bragged about how many hours straight he could plow in subzero temperatures, lectured us on how ill prepared we were for the rigors of life and how likely we were to starve to death. He dismissed my mother's stories as frivolous because unlikely to put food on the table. He always did things the hard way: he refused to see doctors, he acquired everything secondhand, he never conceded a point in an argument no matter how wrong he was. He even refused to cry out when the truck he was working on fell and crushed his leg. He needed to fight; he needed an enemy, something to defeat or at least to resist, so he wouldn't feel helpless. He also needed an audience to witness his victories—that's where we came in.

For all his ferocity, though, he was also the man who fell in love with a photo and made up nonsense songs for his kids. Apropos of nothing, he'd drop to the floor and pump out innumerable push-ups for our amazement. He used to run up and down the block with us dangling from his biceps. He was a shameless poser and show-off and we loved him for it.

Though both my parents, like millions of black Americans, made a conscious choice to thumb their noses at Jim Crow by migrating, in the end only Mama was able to leave her anger at the Mason-Dixon line. Daddy brought Jim Crow with him. He smuggled it in, a stowaway in his heart, an overstuffed duffel bag about to burst at the seams.

ZOO-ZOOS AND LOLLIPOPS

None of us six kids were born down South, but we might as well have been. Beginning in 1948 with JoAnn, followed by Dorothy in 1955, Wina in 1957, me in 1959, Necie in 1960, and ending in 1963 with Bobby, we were Southerners through and through, whatever our Northern address might have told the world about us. We slopped up Karo "serp" with white bread and called it breakfast. We crumbled up cornbread in our buttermilk and called it dessert. We insulted each other's mothers and called it "playin the dozens" without a clue that we were perpetuating the tradition of slave auctioneers comically wholesaling our least desirable forebears by "the dozens" to the steady beat of their wallet-loosening insults. We were country when country wasn't cool.

For all their differences, both parents brought the same country ways from the South, as did everyone else we knew. Most of all, that meant their Southern Baptist fundamentalism. We couldn't play cards (tools of the devil) or games with dice in them (like Monopoly). Nor, for example, could we accuse anyone of lying; instead, they were "tellin a story." Anyone born into a generation before yours was "ma'am" or "sir." If Mama could hear us through the open windows "loud-talkin" (ever the sorceress, she could sort our voices out among all the summer shouting of children), we had to come in from play and sit quietly "like ladies." If she called to us and we answered "What?" or "Yeah?" instead of "Ma'am?" we were, at a minimum, called to her for a smack. The rod was not spared and the child was not spoiled.

We were in church each Wednesday night for choir practice, and from 8 A.M. on Sunday until 3:00 in the afternoon, longer if folks got to shouting. Neighbors we knew as taxi drivers and janitors mounted the pulpit on Sunday to lead flocks sometimes numbering in the hundreds. Few of them were ordained, fewer had any religious instruction at all. Some were illiterate. But all that mattered to us was whether or not Brother So-and-so could preach—and boy could they.

I heard sermons containing impromptu riffs composed entirely of punch lines from commercials ("Jesus'll be yo Cok-Cola: He the real thang!") and pop songs ("Y'all better stop! in the name of His love").

Our church was full of rituals no one could explain. I'd chase the minister down after services full of questions: What does the "Missionary" in Emmanuel Missionary Baptist Church mean? Why ring those bells at those particular moments and what do they signify? Why do we call those funereal, a capella dirgelike hymns that the whole congregation sings together, "Dr. Watts"? During the service, from the choir stand, I had hours to look out over the congregation at the back wall with its mural of a blindingly blond Jesus suffering nobly on the cross, the only white man for miles.

I didn't mind church back then, it was just another of the inexorable rhythms of our closed little world. Poindexter that I was, I even liked Sunday school, if only because it provided me with a second set of kids to compete against. There, I was always the only kid who'd not only done the homework but had gone for extra credit besides. I got pinched a lot when grandmotherly Sister Bibbs wasn't looking.

Our religion went everywhere with us even as it never left our home. When we took our seats for meals, Daddy blessed the table in the same manner each time. He, of course, sat at the head of the table, his back to the sink and window. Mama sat at the opposite end. I sat to his right, Bobby next to me, and Necie next to him. (Bobby was left-handed, so we had elbow wars for many years, but I wouldn't give up my seat next to Daddy.) Dorothy, Wina, and JoAnn sat on Daddy's left.

"HeavenlyFatherwedohumblythankThee [breathe] forwhatwe're abouttoreceive [breathe] forthenourishmentofourbodies [breathe] for Christ's sake Amen."

We'd recited this prayer so many times, the punctuation marks and capital letters had all worn away and the words had rearranged themselves so as to best match Daddy's breathing patterns. When he was away from home, as he often was with his truck on long hauls, Mama designated someone to bless the table. Invariably, they phrased it with all Daddy's worn-away edges, whatever our own natural rhythm might have been. I can't recite that blessing even now without doing it exactly the way Daddy did for so many years.

After Daddy said the magic words, we went around the table and each person recited a Bible verse. Usually, everyone said the shortest one in the Bible: "Jesus wept." Even on a school field trip, you were expected to mumble this incantation over your dried bologna sandwich and shriveled apple. Without reflection, I always did, as did all the other kids in our neighborhood except the pariahs, the ones from slovenly, non-churchgoing homes; where I lived, no one was ever teased for blessing their paper-sack lunch or bag of potato chips. I never doubted the truth of Mama's warning that unblessed food would give us a stomachache. It wasn't a punishment but simple cause and effect: step out into traffic and get hit by a car. Skip the blessing and get a stomachache. But I rarely said "Jesus wept."

I would spend hours with the Bible before dinner, finding long, twisty verses full of archaic language. Then I'd recite them when my turn came to say a verse. No one would dare interrupt a recitation from the Bible, so I got to orate for as long as I liked. At first, I looked up the most common ones, just to make sure the ministers were getting them right. Then I searched for interesting ones about wars or funny stories. But soon, I was interested merely in length and complexity. All around me I could hear stomachs growling and Mama sighing. I was often kicked under the table, but nothing would stop me from "winning" at the verse. Often, I'd end my orations with a vocal flourish and a derisive "Jesus wept."

In the mid-1950s, with JoAnn and Dorothy born, my family was still so new to the North that they had to give up raising pet rabbits in the backyard because the neighbors ate them. The rabbits would have had to go anyway eventually as my father's junk began to take over more and more of the backyard.

He'd long since turned the basement into a dark catacomb filled with long-forgotten crates that, even so, could not be parted with. Ever the orphan required to survive by his wits, what seemed like trash to other people looked like pennies from heaven to him. An irredeemable pack rat and independent trucker always operating on a shoestring, he kept the yard filled with transmissions and dead batteries, cannibalized trucks and cars teetering on bricks, piles of mismatched hubcabs and lots of unidentifiable, greasy gizmos, all of which he was confident he would one day put to use. When *Sanford & Son* aired in the 1970s, the other kids would torment us by humming the theme as my father passed by. But when I was a child, his junk piles were a paradise full of fun stuff to play with and cozy hiding places to curl up in with a book.

Driving anywhere with Daddy was an adventure when I was small. I loved the station wagons he created for us from the varied parts of many other sacrificial cars. We never knew what we'd be riding in, but there were some constants: multicolored bodies with mismatched tires and doors that almost fit. Missing windows replaced with cardboard we thought was there for us to draw on, missing floorboards we could drag our Keds out of when Mama wasn't looking. More often than not, we'd end up getting to play alongside the road while Daddy jogged up the highway to the nearest gas station for water to pour into a radiator on its last legs or ripped up old rags to secure a muffler. People honked and pointed at us as we passed; it felt special, like being part of a circus caravan.

He would pull the car over—whether we were on a side road or jam-packed Highway 70—and pick up any box, bag, or jug that looked likely. Whatever it contained, Daddy would bring it home with us. Whatever its condition, he made us use it. This included a box of key blanks; toilet paper rain-swollen to volleyball size and notebook paper consistency; a shampoo so tarlike and viscous we knew it had been dumped on purpose; an armchair with actual bloodstains and tire marks.

Daddy's finds went far beyond car parts and household goods to include fancy toys discarded by the rich. They kept us in demand as playmates and made Daddy famous as a master magician who could make something from nothing. He loved the spotlight and showed off like a teenage boy deep in the throes of puberty. This he always managed to do in ways that accentuated his towering maleness—like extravagantly romancing his wife.

Many mornings when I was small, he smooched theatrically with my waitress mother before leaving to drive his truck. There in the darkness of our predawn kitchen, he would sneak up on her from the hallway with a soundlessness eerie for such a strapping man. He would sweep her up off her feet and into his arms for a loud, smacky kiss that bent her over backward and lifted her half a foot off the cracked linoleum. He winked at us over her shoulder and, one-handed, shook her gently like a rag doll just to show us that he could. The other hand undid her chaste bun and sent her hair tumbling down her back. Just like the ladies in the movies, Mama would squeak out little helpless protests about the bacon burning or the kids watching, but he never listened and she really didn't seem to mind.

On such a morning, one with big, smoochy kisses, he flipped his spare change at us for penny candy.

"Go get y'all some zoo-zoos and lollipops." Smug, as if he were tossing gold doubloons to filthy urchins from the velvet-curtained windows of a royal coach. Mindless of our dignity, and enchanted by the nonsense words he was always inventing, we swarmed him, shoving for our God-given right to one sixth of any booty. When you're one of six, you snooze? You lose. Pride be damned.

Mama tsk-tsked.

"Eddie, caint you jes divide it up and give it to em?" She tried to swat us apart with her dishcloth.

"Nah. Good for em. In boot camp on Parris Island, they'd lock us in at night one rifle short." He squinted evilly at Mama. "Guess who always had him a rifle come mornin."

So there you have it. Sorcery and happy endings in one ear, fratricide and mortal combat in the other. But the turmoil inherent in these crosscurrents remained dormant then, back in the day. In the early years of my childhood the Dickersons were a happy family.

BACK IN THE DAY

It was always summertime then, in the 1960s. Even my winter memories are warm. Keds and PF Flyers and bicycles whizzing by, drinking straws laced in the spokes for maximum annoyance. Eighty-five percent humidity. Vaseline dripping down bony legs fried charcoal from the sun. Scalp sweat making the edges of hot-combed hair "go back" to nappiness. Mamas in pink waitress, beige custodian, blue nurse's aide uniforms yelling through open windows, spatula in hand, the instant the streetlights came on. Captured fireflies shooting frenetic sparks of light from poorly scrubbed mayonnaise jars. The smell of greens and cornbread, black-eyed peas and cornbread, boiled cabbage and cornbread, butter beans and cornbread, fried green tomatoes and cornbread rumbling our stomachs with anticipatory pleasure as we made for home. Rubber-band rope, rock school, double Dutch. Mega hide-and-go-seek games involving thirty kids or more rolling themselves under cars and crouching on low roofs. Kids everywhere.

Not only did the seasons stay the same in St. Louis, neither did the neighborhood change. In the fifteen years my parents lived together on Terry Avenue, exactly one family moved out, exactly one moved in. Even the Dodds next door, the last white family for miles around, left the neighborhood only for his funeral and her entrance into a nursing home.

Their son Evan was the last white at Beaumont High, which was rapidly turning into one of the toughest schools in the city. He would sit placidly on our porch while we performed racial experiments on him: how red could a pinch make his skin, could his stringy hair be cornrowed, what effect would Vaseline, the Negro ur-unguent, have on it? Evan, a long-haired hippie freak, prowled the neighborhood in the hearse he'd refurbished, a gaggle of us kids stuffed inside. We took turns being the corpse, stretching out in the back while the others imitated the fat old ladies at funerals who bellowed their grief and tried to climb into the casket with the dearly departed.

On our block, no deed, good or bad, went unobserved. No deed, good or bad, went unreported. No village in China kept a closer eye on its inhabitants than did we. After I smarted off to Mr. Banks at the Clark gas station on the corner, my mother was waiting on the porch to slap my face and march me back the half block to apologize. The phone still jangled in its cradle.

On the other side of the Clark station was Kingshighway Avenue, running the length of the city north to south. We were very economical in our approach to it—we only used its northern end. To the south lay white St. Louis, as completely off-limits to us as if there were a second Grand Canyon there where Kingshighway crossed Forest Park. No one had to warn me to stay out of the south side just as no one had to warn me not to touch a hot stove. I didn't really understand that whites lived there, just that we couldn't. The only time we left our neighborhood was on Christmas Eve when Daddy took us to see the displays.

High on homemade sweets and overexcited by the magic of the Christmases Mama conjured for us then, we claimed the streets of our hometown for a night like victorious GIs on town pass. Those Christmas Eves sauntering around downtown St. Louis in the winter chill ogling the dazzling store windows and mechanical Santas were the only times I ever felt like a citizen. It was the only time we had full access to a nonblack neighborhood without having to worry, the only times we saw what the other 99 percent of America looked like and where all our tax dollars were going.

We oohed and aahed, pushed and shoved, fought and made up in the unstable kaleidoscope of alliances and insurgencies, détente and stalemate that demarcate the universe of six siblings required by family law to be all the friends any of us would ever need. Daddy would stay on the fringe of our family stroll, righting a toddler splayed on an icy patch, deputizing the two oldest to get hot chocolates, lifting six-year-old me high enough to see over some other father's fedora. Simultaneously wary and relaxed, like the bodyguard of a minor monarch's third son, he managed to seem both with us and employed by us. Chain-smoking cigarettes he rolled from his ubiquitous Prince Albert can, he nodded and made a measuring eye contact with passersby. Those polite eyes said, "Jes lookin at the lights. Not going to steal anything. Please don't ruin our Christmas." The aggressive tilt of his head, the square of his shoulders, and the promise of a rapid response from the muscles he rippled at will made the "please" revocable.

I never asked to see St. Louis on any other occasion; I knew somehow that our Christmas Eve freedom was a kind of Get Out of Jail Free card, good for one use only. I didn't mind; my world was full. Whites, and the wide-open spaces they occupied, were not real somehow; for me, they only existed on TV, another place we couldn't live. We could watch, though, and I didn't aspire to more. I accepted these things as organic, like humidity and hand-me-downs, and took comfort in our close-knit, all-black world.

Holidays were my mother's especial forte. She spent the entire week leading up to one cooking. At Thanksgiving and Christmas, she got out that big cauldron of a cooking pot she only used for such occasions and started stuffing produce, little leafy sacrifices, into it. The greens varied enough to fill a botany text: mustard, turnip, spinach. Then she'd put in barrels of black-eyed peas, butter beans, and cabbage, and mounds of fatback, salt pork, and ham hocks to season the lot. Then, best of all, while the smell of roasting turkey insidiously infiltrated the house and trenchers of cornbread bubbled, Mama started peeling sweet potatoes into the big silver cook pot for sweet potato pie. That pot was big enough to cook Hansel and Gretel in; big enough to concoct a potion for spell-casting! Days passed as she peeled and peeled, humming her tuneless, bumpy dirges.

Book in hand, I glued myself to a kitchen chair. Hours went by as I watched her hands fly at their work yet still retain the precision of one deactivating a time bomb. After an indeterminate period, without warning, she stopped peeling, slicing, humming, and lined up the pie shells she'd prepared.

"Ma," I asked, "how many potatoes is that?"

"Hmmmm?" she murmured.

Cinnamon, nutmeg, vanilla, coconut, whipped cream—the smells of the all-too-infrequent holidays. The smell of Mama's magic.

"But, Ma," I asked, shivering and tingly at the cosmic forces swirling around us in the aromatic kitchen, "how you know when you done peeled enough?"

As usual, her repetitive motions had lulled her deep into a reverie and she didn't answer. Had she not learned how to detach herself and float away from her crowded home and its never-ending demands, she would never have had any privacy. She was smiling then about something, her hands momentarily still.

"Mama, what you listening to?"

The sound of wailing and warbling in some bizarre language rang tinnily forth from our raggedy radio. Daddy had found it mangled by the roadside and reinforced it with strapping tape all around; it looked mummified. A pale, sickly green, both its casing and its dial were thoroughly cracked. Most significantly, it had no knobs. To change the channel, you could either shake it just right or use a pair of pliers. In neither case could you control where you landed.

When Daddy had brought it home and lovingly bandaged it, bitterly proud of its battered condition, we'd had to swallow our tongues. He gave us females no choice but to accept it into "our" room. Though at first that banged-up radio served only to remind us of all the things we couldn't afford, eventually it became "our" radio. It was our little window on the world, a trapdoor we could escape through when north St. Louis in general, and 4933 Terry Avenue in particular, became too claustrophobic. Because it was often too much trouble to change it, and only likely to land us someplace even weirder, we listened to speeches, the Mamas and the Papas, Lawrence Welk, the emergency warning signal, political debates, bluegrass, big band, foreign languages . . . whatever poured out at us.

In the evenings, when our work was done, we women sat there reading, crocheting, and drinking Lipton tea with lots of lemon and sugar while our valiant little radio entertained and educated us. As a strange side benefit, Wina and I were unbeatable at "Name That Tune."

Apparently, the wobbly sound pouring out at the moment was singing because crashing cymbals and plucky-sounding instruments swelled up to join it. It was so surprising-sounding, like a sudden clash of metal and hundreds of running feet, I couldn't help laughing.

"Ma, why you listening to this? Want me change it?" I held the pliers ready. Much as I'd enjoyed the sounds, I still didn't think they were music. To me then, the radio was like a carnival ride, enjoyable only for its capacity to thrill and quickly past its usefulness. Later, as Daddy cut us off almost completely from the outside world, that radio became our conduit to fresh air, but that day, it was merely a diversion.

She gave me a strange smile. "Leave it be. Them folks could be trying to tell us something special."

So we listened to the radio together while she cooked the potatoes in a trance. She mixed all the wonderful ingredients together in her big fairy-tale pot, never measuring, never counting, never without that otherworldly smile and unfocused eyes.

"Ma, the potatoes," I called. "How you know when to stop peelin?"

I might never have spoken, so small a dent did I make in her reverie.

"Mama? Mama? Mama?"

I thought that was her given name; I liked whispering it there in our gingerbread kitchen like an incantation. When I was nine or ten years old, I would be introduced to the concept of the "maiden name" and that she'd not always been my mother, that we'd not always been "the Dickersons." I became hysterical. But I was happy that day, calling for my mama again and again and again so softly I knew she wouldn't register it consciously but might well weave it into whatever fantasy she was entertaining. Eventually, though, I had to have her back.

"**MA.** How much fillin is that?"

She looked surprised, as if she'd missed her bus stop and didn't recognize the neighborhood. Then, a shrug toward the pie shells lined up on the counter.

"*That* much."

The tone of her voice let me know I'd asked enough questions. The ritual was complete when I got to watch the last drop of sweet potato pie filling exactly fill the last waiting pie shell.

Across Kingshighway, three quarters of a block from our house, was Benton Elementary, where every kid in the neighborhood went. Unless, of course, they were high-seditty and went to one of the handful of black parochial schools. We were not high-seditty. All Benton's students and teachers were black, as was the principal. Its yard was divided in two by a white line on the pavement—girls' side, boys' side. Any girl who crossed the line was "fast" and got whipped; any boy who did was "bold" and got scolded.

Those were old-fashioned days; it would be 1972, my seventh grade, before females could wear pants to school. That included teachers and administrators. We square-danced in gym until the mid-seventies. Chewing gum got you sent to the principal's office and a phone call to your parents. Passing notes or talking in class? A minimum of three lashes with a pointer or yardstick while bent over a desk in front of the whole class. What worse offenses might cost a transgressor I never knew; incorrigibility was held to a minimum in a world where parents came to administer classroom whippings. Any corporal punishment administered at school was given in the full knowledge that it would be repeated at home once the teacher called to alert your parents. Of course, the call just made it official; the news usually made it home before the sore behind did. Teachers, like the Bible, were always right; disputing their version of events would only lengthen and intensify the parental whipping. "Why would a grown woman tell a story on you?" Mama would demand, belt in hand. "Don't you think she got better things to do?" Not that a schmendrick like me ever got in trouble in school. There were no gold stars in that.

It was a very small, very safe, very closed world. It was made even more so for us Dickersons by the fact that we were forbidden to stray beyond a two-block radius in any direction. We were not permitted to listen to adult conversation, nor were we were allowed to watch the news; I was so oblivious to the civil unrest of the 1960s that when a car passed festooned with Freedom Ride banners, I thought Good Samaritans were providing free transportation for the poor. At the Dickersons', the sixties were about tradition and family.

JIM CROW REVISITED

We drove back to Covington as often as we could to visit Daddy's remaining family (Mississippi was deemed too far. Also, Mama was always ambivalent about us going there; I have yet to visit the state). Road trips were high adventure for us kids.

As we got further from St. Louis, the territory became increasingly rural. Daddy avoided interstates (tolls were for suckers, yet another ploy by the masters to deny the masses that freedom which was rightfully theirs), so we bucked and heaved along two-lane roads in varying states of comfort. We exaggerated the bumpiness, flinging ourselves against each other and squealing for joy. We passed farmers and cows, we inhaled skunk stench and watched horses defecate on the run. When Mama confirmed for us that those were indeed cotton fields flying by, we laughed—they seemed unreal, a hayseed panorama staged for our amusement. Daddy listened to talk radio and baseball games and tuned us out, or so we thought.

"Lawsie, Missy Anne," I drawled in my best eight-year-old Sambo to Wina. "Is we gwine fer to milk dis heah cow and skin us'n up soma dis heah possum?" I was smart but not smart enough to realize my own speech pattern was not much different from that which I mocked.

"I don rightly be a-knowin," she responded, eyes round and Rochester'd. "Jes don be fer ta whuppin us'n darkies, Missy. I declares." We giggled and snorted at our own wit.

All at once, Daddy was standing over us, ordering us out of the car.

"You think slavin and cotton pickin is so durn funny, eh? I'm a show y'all jes what our people went through so you could live so high on the hog."

I elbowed Wina and snickered. "High on the hog!"

"Hog!" she snorted back piggily.

He didn't laugh. "Into tha fields. All a y'all. Right now. Pick you some cotton and then tell me how funny it is."

Mama tried to soothe him, but he bum-rushed us from the car to the cotton field in what seemed like a flash. Daddy demonstrated the proper harvesting procedure and then set off down the road, jogging up and down to keep himself awake at the wheel. Defeated, Mama settled herself under a tree with Bobby, the baby. We girls threw ourselves into our labors. We thought it was a game.

Picking cotton is hard.

Quickly, the prickly pods encasing the bolls drew blood. Wina and I conferred and hit upon the bright idea of removing our good-little-girl Sunday school white cotton gloves from the luggage to protect our fingers. Several pairs each were necessary to prevent injury.

Soon, we were chasing each other with clods of sod. We whacked away at each other with thick greenery and clumps of soil. Then we created a suitable plot and dialogue: I was the evil overseer, the others my downtrodden slaves.

"Mammy! I done tol you fer the last time. Now I'se gwine whup'n de tar outta yo wu'thless black hide." I cracked my imaginary whip evilly.

"Please lawd! Don fer tuh whup me. Don whup ol' mammy," Wina wailed bug-eyed. Necie sang "Nobody Knows de Trouble I'se Seed" in the best Paul Robeson she could manage.

And then Daddy was once again standing over us, so furious he was . . . silent. He seethed so intently, he seemed to be going in and out of focus. Then he turned like a robot, got into the car, and drove away.

We ceased our game immediately and trooped back over to Mama, sat down in the shade with her, and waited. Within a few minutes, he was back. We got in, he tuned in another ball game, began whistling to himself, and we drove off. No one spoke for what seemed like hours.

I suppose we learned from television and the movies to see slavery as melodrama. Given that we learned nothing in school about slavery, Reconstruction (except that rapacious carpetbaggers oppressed the virtuous Southerners), or Jim Crow, all our information came from the tube. Sans discussion, we watched Shirley Temple, Bob Hope and Bing Crosby, Charlie Chan, Bette Davis's *Jezebel,* and every other shlocky, apologist rendering of the benign institution of slavery.

The gift my parents' generation gave mine was a double-edged blade: the balm of distance and the curse of ignorance. We couldn't fully appreciate how bad, how systemically bad, things had been, which both freed us and made us insensitive.

We knew virtually no black professionals, politicians, or entrepreneurs. We rarely saw ourselves reflected in the currents of the mainstream; when we did, it was as Rochester, Stepin Fetchit, movie maids and mammies. Our cultural invisibility except as laughingstocks, criminals, entertainers, or athletes produced a sort of schizophrenia in us. We watched—and revered—*Amos and Andy* and any other show featuring blacks, yet we knew sans discussion that many whites viewed these depictions as encyclopedia entries: a lazy white guy named Bob was just a lazy white guy named Bob, but Stepin Fetchit was every black man who ever lived.

"Daddy! Daddy! Whataburger, please, please, Whataburger!" Dorothy, bird dog that she was, pointed with one arm and pounded his headrest with the other. We saw it too and the rest of us set up a chorus. Stopping for their greasy, waxed-paper-wrapped burgers was the high spot of any road trip down South. Given our finances, we rarely ate away from home while at home.

"All right, all right, quit your caterwaulin. Whataburger? Thataburger."

We laughed sycophantically at the joke he told every time Whataburger was mentioned. He laughed hardest; all was forgiven. He pulled across their paved lot out front to the dirt road that ran alongside and behind the restaurant.

Mama gathered all the girls and took us off into the trees to pee and sent Daddy off with Bobby. Daddy was never saddled with a child; looking back, I can see that she must have sent Bobby with him to keep him calm. It wasn't working. His face gray and tight, Daddy disappeared around the back side of the restaurant. Mama stopped us from following him, so soon we were playing tag among the near trees. He reappeared loaded down with bags.

Too concerned with the nearness of Whataburgers to notice his thin lips and shallow breath, we swarmed him for the bags. Soon, Mama had our feast spread out on a blanket across the tailgate. Overstimulated by our strange surroundings, we hopped from foot to foot with our burgers in one hand, shakes in the other. It felt odd to eat standing up. Then Wina threw a fry at me and the war was on. I took off after her, even madder when one of my pickles fell off my Whataburger as I ran.

"Y'all out yo minds?" Mama warned. "Don make me find my belt right out here in the open air. Don think Jesus caint see you."

To our surprise, Daddy cut her off. "Why not?" he said bitterly. "We got to eat outside like heathens, why not act like heathens?"

"Eddie," she soothed, "le's jes make the bes—"

"Oh no!" Necie had fat tears rolling down her cheeks. "We dint say our verse. Now we gon all get stomachaches," she wailed.

My Whataburger turned to lead in my stomach.

We all looked to Mama. She looked to Daddy.

"Damnation!" he fumed, and pounded his fist on the dashboard. Our wailing got louder.

"Damnation!" he croaked again. This time his fist landed on the horn.

We all jumped at the sound. Mama covered her mouth, wide-eyed. Daddy got quiet; his eyes narrowed speculatively. He blew the horn again. White faces appeared at the windows. Moving with alacrity, Mama swept the remnants of our meal back into the bags and shooed us into the car. We were bent over double, sure we could already feel our intestines cramping. Daddy was leaning on the horn now, blaring it like an air-raid warning. Whites, mostly waitresses and cooks in dirty white uniforms, began appearing from the restaurant's back side.

"Drive, Eddie," Mama hissed at him. He stared at the growing crowd and kept blowing the horn. "Close the door, Eddie, and drive."

Wina groaned loudly next to me. "I'm gon be sick," she whimpered.

I alternated between holding my belly and stopping my ears with my fingers. Mama got out, went around to his side, and closed his door. She got back in and turned the key from her side.

A redheaded man with a sweet face inched tentatively toward us. "Y'all need some help? You stuck in the mud? Low on gas?"

Mama slammed her own car door behind her. "Eddie, you drive this car now," she said.

Still blowing the horn, Daddy pulled away, a feral gleam in his eye.

Mama turned to us in the back two rows. "All right now, everybody. Le's all just calm down cause—"

"But we gon be sick," Necie wailed. "*Real* sick, cause we was almost through."

"Listen to me. God knows you forget sometimes and thass all right long as you right quick say your verse. You only get sick when you don bless your food and you know durn well you shoulda. So let's quick everybody say they verse."

She turned to Daddy. "Eddie, whyn't you—" He sped up a little and the car fishtailed.

"I know," Mama recovered. "Dorothy, you start."

"Jesus wep'."

"OK, now you, Debbie."

"The Lord is my shepherd, I shall not want. He maketh me—"

"Good! Now you, Wina. Sit up straight, that's right."

Wina struggled herself upright and puked in both directions like a lawn sprinkler, drenching me and Necie. I looked down at myself, over at my sisters. Necie's eyes met mine, and we puked in unison. Mama faced forward again and slumped in her seat.

"Eddie," she said, her voice drained. "Pull off so we can find a Laundromat."

I read aloud every sign we passed. Miserable I certainly was, but I still needed to be the first to find the Laundromat.

"'Bakery.' 'Joe's Auto Body.' 'Benjamin Franklin.' Hey. There it is, 'Wash-a-teria.' Daddy. Daddy?"

He and Mama exchanged looks. The car never slowed.

"Whites only. What that mean?" No one answered. "Aint we gon stop?" Still nothing.

Then, I got it. Our clothes were colored, not white. Had we used that place, our clothes would have faded.

Daddy finally spotted a lake and pulled over. Mama stripped us, squatted on the bank, and rinsed our clothes out by hand. Daddy smoked in squint-eyed silence.

He surveyed the bucolic meadow we occupied as if planning its invasion. When he seemed to have finished committing the area's topographic features to memory, he settled back to blow smoke rings.

"After the fighting was over on Okinawa," he began, apropos of nothing, "we start agitatin for better rations. Lord God was we sick of them canned goods. So, the CO—a white boy but one a them with fire in the belly—he sent us on down the road to the Air Corps boys. You know what them white boys said to us? 'No. This here meat for white folk' and for us not to get no fancy ideas just cause a the war. So, we jes goes back to camp. Empty-handed." He paused for a moment, cleared his throat.

"So, anyway, the major see us without the meat and don'chou know he spit on our boots! 'Marines. Don't. Lose.' As loud as he could yell it. When he said 'lose'? He sucker-punched each and every one of us. Then he tol us to get outta his sight, like he was sicka tha stomach.

"We went back and took that place apart. Tore up every quonset in they camp and took all they food!"

By this time, he was pacing back and forth along the bank, our eyes riveted to him. His pace slowed and he stood staring back down the road we'd come along, that same feral gleam in his eyes. I had no doubt he was visualizing a horizon in flames.

"Marines. Don't. Lose." He barked it confidently, like a password or a secret code. As if magic portals might open and mounted warriors lunge forward to do his bidding. Then, turning on a dime, he began again.

"Another time, we was on pass back stateside when—"

The sun went down while Mama scrubbed our clothes on a rock by a lake and Daddy brayed defiant warrior stories at a town that didn't even know he existed.

THE MAN OF THE FAMILY

Since the home we grew up in was strict and fundamentalist Protestant, it was also strictly patriarchal; our father ruled with an iron fist. So, given both those circumstances, my brother was treated by us women—by my mother especially—like a young prince.

In addition to being the baby, Bobby was a beautiful child. He had a baby's lisp, thick curly hair, and long eyelashes. He was so attractive he was often mistaken for a girl. From the moment of his birth, Bobby was special. Because he was the baby, because he was to be the last of us, because he was so beautiful—but mostly because he was a boy.

In our world of fundamentalist sharecroppers, nobody bothered to deny the double standard of male privilege. That would have been like denying the double standard of white privilege. Sex roles were presumed to have been ordained by God. Men had to work if they wanted to be thought of as men, but once the workday was through, so was their toil. For women, once the workday was through, their night jobs began at home; few could afford to be housewives. When my father made it home after a grueling day in his truck, he disappeared to tinker with his junk in the basement or in the backyard, Bobby with him.

My mother's day started anew when she came home. Fortunately for her, she had five daughters. By the time I could reach the stovetop, I was making meals for eight. Each Sunday, I dismembered and fried a minimum of two chickens, as many as five if relatives were expected; I had burn marks up and down my arms from splattering grease that didn't fade until my teens. Even so, I volunteered for extra duty, racing to beat my sisters to tasks, redoing work that had not been done to my satisfaction. The more work I did, the more approval I got, so I did all I could.

Given the Marine Corps standards by which the house had to be kept, there was more than enough work for us girls. Daddy's job was mainly to exist as a disciplinary threat. He was responsible for mechanical maintenance but such work proceeded at whatever pace he deemed appropriate; there was no questioning his decision that the grass wasn't long enough yet, or to leave the car up on blocks for weeks, or to let the roof leak until he happened upon some building materials at a job site. In any particular room of our house, the walls were part wallpaper, part paneling, part paint, and in all the different colors of the rainbow based on whatever my father found as he scoured the streets of St. Louis. Our embarrassment meant nothing to him, except, of course, as proof of our unfitness for such a cruel world. But if dinner was late, or a floor dirty, our female souls were in mortal peril.

These were community-wide standards, but my father took this further than most. He saw waste and disorder, no matter how minor, as directly related to sin and damnation. A poor, uneducated black man in 1960s America, he patrolled his home, his one area of power and authority, with constant vigilance. Whatever Mama might have thought, she backed him up; throughout my childhood, she promised to haunt me if I ever kept a dirty house, just as her mother had her. Murder? All right, just be sure to clean up thoroughly afterward.

So, we swept clean floors and scrubbed trash cans which never knew trash for longer than an hour between emptyings. If Daddy found potato peelings that were too thick, or a "filthy" container (one which had not been rinsed clean) in the kitchen trash can, there'd be hell to pay. Gone in a flash was the man who made funny shaving faces and let us swing from his biceps; he had been replaced by the humorless white-gloved inspector who determined our worthiness by our cleanliness. And to answer back, even in jest, especially in jest, would signal a disrespect that was not tolerated among God-fearing folk.

But if we were lucky, if we could all manage to seem chastened enough, we'd get off without a whipping. Though he would not shirk from what he saw as his duty, Daddy preferred to leave his daughters' punishment to our mother, usually confining himself to thunderous sermons and a swat on the back of the legs. In any case, it did not take us girls long to understand how to avoid his whippings: abject, energetic submission. Another community-wide standard carried to an extreme by a man desperate to feel himself in control.

There was so much to be done that as soon as Bobby had enough manual dexterity, we put him to work. It seemed only fair; since he was the only one (besides Daddy) not required to do housework, he was the only one who made messes. We'd certainly known it was he who thoughtlessly put unrinsed cans and the telltale (too thick) potato peels in the trash; we knew better. When we bent Daddy's rules, we did so with all the stealth of escaping slaves following the North Star. So we determined to train him, as we'd been, and keep Daddy joking and peace in the house.

When Mama found Bobby performing some household task I'd delegated to him, she simply called him to her and sent him indulgently on his way. As soon as she turned her back, I put him back to work. I didn't yet understand the full extent of gender stereotyping. I understood that Daddy didn't do housework and was never in the kitchen for longer than it took to eat and critique our labors, but I thought that was because he was Daddy. I didn't understand that it was because he was male. At least I didn't until he came home and found five-year-old Bobby standing on a chair placidly washing dishes with a large towel covering him from chin to Keds.

I was cleaning the refrigerator, my back to the sink, when Daddy came in. I hadn't even heard him.

"What on God's green—" It was the incredulous disbelief in Daddy's voice that got my attention.

"This a dress? You wearing a dress, boy!" I turned and saw him holding Bobby by the shoulders, shaking him and staring in disbelief at the towel flapping around him.

Bobby didn't say a word, his face devoid of understanding.

"Boy, whachou think you doin acting like a li'l girl! I won't have it, swear fore God I kill you fore I see you like this."

Thank God Mama appeared from somewhere. All I could think was that I was the one who'd made him do the dishes.

She pried Bobby loose from Daddy's grip. Bobby still hadn't made a sound, though he wrapped himself around her like a garden vine.

"Johnnie, I won have that boy actin like a girl." Daddy's eyes had that narrow glint.

I spun back around to scrub the refrigerator at top speed, terrified he'd vent his steam on me. Mad as he was now, he would fulminate for at least a half hour while I would have to stand in feigned awe and humility, praying it wouldn't end with a whipping. Thankfully, he followed Mama and Bobby out of the kitchen, still bellowing.

After that, I noticed Daddy eyeing Bobby quietly for long minutes, as if seeing him anew. He took him for frequent haircuts to downplay its curly voluptuousness; he growled and ground his teeth at Bobby's lisp; he bit the head off anyone unfortunate enough to mistake him for a girl in his hearing. Bobby couldn't play with us at all anymore; if Daddy found him even in the same room where we played with dolls or cleaned, he'd thunder at him to come away. Confused, we'd watch Bobby scamper away and disappear with Daddy to hunt or use tools. We wouldn't even let him carry his own dishes to the sink, a mere two feet from the table, for fear Daddy wouldn't like it.

From the age of ten or so, at family events, I began to notice the same sort of sexual divisions: the males lounged while the females cooked and cleaned with babies on their hips. Girls got reprimanded for the most minor breaches of decorum; the boys had significantly more leeway. At one of our backyard cookouts, a gang of male cousins destroyed our backyard swimming pool with firecrackers. One of Daddy's finds, the mangy pool was on its last legs, but still, they made it unusable. At the same time, a bunch of girl cousins were cleaning up in the kitchen. A spontaneous dishtowel volleyball game broke out. All we were doing was swatting it around and laughing; we knew better than to break anything. Mama fussed at the boys; she hit us girls. Even when we got into coed mayhem, the girls were "supposed to know better" and, at a minimum, lectured, while the boys were shooed away indulgently. I noticed all these things, but didn't have the imagination to consciously resent them any more than I consciously resented whites or our inner-city cloister; it didn't occur to me that these were things that could be changed.

I thought Bobby was special, too, simply because he was a boy; I also wanted to help him stay out of trouble. I was jealous of my mother's special affection for him, but I was just as jealous of my sisters; vying for her attention was just another of life's inconveniences. I mothered Bobby as much as Mama did. All us girls did; from the very beginning, he'd intrigued us all with his comedic skills and silly wordplay. In any event, he was just a baby. Just as we'd learned to submit to Daddy's will, we learned to indulge and protect Bobby. And there was peace.

THAT VV SMELL

It was 1967; I was starting the fifth grade. We were on our way to Veteran's Village, a secondhand store where Daddy made us buy most of our clothes. (Except Easter clothes: even for him, these had to be store-bought new or one faced expulsion from the race.) When playing the dozens at school, it was a potent insult to "jone" on an opponent by saying he dressed from Veteran's Village. In reality, lots of kids at Benton wore secondhand clothes, but it was only insulting to look as if one did, wearing ill-fitting or stained and torn clothing. Even so, I preferred having no new clothes to these ragged hand-me-downs from strangers; toys from the roadside were one thing, but this was just too much. On top of everything else, they smelled of that nasty disinfectant they sprayed everything with; this was what usually gave you away at school. Everyone knew the VV smell.

Given Daddy's thrift and bleak outlook on the pleasures of life, my attitude was unacceptable. He loved any kind of salvage operation. He never enjoyed anything much unless he had a story about how little it cost him and what adversity he'd had to overcome to acquire it for free. Were we to seem uninterested and unappreciative at the VV, we could expect at minimum a severe sermon on our ingratitude and how ill prepared we were, blah blah. At worst, a whipping. So we had to move the hangers around the racks with feigned enthusiasm while simultaneously not holding our noses against the disinfectant smell. Eventually, we had to produce about three dollars worth of "new" clothes each or face his unpredictable anger.

As excited as a kid, Daddy attacked the boxes jumbled everywhere and began clearing a path for an aisle. Like his children on Christmas morning, he couldn't stop himself from whistling and holding random boxes up to his ear, shaking them to divine the treasures they contained. He was happy. I watched him scout the room for unexplored piles and cartons to conquer, and thought about how some of the kids called him a "junk man." Looking around me at the tumbled mounds of broken toys and scarred cupboards without handles—most of it *was* junk.

I tried thinking about Oliver Twist and how suffering had ennobled him. But as exhausted-looking women with head scarves and pink curlers dandled wailing babies on their hips and foraged among the shopworn merchandise, I could only remember Oliver's poverty. So I tried to imagine the VV as the Old Curiosity Shop filled with wondrous objects, and the snoring, obese clerk as fragile Little Nell. Wina jostled me pointedly from behind—Daddy was coming. Too late, I noticed that everyone else had finished picking out their annual complement of new school clothes—three skirts, three white blouses, and a pair each of sneakers and church shoes.

Daddy was behind me. I heard him suck his teeth in that way that communicated his annoyance.

"You gotta problem, good sista?" "Good sista" was dangerous, that (and "heathen") was what he called us while sermonizing or whipping.

I forced myself to sound cheerful. "No sir, it jes hard to choose. They so many."

Ever efficient, Daddy held up a brown plaid jumper. There was a crudely lettered price tag attached by a dirty piece of yarn. The jumper cost twenty-five cents. The cents sign was backward.

I hated it.

"'S broke," I said, holding it up by the cheap, flaking chains that connected the front with the back across the shoulders. "See?" I wiggled it a little. The chains came loose and I caught the jumper just before it hit the ground.

"I can fix that," he said, inspecting the chain. "Jes take my pliers to em. Good as new." He grinned; he was happy knowing that the nearly free dress would require labor and tool usage.

"Yes sir," I said, and dutifully draped the dress across my arm. It was important not to sigh, not to give any sign of unhappiness. Suspicious, he was still watching me, so, nonchalantly, I picked the rest of my clothes at random from the next three rows and added them to my load.

"Finish," I said in his general direction, and dropped my new school clothes in our cart.

The shoes were the worst part. For some reason, I was much harder on shoes than anybody else. This pair was expected to last the school year, but by spring the area surrounding my big toes would wear through down to my socks; next, the entire soles would flap free. For weeks, months, Daddy would refuse to buy me a second pair; he said my walk was slovenly and that I just needed to concentrate on doing it correctly.

Desperate, I burrowed down to the bottom of the big refrigerator box the shoes were in and found a pair that seemed barely worn. They were a little too small but I could get them on. With perseverance and practice, I was sure I could stretch them and make it through the fourth grade without my socks showing through. I added the least worn pair of everyday, nonsneaker shoes I could find and dumped my new shoes in the baskets Daddy had commandeered. When he wasn't watching, I ran to the car to claim a window for the ride home and finish *The Old Curiosity Shop.* Hot as it was, I went around and closed all the windows to block out the VV, the smell, the neighborhood.

On the way home, Daddy was feeling good.

"I figger we done saved ourselves at least twenty-five dollars. Shoot, maybe more! Don't make no sense payin full price for the same stuff these fools payin top dollar for down to Sears. All we gots to be is patient."

He shook his fist at the big Sears at Kingshighway and Page as we passed. A car pulled up next to us filled with huge Afros and covered with political posters.

They raised their fists back at Daddy and yelled: "Power to the People." "Capitalism Must Go!"

They had mistaken Daddy's hatred of Sears, and the full prices it represented, for the black power salute. Daddy nearly killed us all trying to catch up with them and give them a piece of his mind.

TROUBLE

By the time I was nine or ten, I knew that our home was not a happy one. The bad times became less isolated events, the good times began to take on the hazy quality of dreams. I can remember us all lingering at the table long after it was cleared, begging Daddy for more stories, more jokes, more silliness on those rare evenings when he was his old self and preening for our approval rather than swaggering jackbooted through our fear. I couldn't have put my finger on exactly when the decay began, but I knew that things were falling apart. I knew it for sure the Thanksgiving I was nine when I walked with Paw Paw to the liquor store (my old granddad pretty much lived on Old Grand-Dad and Kool cigarettes the last twenty-five years of his life). In one of only two or three serious conversations we ever had, he quizzed me about our household, about whether my father ever hit my mother (he did not), and whether or not my mother ever talked about leaving (she did not. Not yet). He wouldn't answer any of my questions, but that settled what had been taking shape in my mind: something was wrong with our family. I didn't have a name for it, I didn't know where we were headed, I just knew trouble was in the air. On top of it all, I had my own problems.

By first grade, I was the designated "brainiac" and good girl. I loved school, I loved teachers, and I loved books. If I didn't exactly love rules, I did accept them as a fact of life and focused on mastering, rather than resisting, them.

If I was kept home with a cold, I'd beg to go to school; if extra credit was offered, I went for it. I was always tracked Group I, always got E's (Excellent), even in conduct and citizenship; and I was never, ever sent to the principal's office. Learning was everything.

It was books that did it to me. In every spare moment, I begged permission to light out for the neighborhood library, grimy and substandard even then but a treasure room to me. I can remember it pulling me, even across full-humidity, scorching St. Louis summer middays. Standing in the foyer looking in at all the books and maps and encyclopedias and microfiche and Dewey decimals, I felt a giddy rush of pleasure.

I was always the star of the reading program: the only name in ink, mine was always first on the bulletin-board rankings. Following it was what looked like an intergalactic explosion. Many stars (all gold, even during my week of chicken pox) followed it; the librarians had given up on neatness and snuggled them in wherever they could.

Hours later, I'd struggle home with my load of hardbacks and fan my new books out in front of me. I'd open each book and sniff the pages. Most of them hadn't been opened in years; these had an intoxicating, loamy smell I craved almost as much as the printed words themselves.

I rubbed my face in them and imagined that undiscovered tombs had this smell, the smell of papyrus scrolls inscribed with the musings of ancients, lost under shifting desert sands. The places I encountered in these books were no less otherworldly to me. Going to the library was like happening upon the keys to the enemy's storehouse. I couldn't believe they just gave them to me.

I would lay the books out alphabetically by title, then alphabetically by author's name, next by publication date (I adored the administrative fine print in books), finally by subject matter. The ritual complete, I solemnly eenie-meenie-miney-moed to see which went first. Back against the door, drunk with anticipation, I'd dive into *The Once and Future King* or *The House of the Seven Gables.* 4933 Terry Avenue slipped farther and farther away.

THE PROMISED LAND

I wanted gifted school so badly I couldn't sleep at night. Much as I loved school, I had come to dislike Benton. The classes had long since ceased to be challenging; the teachers resented me because I corrected them and asked questions they couldn't answer; the other kids hated me. I was such a nebbish, even my own siblings had taken to disowning me in public. But my father didn't want me going to school with whites and my mother opposed busing. She also wouldn't allow me to skip any grades, primarily, I believe, because it offended her sense of order. But I begged and begged and begged.

I wanted that special knowledge to which only whites had access. I knew that if I stayed at Benton, stayed in my neighborhood, I'd only know what whites wanted me to know. If I went to their school, though, I'd know what they knew. This was not a political act. I wasn't concerned that black people in general gain access to this special knowledge. I didn't intend to work for revolution or to help my people or cure cancer. I just wanted more.

In the end, I wore my parents out with my begging. They let me go. I left black north St. Louis and began my many years of long bus commutes. At nine, starting in the fifth grade, I went from an entirely black world to being one of only a handful of blacks, for the first time a practical rather than just a statistical minority. Gifted school was wonderful. Gifted school was awful.

At Wade Elementary, the classwork was as rewarding as I could have hoped; Harvard Law School included, I have yet to have a more intellectually stimulating experience. Early in the fifth grade, Miss Albrecht brought tears of nerdy joy to my eyes. We were studying the Latinate roots of English; without any previous instruction, I was nailing those prefixes and suffixes left and right. When she got to "-ject" and I yelled out "to throw!" we shared a wordless moment of egghead bonding. In front of the entire class, she came over, took my hands, and looked me in the eye. "Young lady," she said, "you are going to learn so many words this year." I accepted that as a blessing. That fifth-grade experience sustains me still.

The problem was spiritual survival. White-girl hair alone nearly made me beg to go back to Benton.

The pressing comb was an implement Mama, a master of the sewing and crochet needles, the spatula, the spoken word, and mechanic's tools of any arcane type, never conquered. She'd never "had" to use one either on herself or her two eldest daughters, but Wina, Necie, and I had thick, unruly "bad" hair that left her perplexed and our ears and necks scabbed.

Worse than the pressing comb was the actual process of washing our hair. We had neither a shower nor shampoo (unless Daddy found some), so we washed our hair with bar soap in the sink. Conditioner, like lotion, was a white folks' luxury I never even heard of until my mid-teens. So my hair was a bushy, tangled mess nearly impossible to comb unless I was clamped, howling, between Mama's legs. We lost enough hair in the process to make wigs for a whole chemotherapy ward. She'd put my hair in pickaninny braids because it took a full day for my mangy mop to air-dry, during which time I couldn't leave the house because of my shameful braids. Woe betide the girl who tried to press damp hair—it sizzles and fries like bacon.

Finally, when it was dry, we got to sit in a kitchen chair next to the stove while Mama slathered on more Vaseline and dragged a heavy metal comb, red-hot from lying in the gas burner, through it, essentially frying our hair. Like most of my generation, I spent my girlhood with burns on my forehead, ears, and the nape of my neck. The least moisture makes African-type hair shrink and shrivel, so often after only one sweaty day's play in the humid air, it would "go back" to its natural state. Rain was my fiercest enemy. Fat, tangled, nappy roots swelled and bulged and made me hate myself. This battle black women fight with our hair is a large part of the reason why so few black women over the age of thirty can swim—chemical relaxers had yet to be invented and we simply would not subject ourselves to the public humiliation of nappy hair.

Washing and pressing my hair was a childhood trauma I still shiver over. I learned to hate it when the white kids at school would sniff the air and try to trace the source of the smoky smell while their own hair wafted on the breeze. I didn't hate them. I hated that part of us that was so deficient as to require the application of fire. I finally came to fake washing my hair. I'd just dip my two or three braids in water, maybe lather them up a little with soapsuds, then let Mama press my filthy, soap-scummy hair. But my hair, our hair, was only one of the many things to be ashamed of. My big, fat nigger nose. Ugly, gnarled nigger toes. Blackened elbows and knees. The ashiness that threatened to envelop my entire body unless I coated myself with Vaseline every moment, it seemed. I envied the women of Saudi Arabia those handy veils they wore. Being deprived, I had to settle for long sleeves, closed shoes, and knee-length skirts regardless of the weather. A hand to cover my smile and the spreading nigger nose it produced. Habits I couldn't break until my thirties.

I learned many things at Wade. The first was that I was poor. The second, that I was low class. I learned that some mothers stayed home and that some fathers wore suits to work. It turned out that not everyone wore used clothes from Veteran's Village. Some folks didn't even roll in the aisles at church and scream at Jesus.

I learned to marvel at how multifaceted a thing it is to be poor; it's much, much more than the mere absence of money. I heard snatches of conversations about summer science camps, I heard parents lay out their children's progress ten, fifteen years into the future. Mine never discussed the future except to hope that things would be generally better then: poor folks can only afford the present tense. I'd known that the middle- and upper-class lifestyle was book true, TV true . . . but in real life people ate in fancy restaurants, took European vacations?

I also learned that I didn't really speak English.

During a boisterous classroom discussion that first year, someone said something with which I heartily agreed, so I blurted out, "Sho nuff!"

The black kids froze, mid-laugh, and sealed their faces off. The whites giggled and scooted around in their chairs to pinpoint the source of the funny words.

The teacher laughed appreciatively. "Who's the li'l ol' Southern honey chile?" she mock-drawled.

I collapsed into myself and sunk down into my seat. I never admitted to having sho-nuffed, though all the other blacks knew. "That was real black, heifer," one said to me at recess.

Saying "sink" in the neighborhood made me an Oreo. "Zink" at school made the white teachers patient with missionary zeal. "'Tin' is a metal, dear," our English teacher said in front of the whole class while I stood wishing to die. "If you're referring to the number that comes after nine, it's pronounced 'ten.'" One day, we black kids would chastise each other for using black English, the next day for not using it. A quick dictionary check, to me, settled the matter.

I began to cringe when elders spoke of the "horse-pital" or preferred "the new-monia" to the infinitely worse "old-monia," which would make you as crazy as the "bessie bugs" I could find nowhere in the encyclopedia. I tried not to grimace when my mother opened the "winder" or threw the rotten "poke chop" in the "ga'bage." Once, when an earache earned me her rare full attention, my moment in the sun was ruined when she asked "which un?" I began to correct my elders; having Mama slap my face on the spot of the transgression broke me of that habit. Street fights cured me with my peers. So I kept my knowledge to myself and wondered why people wouldn't rather know. I thought I was helping.

But at some point, I discovered that I could wield my knowledge like a sword when needed. One day, I had again been chased home from the special bus for "talkin all proper and thinkin you's better than erbody." This had happened nearly every day for the first few weeks of Wade; that day, my mother locked the screen door against me and forced me to face them. During the preliminary "dozens" session, I claimed the power of my special knowledge.

Usually, the neighborhood understanding that anyone who wanted to fight a Dickerson had to fight all of us seriatim was enough to stop a disagreement at the name-calling stage, but Rochelle, Queen of Group III . . . she was a special kind of tough. Once, the year before, I'd kicked at her dismissively from a foot away when she called me "fatso." She'd caught my foot and hopped me around the schoolyard one-legged for a week. Knowing that I would have to fight her, no matter how well I acquitted myself in the "dozens" preliminaries, tinged my words with hysteria.

I began with a promise to "reduce her head to lowest terms." I opined that her mama's head was biiiiiig, really, really big. As a matter of fact, her hat size was 10 to the twelfth power. It was so big, it was "bullish on America." I pointed out to Rochelle that since she had so little idea of who her father was, when he died, he'd have to be buried in the Tomb of the Unknown Daddies.

Afire, I let loose with a brier patch of French nouns, names from Greco-Roman mythology, and elements from the periodic table adjectivized and anthropomorphized into a venom that surprised even me as it spewed forth willy-nilly from my frightened fury. Gobbledygook for the most part, but it served its humiliative purpose. The crowd was mine. I still had to fight, but Rochelle's blank face had admitted defeat in the preliminaries and the crowd had to support me and my lethal tongue. It also took the gusto out of her assault on me; she just smacked me around a little, then wandered off to the crowd's catcalls. This experience was so successful, I repeated it over and over until I could verbally ice any potential opponent. No one wanted to face me in a verbal joust, but everyone wanted to watch me eviscerate someone, so potential opponents took the long way around. Soon, I had what I wanted: invisibility. I was safe. Safe, but completely separate.

It's hard to say which had more to do with my isolation—my special schooling or my self-imposed physical distance. My mother used to have to order me outside to play. She'd send me outdoors, only to knock me flat onto the back porch when she opened the door to hang out the wash; I'd be leaning back against the door reading a book, technically outside but as close as possible to the safety of the house.

When I tried to be a part of neighborhood goings-on, I floundered. St. Louis was firmly racially segregated in those days. Perversely, Jim Crow functioned as a kind of social shorthand for blacks then; it filled in the gaps of nearly any social situation. Our civic and social options were so few, knowing where someone lived told you just about everything you needed to know about that person. So, my living at the corner of Terry and Kingshighway but not going to Benton with everyone else made me strange. More than that, it made me suspect. I was a dropped stitch in the fabric of black St. Louis life; I kept tripping everyone up.

Meanwhile, at school I was just as much on the fringes as in my own community. We blacks in the gifted program were like Cinderella at the ball; the party was over when our special bus arrived to whisk us back to the ghetto. Our inclusion in the mainstream only lasted the duration of the school day and within the confines of the school building. We "bused kids" were not allowed off the school grounds before or after school nor during lunch. Because of the logistical difficulties of having students from all over the city, there were few after-school activities; even when there were, my father forbade me to associate with whites beyond my schooling. So I spent those years alone with my books, increasingly mad at the world—and increasingly fearful of my father.

One morning, sometime after I started at Wade, I was scrubbing the kitchen table. Since it was already clean, as everything else in our house was required to be at all times, my strokes were overbroad, leaving wide, unwiped swaths visible among the wet streaks.

Daddy chuckled. "Girl, you won't never make no good waitress."

"'S OK by me, I don wanna be no waitress," I rejoined.

"Watch that tone, good sister. See that stain right there? Why you leave that there, 's triflin."

"But, sir, 's under the surface. It been there forever; it aint gon come out." I'd wiped this table often enough to know.

He sucked his teeth and took a disgusted breath. "When I was on Parris Island . . ."

Not boot camp again.

". . . they had us digging foxholes just before we was to ship out for Okinawa. It was about two hundred degrees and 700 percent humidity, so, way we dug em, them foxholes was only yea deep. We was goin off to fight the Japs in two days, we figure, what else can happen to us now? Drill sergeant tryin to make us understand how deep them holes need to be, so they can protect us. We figger we just wait till Okinawa to get em deep enough. So, OK, drill sergeant says. Fine. Them holes jes fine. Now get in em, he say, so we do. Bless God if drill sergeant don start drivin his jeep right over our holes. Right over our heads! Since I'm right here talkin to you, I guess you believe I got my foxhole nice and deep fore drill sergeant got to me."

"But, Daddy, cu'nt folks a got hurt?"

He slapped the slick tabletop. "And aint that just the very point." He barked, "If we'da done it right the first time, nobody wudda got hurt, would they a? Them that did had it comin. You think the Japs cared about how tired we was? How scared we mighta been? Erthin aint no picnic, good sister."

"Yes sir; you right, erthin aint no picnic," I soothed before he could get worked up to full sermon steam. "'S just that I rather not be a waitress if you don mind."

"OK, Miss High-Seditty, jes what is it you think you gon be?"

"A lawyer," I bluffed. My aspirations changed with every book I read and I'd just finished *To Kill a Mockingbird.*

Halfway through an inhalation of Belair smoke, the absurdity of this caught Daddy by surprise. He doubled over laughing.

"A lawyer, eh? Girl, don't you know you's Negro? You think the white folks calling you 'gifted' or all that book-readin change that?" Still chuckling, Daddy left me alone with my chores.

I got mad—and then I got worried.

Daddy was the first person to tell me I couldn't do something because of my race, but I took it personally. I thought he meant I couldn't do it because I was *me,* Debra Dickerson. Who should know better than he what I was and was not capable of? And I, the fragile little fifth grader just beginning to test her own limits, believed him; it occurred to me for the first time that some things, important things, might just be beyond me.

Later, I came to understand that he both expected and needed blacks to fail, otherwise there was no proof of white perfidy and soullessness. He never understood that his fatalism was a self-fulfilling, self-defeating prophecy. He never considered that he had to believe, at some level, that whites were superior since he believed blacks had no chance whatsoever in life—but probably, he would have attributed that to the transcendent power of whites' innate evil. Among ourselves, we say "the white man's ice is colder" to describe the many of us who won't believe or value anything unless it comes from white people. The worse off some blacks are, the more magical whites seem, albeit an evil magic.

So my father, like many other blacks, did the oppressor's job for him; he taught me to do the same. This was the moment that I began to close doors on myself. Perhaps whites would have been happy to take that task on themselves, but they rarely had to. Whites didn't have to place barriers in my path, I did it myself by "accepting" my preordained place at the end of every line. Racism and systematic inequality are very real forces in all our lives, but so is fatalism and a perverse exaltation of oppression.

I attended Wade Elementary School seething with the knowledge that doing so would have no bearing on my future. Illogically, but implicitly, I saw my presence there as merely one of an invited observer soon to rejoin her proletarian peers. My homeroom and math teacher did everything she could to fortify this belief in me.

Miserable and an inveterate daydreamer, I'd tune out repeatedly during class, lost in my own imaginings. As soon as I did, she'd pounce on me. I could catch up on my own in English, French, and history. But math . . . She'd send me to the board and heckle me as I struggled to concentrate. Whether I knew the answer or not, I'd just stand there facing the board till she sent me back to my seat. Eventually, she told me there was no point in my attempting the work and that I, along with her other designated math dummies, could just read a book while the others did problems. But look on the bright side, she'd say, you'll make a fine secretary some day. When our Iowa Basic Skills Test scores came back, she called us to her one by one to show us ours. She preened like a whorehouse madam over Tracey Nash, the latest in a long family line of high-yellow doctors, and Nevels Scott, the son of black engineers. While I stood beside her, in front of the class, she expected me to laugh with her at my low spatial-relationships score. Don't pout, she said, secretaries don't need to understand these things.

I had a lot to think about as I emptied trash cans with Mama at her second job. I thought and thought as I perfected the arts of frying chicken, mopping floors, and anticipating others' needs. I was an honor student adept at crooning "yes sir" with just the perfect amount of placidity while inwardly I boiled.

Little did I know what good training those skills would be for the next twenty or so years of my life.

THE BAD YEARS: THINGS FALL APART

What made the situation at home a powder keg for me was my introduction of "the white man" through my education and far-flung reading. What made this situation a powder keg for the entire family was the simple act of our growing up.

As his teenage wife and adoring moppets grew into autonomous individuals, my father must have felt himself minimized and second-guessed at every turn—especially by me and by the timid wife who turned out to be every bit as capable as he was.

Before he frightened me into silence, we used to have after-dinner debates the way others had after-dinner mints. I once argued with him that the Fourteenth and Fifteenth amendments guaranteed equality of treatment for all, and therefore, there was no discrimination. He almost had an aneurysm but he couldn't convince me it wasn't so. It was written in black and white and if I couldn't trust books, I couldn't trust anything. Even my mother, who rarely railed against the system, lost patience when I refused to acknowledge the existence of either discrimination or disadvantage. All I knew was, blacks were free and equal because it said so on paper. I wasn't smart enough then to follow that thought through to its logical conclusion—so why were we so much worse off as a group?

What I didn't factor in until I was a grown woman was what must have been going on behind closed doors between my parents. What happened between them is their story to tell, so I can't say which came first—his ever-tightening grip on his family or the deterioration of their marriage—but the result was the same for us all. The shy, nineteen-year-old bride's development of the Gooch rapid-fire wit did not help matters. Soon, the simplest things would set him off and his unpredictability made our home a prison camp.

"Why you need erthing to be so hard, Eddie?" I heard my sad mother ask him once after he'd put us all through some unnecessary hardship, like keeping us home from a party or refusing to make a repair which would add to our comfort but not our character.

Apparently, he was unfamiliar with the concept of the rhetorical question, because he answered her, albeit with a non sequitur. He told her, with prim righteousness, that she was going to hell. The Bible said women were supposed to act a certain way and he had firsthand knowledge that she, in fact, did not. His real fear, as a concerned father, was that she was putting his daughters' mortal souls in peril with her heathenish example.

Mama gasped.

"Eddie," she finally said, "I know bout how the husband and the wife spozed to be as one and all—but why is it we always got to be you?"

Daddy stormed off to his basement and stayed there for nearly thirty minutes while we waited at the table. As he well knew, no meal could start without him.

The next morning, Saturday, he woke us at 6 A.M. with a drill sergeant's cold purpose, as had become his practice over the last few months. From the early morning, we girls were required to clean without ceasing until the late afternoon. This, in a house which was never allowed to be dirty. He wouldn't even allow us to listen to the radio while we worked because "this aint no party." Jeeps rumbled overhead.

He passed by on an inspection sweep whistling "Precious Lord, Take My Hand." It was one of my favorite hymns, so I joined in. Briskly, he stuck his head in and informed me that I, too, was going to hell.

I stopped mid-whistle.

Hell was as real a place to us as our house at 4933 Terry. Daddy was always pointing out people who were going there and I had never doubted either their going or the justice of that disposition. But me? Screaming in agony for all time as I burned but was never consumed in hideous flame?

He recited priggishly:

A whistling woman
and a crowing hen
both come
to a bad end.

His shrug said, Sorry, not my rule.

"I thought hens had to crow," I said stupidly. He seemed so calm about my eternal damnation; I was more disturbed by his easy abandonment of me than anything else.

He was quickly exasperated. "Y'all don't never learn nothin in the country. Roosters. 'S roosters that crow. Males. Women got they jobs and men got they's. Decent women don't whistle. Just like they don't cut they hair, wear pants, or answer back. 'S mannish. The Bible say."

Bored with cleaning, this caught my fancy. I loved indices, tables of contents, appendices, footnotes, encyclopedias, almanacs, dictionaries, atlases—I adored fact-checking. When the ministers gave chapter and verse in church, I raced the old ladies around us to find it first. Daddy had always been proud of that. I wanted to track this down, too. I accepted everything I read at face value and knew women were second-class citizens. It didn't occur to me to object to this stricture; I did, however, want to see it in print. Old Testament or New? I wondered. Knowing my Daddy, it had to be Old.

So I asked him, "Where?"

His lips thinned.

I was "quizzin" him, calling him a fool. He turned on his heel and left. Nastily, I thought to myself: At least I won't be lonely in hell; Mama'll be with me.

It was well into the afternoon and we'd been cleaning nonstop. Since he was so stealthy, it was hard to know exactly where he was in the house. He was always sneaking up on us, poking his head through doorways and appearing from corners to keep us off-balance. He'd appear on top of us from a shadow and exult in our gasps and frightened exclamations. Then, he'd say something like "Had I a been a sniper, you be dead." After all, there was no one else to use for target practice.

Bored with my dustrag, my mind wandered to the new book I was reading. I tiptoed over to flip through it; I never meant to actually read it right then. But somehow, I found myself stretched across my hospital-cornered bed, lost in *Little Women*.

The next thing I knew, Daddy's razor strap had me pinned, whimpering and disoriented, to the covers. The whole time, he kept up the question-and-answer session with which every African-American of my generation is so familiar.

"Didn't . . . I tell you . . . [WHAP] . . . to . . . [WHAP WHAP] redo those mirrors?" WHAP!

"Yes sir . . . [WHIMPER] . . . you told . . . [WHIMPER] . . . me you . . . [BLUBBER] . . . told me."

WHAP. "Next time . . . [WHAP] . . . you gon . . . do . . . [WHAP] what I say . . . ?" WHAPWHAPWHAP.

CRINGE. "Yes . . . [WHIMPER] . . . sir."

"I [WHAP] know [WHAP] you aint [WHAP] crying. [WHAP] Shut up that [WHAP] . . . noise . . . [WHAP] fore I give you [WHAP] . . . something to cry . . . [WHAP] . . . about!"

Silly me. I thought you just did.

I flooded my mind with a million similarly caustic one-liners to stop myself from crying. It was imperative to stop because he'd beat me as long as I cried. Why? Because he'd told me to stop.

We cleaned pretty much straight through until dinner with a lunch break only long enough for a peanut butter and jelly sandwich. I was starved. My stomach rumbled and gurgled through Daddy's blessing. There was grape Kool-Aid, fried chicken, black-eyed peas with cornbread, and fresh tomatoes from our garden, my favorite meal. Mama was trying to cheer us up after a day in the salt mines. More hungry than neurotic for once, I opted for simplicity. So, when Daddy finished, I lowered my standards and mumbled a fairly commonplace "Come unto Me, all ye that labor and are heavy laden, and I will give you rest": overused and less than a tenth of my usual performance but still probably twice as long as anything anyone else was going to say. It was "Jesus wep"'s all around. I won.

Daddy began lecturing on the evils of white people—how they couldn't sleep at night unless they'd harassed somebody that day, how deep down in their hearts they knew other folks were just as good, if not better. That was what kept them so mean and hateful all the time. I understood that by "white people" he meant the rich and powerful, the college-educated, the movie stars, and, by all means, the Jews—the haves, in other words—not just the merely Caucasian. "Other folks" really meant the poor, the sickly, the workers of the world: the have-nots.

Something in the paper had set him off. He screeched his chair back from the table and thumped the paper down in his lap. He began tearing through it and shouting about how, if a white man manages to blow his nose, they quick run out and put him on TV. He held up a random picture filled with whites as if written above their heads by the finger of God was the word GUILTY! We shammed studying it intently, non sequitur that it was. Humoring him was our only hope of returning to a quiet dinner. But he'd already whipped himself up into a class-based, race-enhanced frenzy.

Waving a portion of the paper over his head, he shouted, "I dare you to show me colored folk in any of these fancy pictures!"

He flung the paper down so it landed just off to my side on the floor. The advertisement section opened to an ad featuring four women; three white, one black. The sister was right up front.

I looked down at it for a nanosecond too long. I knew when I raised my head that Daddy would be staring me down. I said nothing, kept my face blank. Looking away might well be considered back-talking. I held my breath and held his gaze, trying to look as stupid as possible. Forks clinked faster and faster against our VV plates. No one spoke. Finally Mama cleared her throat and sent me upstairs to make sure there was toilet paper in the bathroom.

I stretched out on the floor for as long as I dared. Bleak as my immediate future was, I enjoyed knowing that, for once, no one would bang on the door and invade my privacy. I did what I always did when I managed to be in a room alone back then; I recited passages from the books I loved. Dickens was my current favorite. I recited the beheading scene from *A Tale of Two Cities,* just to make sure that the good twin's bravery would still bring tears to my eyes even as I faced my own angry mob. It did. I went back to dig my way out of that half-assed foxhole I'd dug.

When I returned, Daddy looked calm. I sat silently for a minute in case he had something to say, then resumed eating. Or tried to. My fork was gone. For a comically long time, I looked around for it on the floor, even though I knew where it had to be.

For the rest of the meal, he never looked at me. He made chirpy small talk to which everyone responded with extreme caution. They needn't have worried; he was charming. Even so, when he reached past me for the cornbread, Bobby flinched. I watched my fork there on the far side of his plate with my hands in my lap.

After he'd finished eating, he did what he always did: with the last of Mama's homemade biscuit, he scraped the last morsel of food away so the plate looked scoured clean even before washing, then began chain-smoking neat piles of Belair cigarette ashes into it. He held forth on the stupidity of every person he'd come into contact with that day. Across from him, Mama gazed somewhere through and beyond the window behind him. Though she seemed far away, as each of my siblings made it furtively known that they wanted to leave, she nodded permission. Finally, just the three of us were left. Without one clever thought in my head, I did what I had to. I let the tears roll down my face.

Sometimes you had to stop crying. Sometimes you had to start. His call.

"Clean up this kitchen and git to bed," he said, and left.

My stomach roared with hunger. My tears disgusted me. I wanted to slam a door or throw something at the wall. I squeezed my eyes shut and pictured myself answering Daddy back with big words he wouldn't understand, but my fantasy's very dreamlike quality made it just that much more frustrating. Dangerously, I tossed a plate from hand to hand and made faces at the hallway, knowing I'd never have the nerve to drop it. Daddy would see that for what it was: defiance. At the best of times, a broken dish would earn you a thunderous sermon on your ingratitude and sloth. This was hardly the best of times.

I knew which book I was going to start as soon as I finished with Louisa May Alcott—*The Lion, the Witch, and the Wardrobe*—and I couldn't wait. Reliving dinner again and again, I hated myself for not simply asking for my fork or for not having just gotten another from the drawer. But I'd been too scared. Too scared of what Daddy might do. My anger gave way to confusion. What happened to the zoo-zoos and lollipops? What was I doing wrong that he didn't like me anymore?

Crying and hiccuping, I lifted the dishpan to empty it down the drain just as my knees gave out in a blinding swirl of pain. Dirty, greasy water from the upended dishpan drenched me as the doubled-over extension cord cut into the back of my legs again. Daddy's strong arms pinned my face to the faucet by the scruff of my neck and kept me from falling down. I hadn't heard him coming.

"I'm a give you somethin to cry about," he snarled. "I'm a teach you about back talk if it kills me." His voice was a hiss in my ear.

Ah, tears were such a complicated phenomenon. Tears of submission were acceptable, the proto-lawyer in me had the time to conclude, while tears of sadness and blame were not. I'd better get this right pretty soon or there wasn't going to be much left of me.

Of all the things to be whipped with—bare hands, tree switches, belts, hairbrushes, razor straps—extension cords were the worst. They made a sickening whistling sound as they whipped toward your bare flesh which, no matter how you steeled yourself, squeezed agonized, anticipatory moans from you. When it landed, it cut a strip of skin away and seared the very air from your lungs. The sting of an extension cord robbed you of all coherent thought except this lone sentence: I cannot survive this. It left painful welts that took as much as a week to heal; they were visible for far longer. Females could not wear pants to school in those days, but even if you could, you could not bear the pain of cloth touching the welts. Tights were a special form of torture. When the entire schoolyard is snickering because you have to sit on the edge of your seat, humiliation is a word that just isn't deep enough. In the hood, extension cord whippings were like VV clothes: everyone got them but we all pretended to be unacquainted with them.

The world went white with pain and fury while he used the extension cord on me. I heard Mama yelling something but was never able to make it out. It was probably what she always said when he whipped us:

"That's enough, Eddie. That's enough, Eddie."

He beat me and he beat me and he beat me. Sweat dropped from his face onto the back of my neck and his breathing was ragged. The hand squeezing my throat against the fixtures closed and opened spasmodically. By then, I was clinging to the faucet as if it were a life preserver while the rest of my body bucked and thrashed, unable to escape either Daddy's grip or the cord's reach. I rubbed my face wantonly against the faucet's coolness while colored lights flashed behind my eyelids. I babbled little prayers to it—my smooth metal tether to an unwhipped world—that I only heard once the whistle of the extension cord went away.

"PleaseGod, pleaseGod, pleaseGod, pleaseGod, pleaseGod," I begged, understanding for once the full extent of the humility the preachers were always lecturing about in church. Please God make it stop. I'd left the last three words off, but I was sure He knew what I was talking about.

Daddy dropped both me and the cord as if we suddenly weighed a ton.

"Put that up," he spat. With my face still at sink level, I could only assume he meant the cord I could see coiled up like a sudden snake at his feet.

"Clean yourself up and git to bed like I done told you." His voice shook. Somehow, I found myself standing at the foot of my twin bed. I chose not to remember how long it took me to climb the stairs. A sweltering fall night, Necie was a stone mound swaddled in blankets against the far wall next to her bed. She was whimpering. I had nothing to say to her.

In the center of my bed lay the big family Bible. Behind me, Daddy was saying that I'd done read enough about white ladies in long dresses carryin on. I needed to get right with the Lord, good sista. I had not heard him coming this time either.

Something fell on my sneaker. I looked down and there was the extension cord again. I must have picked it up. I wondered if I'd get in trouble for not putting it back like he said, but he must have melted away.

My neck was excruciatingly sore, but even so I forced my head around to check the dresser top. As I'd suspected, my pile of library books was gone. My legs bloody, my pride gone, I determined to start hiding my books. That way, as long as I hid them well, he could only take them away one at a time. We would soon know if I had inherited the Dickerson stealth.

I struggled into my (too large, one arm shorter than the other) nightgown, moaning and rocking myself like an old lady to finesse the pain. Sleeping bottomless, let alone naked, was indecent, out of the question. Necie's mound never moved. I de-hospital-cornered my bed just enough to slip into it, hit the light switch, and collapsed face first on my thin pillow. I sighed, knowing I'd be awake all night, then cut it off in terror before the sigh could become tears. God help me if I cried again.

I ached for C. S. Lewis, or Dickens. Even a Brontë. Then I remembered the Bible I'd let tumble to the floor. I lay on my stomach waiting for the house to settle. Daddy began snoring within a half hour of my turning out the lights. Within a half hour of that, I heard the mice begin their night's work in the back of our dresser drawers and scurrying along the floorboards.

After Daddy'd snored for a continuous hour, I knew it was safe to get out my flashlight (scavenged from a roadside when he wasn't looking) and start in on the Bible.

I was the first one at the table the next morning, simple enough given that I'd hardly slept. When my turn came to say a verse, I recited all sixty-seven books of the Bible in order. There was an impressed silence. Just as Bobby began "Jes—" I interrupted him and recited them again. Backwards.

Daddy leaned back expansively in his chair once the table was blessed and beamed at me. He lectured my siblings; let "that" be a lesson to them all. The threat in his voice and the pride he took in his handiwork on the back of my legs was clear.

I said nothing. My legs were on fire and I'd woken up with charley horses again; both calves. For the rest of the time we lived with him, I'd wake four mornings out of seven with my calves in a vicious knot.

Through the six hours of church, I kept my head buried in the Bible and ignored Wina when she tried to commiserate with me. Back at home, I lugged the Bible from room to room, trying to find a quiet spot. When we sat down to dinner, I noted that Mama had made Daddy's favorites—deep-fried pork chops, boiled cabbage, butter beans with spicy hot chow-chow, fried green tomatoes from the garden, cornbread and lots of buttermilk to crumble it into. He sat down, rubbing his hands in high good spirits. He blessed the table and I began reciting the mind-numbing lists of names from the second census of the Israelites in the twenty-sixth chapter of Numbers:

> *These were the Israelites who came out of Egypt:*
>
> *The descendants of Reuben, the firstborn son of Israel, were: through Hanoch, the Hanochite clan; through Pallu, the Palluite clan; through Hezron, the Hezronite clan; through Carmi, the Carmite clan. These were the clans of Reuben; those numbered were 43,730. . . .*

I did this for three and a half minutes.

I went on so long at breakfast the next morning, Mama had to wrap Daddy's breakfast for him to take with him. Since I was still sitting on the edge of my seat, I could feel his feet tapping impatiently as I filibustered my family. I orated for another five minutes at dinner—more lists from Numbers. When I finished, Daddy faked a hearty "Amen," his fists clenching and unclenching in confused frustration. The table once blessed, I never raised my eyes from my plate, never spoke again. I only had so much energy.

On the third day, the Bible disappeared. I went across the street to the Reverend's. He was only too happy to give me another one.

On the fourth day, I began with Song of Songs, second chapter, sixteenth verse:

My lover is mine and I am his;
he browses among the lilies.
Until the day breaks and the shadows flee,
turn, my lover,
and be like a gazelle or like a young stag
on the rugged hills.
All night long on my bed
I looked for the one my heart loves;
I lo—

Daddy gasped. That shocked me so, I stopped speaking. Daddy was speechless but powerless to bring down God's wrath by interrupting and disapproving of His Word. I had him right where I wanted him. Daddy, who had probably never read an actual page of the Bible, both dreaded and longed to hear what I would say next. I peeked up from my lowered eyes and saw him breathing through his mouth in abject, but approving, surrender. He was impressed. Bobby began to whimper. Suddenly, I was exhausted. Tonight, at last, I knew I'd sleep.

"Jesus wept," I said.

The next day, after I'd gotten my first night's sleep since the beating, I wore my "new" brown plaid jumper, the one Daddy'd taken his pliers to. Even though it was still too warm for it, it was perfect for hiding the scars on my legs because of its length and the stiff way it belled around me like a hoop skirt. After some practice, I learned to walk so that it never made contact with the backs of my legs. Sitting was torture, given the scratchy corduroy, but sacrifices had to be made. Matched with my longest kneesocks, virtually none of the extension cord marks showed.

As we recited the Pledge of Allegiance, I thought back to breakfast. Daddy might even be proud of the way I'd outflanked him. Confused, angry, sad, and sore, I wanted nothing more than to have things back the way they used to be when I could sit on his lap and watch him laugh. Then I tried to sit down.

My feet were pinned in place. Sometime during the Pledge, the pliered chains had come loose and my dress had fallen off. It was garlanded around my stained white plastic go-go boots with back zippers (only one of which was operational when Daddy'd found them). I stood in the middle of my classroom wearing nothing but a too-small-to-button-below-the-sternum secondhand white blouse, white panties, white kneesocks, and raggedy white boots.

My extension cord scars would be visible to everyone behind me. Since, as the most trusted room monitor with the most gold stars, I sat right up front at the teacher's right hand, everyone could see my criss-crossed legs as I stood there in my hand-me-down underwear, worse than naked. As the tittering washed over me, I could only stand with my face in my hands.

After about a decade, Mrs. Washington, our substitute teacher, came over and draped her white angora sweater around me. Then she took me to the teachers' lounge. I waited there for Mama to come get me.

THE MAN OF THE FAMILY GROWS UP

As we females battled in our own ways against our father, Bobby, four years my junior, began to show scars. At four or five, he would flinch if you reached toward him. At the dinner table, a simple move toward a platter would make him cower, cover his head. He developed bizarre facial tics and a nervous blink that so distorted his face he looked like a tiny stroke victim. He baffled and worried us women, but he infuriated our father. He interpreted all these symptoms as signs of weakness. It never occurred to him that he might be the source.

By six or seven, Bobby was stuttering, cutting holes in the curtains and towels, setting small fires. Even when directly observed, even when he saw you watching him, he'd lie. Soon, he was lying about everything, no matter how minor, terrified that he was in trouble. Speaking directly to him started him shivering and stammering. He was afraid of his own shadow. Daddy just kept trying to toughen him up.

His mortal fear of everything notwithstanding, Bobby exhibited some behavior I now see as desperately defiant. Our father had many ways of cutting us off from the rest of the world; one was to never allow us any money. So, one day when he was about eight, Bobby broke into my father's desk and stole fifty cents. Then he gorged himself on candy. He'd had to gouge the drawer open with a screwdriver; it was completely ruined. When confronted, he stuttered that he'd found the money in the backyard. A "big white man" had broken in and ransacked the desk.

We women never challenged my father in such direct ways. Our skirmishes against him were clandestine. For instance, we'd manipulate him into doing something he wouldn't have done, even though it was necessary, just so he could show us who was in charge. In particular, my response to my father's tyranny was to develop a strongly passive-aggressive streak. I made sure that my defiance wouldn't get me razor-strapped.

In fact, I ensured that my defiance could never be acknowledged for what it actually was. I delighted in finding ways of setting Daddy up to say ignorant things, knowing he'd be too proud to back down. I'd speak as "white" as I possibly could around him, using archaic words mined from the hours I spent lost in the dictionary. I'd answer a sibling in French within his earshot and then grandly translate. It was all I was brave enough for. And in the end, in our very unhealthy Dickersonian way, I "won." He figured out how to keep me mute: he stopped taking away my books. He even brought them home to me whenever he found some, knowing it would keep me occupied and silent. But Bobby just kept making flagrant, doomed gestures that kept him cringing under my father's belt.

It wasn't just my father Bobby felt impelled to defy. We, his sisters, were always running to help him fight the neighbors and strangers he was always at odds with. If one of us fought, we all had to, but the problem was that he was the only Dickerson who ever had to be saved because he was always provoking fights, often with boys much larger than he.

We were always running pell-mell to find him at the center of a group of gawkers, barely defending himself from at least one teenage boy. He'd be taking their punches while keeping up a running stream of mama jokes and personal insults. The crowd was rolling on the pavement at his patter, which would infuriate the bigger boys he was "fighting," and intensify their attack. Invariably, our arrival would disperse the combatants: no boy wanted to hit one of us girls and face Eddie Mack. Also, they knew we Dickerson girls fought like marines and, against boys, would use the sticks and stones that no self-respecting boy could. But Bobby was vilified for having to hide behind his sisters. After his opponents smacked him around, we often would, too, for making us fight all the time. And within days, he'd just instigate a new argument with even bigger boys and take his licks until we got there to both help and humiliate him.

My brother was being trained in his father's image. While Daddy insisted we girls be meticulously trained in women's ways, Daddy set about making my brother a man. Long past the age where we were still getting whippings, my father was still teaching my brother his limits. Unlike us, my brother kept testing him.

But Bobby decided on his own definition of manhood and stuck to it. He went out when told to stay in, he spoke when told to be quiet, he broke nearly everything he touched, his teachers couldn't contain his high spirits—his every move seemed designed to infuriate our father. I thought he was mildly retarded.

But for all this, it was in our sharecroppers' blood to pull together as a family. It was impossible not to feel the pull of that blood when an outsider threatened one of us. It was no less impossible to ignore the call of that blood when the threat was inside our own house. Every whipping our father gave him drove a wedge between us women and Daddy. We knew every whipping the son got was one the daughters had only avoided by biting our tongues and knuckling under. Because we were well-trained, God-fearing Southern Baptist women fresh from the cotton fields, we didn't fight back. That wasn't a reasonable option. We saw no dishonor in living to fight another day whole and in one piece. But times had changed. This was the 1970s up North in St. Louis, not Webb, Mississippi, nor Covington, Tennessee. There was no cotton to pick, no back of the bus, no more Mistah Charlie. We owned our own home, I went to school with white kids. Women were burning their bras and demanding to be heard. We were too old-fashioned for that, but revolution was definitely in the air.

But Daddy was still on Old Testament time. A son stole fifty cents, so the patriarch beat him all over the house. From where we cowered in the attic, we girls could hear my mother calling, "That's enough Eddie. That's enough Eddie. That's . . ." Bobby just kept screaming and running. Afterward, the furniture in nearly every room of the first floor was overturned, upended, scored by Daddy's belt buckle. My cousin Nicky was staying with us that week. She secretly phoned our uncle to come get her and waited on the porch until he arrived.

After that, we were almost completely isolated from the family. We'd been cut off from our friends for a long time. The embarrassing half-paneled, half-painted walls and hand-me-down everything were one part of the problem; the other was Daddy's tendency for mayhem. Once, when we'd thought him away, he'd snuck up on a group of us playing gin rummy, that game of de debil. He passed through, seeming unconcerned. But that was just a diversion. He slipped upstairs, ran back down with his belt, and beat us all. The cousins and neighbors ran, but not us Dickersons. We knew that running was defiance, crying was contradiction. We'd gritted our teeth and took our blows like men, like marines, like Dickersons. No one came to our house after that; we wouldn't have let them if they'd tried.

The whipping Bobby got for the desk caper was a turning point for Mama. Though I'd begged, though her sisters had begged, she would not discuss leaving. What God had joined together . . . But Mama overheard Wina and me laying plans to run away and accepted that it had to end. That she had to leave this foolish, doomed man who could not tell the difference between fear and respect.

In the spring of 1973, while he was away driving his truck, we moved across town to a safe house. Safe, because he wasn't there.

CHAPTER TWO

WHISTLING WOMEN

It was raining the day we left.

It was spring but still early yet, and the last of winter's chill seeped in through the big crack in my bedroom window. Through the connecting door, I could hear Mama moving around. Eyes still closed, my ears strained, but no use. He didn't want to be located. No telling where he was.

Wordlessly, we finished our morning tasks and took the breakfast seats we'd occupied forever, then waited for him to sit so we could eat. Ignoring us, he finished making his lunch, fumbled around at his desk in the hall, spent a few minutes in his basement. His point proved, we sat and waited. Finally, he sauntered back in, sat, and blessed the table.

Sitting to his left, my sister Dorothy said a Bible verse and everyone followed suit clockwise around the table. Then it was my turn. There was a long silence.

My heart was so full of bitterness I thought I might choke. I contemplated speaking from my heart on this last day under his thumb, as I had fantasized about so often. A million things—curses, pleas, memories, confessions, questions, all the things I might have said, all the things I would never say—coursed through my mind. I watched the ever-present storm clouds of his hellish temper gather on his face as I wasted his precious time.

We're leaving, you crazy bastard! I thought, and I knew my eyes were dangerous.

Mama cleared her throat. She was right. I couldn't risk pushing him too far, not today.

"Jesus wept," I said with all the authority I could muster.

Then, all of a sudden, breakfast was over and he was gone. I have been fatherless ever since.

My mother managed pretty well that day for a woman who was dooming herself to eternal damnation. We flew all over the house, my mother, Dorothy, Wina, and I, carting off the few possessions we'd be taking with us. We'd been stockpiling castoffs in preparation for this day. This time, I hadn't minded scavenging through the piles at the VV; now, we had a reason to settle for others' discards. Given the sin she was already committing in leaving her husband, my mother would not compound it by absconding with one whit more than necessary. We left him the furniture, the dishes, the pots and pans, the bedding. The house.

For all my righteous anger, once our labors began I found myself feeling sorry for my father. Then I found myself feeling angry for pitying him. Then I didn't know what I was feeling, just that I felt bad.

I had begged my mother to tell him we were leaving. The thought of my father coming home to a house empty of his wife and children broke my bitter little heart. How could he help knowing the truth, that those he saw himself as protecting had fled him like a pestilence. I knew just how desperate I was to be away from him, and the knowledge that he would know it, too, made me want to howl with sympathy for him.

I couldn't stop imagining what it would be like to walk through the front door that day and find my world turned upside down. So I had pestered my mother, with increasing hysteria, to tell him. I guess I thought that a polite notification would have made our leaving him a mere inconvenience he could have planned his week around. I even lectured her that it was un-Christian, lying almost, to run off while his back was turned. She forbade me to broach the subject again. "You'll understand by and by," she said. As always, she was right.

As the day progressed, I continued to lurch between emotions. Like good little Dickersons, we didn't discuss our feelings or try to comfort each other. We just scurried around avoiding eye contact, each lost in her own private misery, each stoic as hell.

Her arms full of clothes from our clothesline, Mama regarded me strangely as I stood in the middle of the hallway, trying to decide how I felt seeing these walls, these rooms, for the last time.

"You run out of stuff to do?" she asked.

"Look at these walls. He never finish nothin, do he?" I sneered. I had no idea I was going to say that.

Mama followed my gaze around the room. "Huh?"

"Look, there." I pointed at the base of the staircase. "Look at all the mouse holes. Why cu'nt he jes plug em?"

"Debbie, stop," she warned, still confused but figuring it out. Children had no business criticizing anyone, let alone their father.

"Look up, Ma," I said, straining my head toward the watermarked, cracked ceiling. "I guess he jes waitin for the roof to fall right in on us. Triflin."

"Stop, Debbie."

"Triflin. 'Sall he is."

She slapped me. I insulted him again. She slapped me again. I opened my mouth and she turned on her heel, but I followed her, spewing insults. On the trot, she turned and slapped me again, then slammed the kitchen door in my face so she wouldn't have to slap me anymore.

I ran out of steam and lurched back to sadness. That's how Mama found me a few moments later. Sad. I was emptying the hamper, separating his clothes from ours. She found me there at the top of the stairs weeping into one of his work shirts. It was the VV smell his clothes never seemed to lose that got me.

The strain of our escape plan had been nearly unbearable. We were racked with worry and guilt, especially our mother. It all went over Bobby's head; we picked him and Necie up from school and brought them to a new home. He hadn't had to do any work, he hadn't had to bear any guilt, he bore no responsibility. He had no choice. He was eight and I was twelve. Incongruously, he was excited over the new house. He didn't get it; he didn't realize his life had changed forever. All he knew was that he had a cool new bedroom while his sisters had to share the basement. He couldn't fathom our gloom.

Daddy showed up after work and I watched through our new front window as he searched out addresses. He squinted back and forth from the letter in his hand to the house before him, as if a wrong address would bring his family back to him. Eddie Mack looked cowed, something I had never seen before. The look on his face made me drop the curtain and back away. He marched himself in and we stood around mute and agonized; a lifetime spent together and we still had no idea how to reach each other.

Bobby ran around waving a chair in the air in his excitement and broke the dining room chandelier. My father moved automatically to give him a smack, then stopped himself. It was as if we'd been granted asylum in some foreign country where he had no authority. I hovered close to my mother while he was there; even had they been capable of talking, they wouldn't with me present. They couldn't even look at each other; they fidgeted and bobbed from foot to foot and continued failing each other. Twenty-five years of marriage just slipped away from them that day and came to nothing but their six kids, only two of whom—JoAnn, who was across town with her own family, and the inexplicable Bobby—could abide their father.

ON OUR OWN

My mother and I became ever closer in those lean years on her single income. Those years were grim, grim but good. We were too poor to pay attention, but at least there was no fear; we never considered going back, though the privation of those years nearly broke us. It's hard to say which made me stronger: living with Eddie Mack Dickerson or living without him.

My sharpest memory of those years is of watching my mother calculate the bills each payday. Still uniformed, she'd sit at the kitchen table every Friday afternoon clucking fretfully to herself, biting her lips while she rifled through the shopping bag which held our household accounts. She'd organize, then reorganize, the little envelopes with their cellophane windows. Invariably, some bills went back into the shopping bag to be attempted again next time around.

Afterward, Wina and I would head to our little branch bank in the Riverview Circle with a list of money orders. Like many poor people, my mother had no bank accounts except for a frequently raided Christmas club. I'd hand over that list written in my mother's crabbed hand on the back of a receipt or a tear of paper bag and watch the teller roll her eyes heavenward at the tedious prospect of preparing yet another raft of piddling money orders: $10.00, $13.47, $10.00, $18.18,

$22.14, $10.00, $10.00, $10.00. Ten dollars, the minimum payment for most of her debts, was the money order amount most frequently represented on Mama's list.

That sad list of forlorn numbers fascinated me. I still have a pile of them, those scraps of paper bearing the symbols of her toil, of her love for her children. I knew they identified her as a slave. A slave to her job, a slave to debt, a slave to the nearest grocery store. For better or worse, a love slave to her kids.

The early seventies were a time of inflation, recession, and job instability; not a good time for a major lifestyle change. Mama switched from waitressing to a factory job and things improved. Daddy gave us what he gave us and we never asked for more. Then it all fell apart. There was a blur of bad times: her union went on strike, or she was laid off, or she'd had that surgery. Take your pick, each of those occurrences sent us into a tailspin. She waitressed when she could, cleaned offices and homes, but it wasn't enough. With so many out of work, wages were a joke and full-time work unavailable. We started dumping the bills, unopened, into the shopping bag. Wina and I invented the tea and crumpet game then. The only things we could count on eating were tea and toast, fried potatoes, canned pork and beans, or meatless spaghetti. The game was to fill up on Lipton's and toast while reenacting what we assumed was high tea as culled from my reading. We did our best English accents, said "dah-ling" and "rahthuh." This bit of toast became a cucumber sandwich, that one a hot buttered scone. There were free lunches at school and something, if only "tea and crumpets," for breakfast and dinner. Mama would remind us that "you go to sleep, you won't know you hungry." She was right.

In the evenings, we'd huddle together in the kitchen, the only warm room, and talk, crochet, read, do our homework, each other's hair. Since we had nothing but each other, that's what we made use of, especially after the TV broke and we could afford to neither replace nor repair it.

Regardless of all the things we did without, no one complained; we knew there were worse things than hunger or a lack of sitcoms. Charity, for instance. Hard as I argued against it, the day came when Mama and I drove, grim and miserable, to the welfare office. Sick with the shame of it, I told her: "I'd rather starve. The rest would, too." Distracted and sad, she mumbled, "Guess I rather y'all wun't." Forbade to speak further on the subject, I just stewed—but wouldn't let her go to that shameful place alone.

I behaved badly at the welfare office. I sniffed at the other women and their surely illegitimate children. I refused to sit on the germ-ridden chairs. I corrected the English of every social worker who spoke to us. We didn't belong there. Mama was too dispirited to give me the throttling I deserved. And then we were told we were not in financial need.

Stunned, we left without another word. Back in the car, we sat there staring at each other openmouthed, the keys still in Mama's hand. Focused on dealing with the shame of charity—Mama in quiet contemplation, me in feigned contempt—we had not imagined such an outcome.

Simultaneously, we broke into sniggers. They escalated into outright guffaws. We had no idea how we were going to manage until the factory reopened/the strike ended/she recovered from her surgery, but laughing at the absurdity of it all was what we most needed. Since we didn't starve to death, didn't lose the house, didn't die of hypothermia, I guess our beloved civil servants were right. No matter how dire our circumstances after that, never again would we consider public assistance. I was even more contemptuous of welfare recipients after this than I had been before. They couldn't be any worse off than we were and we'd made do "without accepting" handouts, so, I concluded relentlessly, anyone could.

My relief at not going on welfare and my contempt for its recipients coexisted with a subconscious fury at the impersonal government which taxed us but failed to take an affirmative interest in our well-being. Like most poor minorities, my mother had an unexamined fear of the government not unlike her fear of our neighborhood strongmen. She dreaded drawing its attention.

As late as the 1980s, I had to come home on leave to drag my mother to the Social Security office to collect her widow's benefits. She wouldn't be eligible in her own right until sixty-five, and with her peasant's inbred low profile, she just knew the government would find a way to punish her for stepping into its gaze; help for a working-class widow who'd raised five kids alone just seemed too good to be true to her. I couldn't even get her to articulate the fear that cost her nearly a year of benefits. Mama held her breath for months and hoarded the money, waiting for the other governmental shoe to drop. No, we Dickersons didn't fight the power, we sought the shadows. We were oriented toward evading blows, not striking them. It never occurred to us to protest the denial of our benefits. It didn't even occur to us to be angry. We didn't think our good citizenship meant anything; we didn't see ourselves as served by the government, but rather as subservient to it. Taxes, for us, were a form of protection money; all we asked in return was not to be crushed under the bootheel of government. We expected, demanded, nothing, and that's exactly what we got.

Our new home life, compared to what had preceded it, was a haven. Outside it, however, I was still a stranger in a strange land. Every adolescent is, of course, but I had no way of knowing that.

Puberty crushed me. My stinky hair, my electrical-taped glasses, my pizza face, the home I wouldn't allow anyone to see—I was a social outcast at Wade. I hung with the uncool, unbeautiful people. Darlene was fat. Beverly was tormented for coming to school dirty and hungry: they called her "Snow Monkey." Wanda: dark skin, bad hair, bad neighborhood. Karen was a grade ahead but had committed some social faux pas that made her classmates torture her. On the bright side, Valencia was beautiful, stacked, and athletic, but considered "country" because she came from Wanda's same bad neighborhood but refused to be ashamed of it. They'd sneer about the slaughterhouse a block away from her home and the foul fumes it spewed into the air. She'd kick their ass. The voluptuous Valencia brooked no disrespect.

On a field trip once in fifth or sixth grade, Wanda, Beverly, and I were in an alcove looking at an exhibit. Timmy, one of the cool kids, walked in, stopped on his toes in horror, and backed out saying, "Yeech. Wanda, Beverly, and Debra. All in one room." We were geeks and we huddled together for protection. Every school picture showed me with my bangs standing at attention, my nasty braids sticking straight out at ninety-degree angles. When I tried a more sophisticated look—two braids pinned across the top of my head, one in back—invariably, one would spring loose, and point straight heavenward for days before the snickering alerted me. I talked to myself, I walked into walls daydreaming, I developed a slouch-walk that kept my feet from leaving the ground so the soles of my ragged shoes wouldn't flap. I was a mess.

The summer between my seventh and eighth grades, Dorothy couldn't take it anymore. An inveterate glamour-puss even while a rowdy tomboy, she made me over. She put me in an Afro and a hooded two-piece layered-look 4-H pantsuit she'd made à la Thelma on *Good Times*. We dried up most of my zits with undiluted alcohol (praise God, Daddy'd found a case of it). She let me borrow her shoes. I learned to walk like a normal person except that now I walked into walls not only from daydreaming but also because I refused to wear my glasses.

I showed up for the first day of school and the boys' eyes went wide. Girls invited me to their slumber parties. I was cool. I was in. I was disgusted.

I was the same person I'd always been, but now, because of new clothes and a new hairstyle, I was a different person, a person worthy of inclusion. I let Timmy be my boyfriend (how else to torture him for the museum comment?), but just for a little while. Regardless of the cool crowd's disgust, I kept my old friends, my real friends. I knew my forays into uncoolness were dangerous and might slam the door behind me, but I didn't care; it was the only area of my life in which I was brave.

Fraught with anxiety as they were, gender issues were the same for me as they were for everyone else. Racial issues still made me the most miserable—specifically, my relationships with other blacks.

Most activities in those days were neighborhood-based, but local goings-on didn't include me because I spent so much time out of the neighborhood. I missed the boat on the new slang, the new dances. That was just as well because I rarely got to use them. As soon as a boy at a neighborhood party forced me to admit where I went to school, he'd draw back and sneer, "So, you be likin them white boys, huh?"

"Were that the case," I sniffed with the chilly contempt I practiced in the mirror, "would I be here?"

I have always had a misplaced faith in logic. I can see now the flaw in this strategy, but what was a sixth grader to do?

By the end of sixth grade, I wouldn't touch a neighborhood party with a ten-foot pole for fear of being ostracized. I remember my final few neighborhood events as gauntlets of ravenous prepubescents waiting in line to challenge my Négritude, anxious to reject me before I could reject them.

I had learned at Wade to be ashamed of who and what I was, what we all were. No one ever directly assaulted the black way of life; to the contrary, I recall no racial incidents at all. (Class issues undergird many a tense moment, but Americans have always been loath to call those by their proper name. I graduated as intimidated by the few black doctors' and judges' kids as by the white ones. Without a doubt, our teachers differentiated among us by class.) The shame came from the drip-drip-drip of their way, the white way, or no way at all. No other ways existed. Everything we low-class black kids did, said, or thought was wrong. On the rare occasions when one of us suggested an alternative to the mainstream, our teachers would appear merely puzzled and mark the attempt "wrong." Minus five points. If you wanted to pass, you did things the white way. You thought the white way. I remember a neighbor kid venting his frustration over his score on the Iowa Basic Skills Test we took every year and which had so much to say about the direction our lives would take.

"'Cup and table' be right!" he spat, furious. "Who be usin a cup and saucer round here?"

Wade wore me down and I bought into it. I accepted that the black way was the wrong way. I learned from my reading, exemplified in the high teas I reenacted with Wina, to automatically substitute whites' experience for my own. Without having to be told, I knew that my world was just that—mine and something to be overcome.

I was the queen of internalized oppression. Every split infinitive, every sentence ended with a preposition, every act of seemingly willful ignorance maddened me. It seemed to me that blacks were trying to fail, especially as I entered my teens and saw true decline all around me. People dropped out of school, used drugs, committed crimes, and, of course, there was the never-ending tide of illegitimate babies. These self-destructive behaviors baffled me. The people who spent the most time railing against "the man"'s refusal to let us get ahead were the same ones living in their mother's basements watching eight hours of television a day on huge televisions rented at astronomical rates. Logic told me that racism was not their only problem. It wasn't even their biggest problem.

I began to believe that poor people bring most of their problems on themselves. I understood that oppression was a real force in our lives, but surely the answer was not willy-nilly procreation, drug use, sloppy work habits. The answer was to work hard, be smart. Like me.

Black people had begun to make me nervous, so I stayed away from them, family included.

I was almost out of elementary school before I discovered the huge central library downtown and saw my first book by a black person: *I Know Why the Caged Bird Sings* by Maya Angelou. I read it five times. It had never occurred to me that blacks could write books.

With this discovery, my desire for serious modern literature burst into flame. I lost myself in the Harlem Renaissance. Dabbled in sixties protest and non-Western literature . . . lost interest. I always came back to the canon, those Dead White Men who got me through my childhood: Dickens, Maugham, Melville, Steinbeck, Balzac.

Eventually, I came to see that the knowledge I garnered from my reading gave me power with, if not over, whites. The offhand reference to Scott and Zelda, I soon learned, rescued me from personal invisibility even as I became increasingly aware of my literary invisibility. No high tea on the moors for folks named Eula Mae, no Afros blowing in South Sea breezes. I loved these books but they made me so mournful. I knew they were meant to specifically exclude me.

But I couldn't help myself. I read everywhere. I spent hours with the dictionary and atlases. On the toilet, tripping up and down the stairs. I read at the table until my mother put a stop to that, but I just read the cereal boxes and catsup jars instead.

Poorly educated herself, my mother made no attempt to guide or censor my reading. She assumed that, since it was written down and properly bound, it must be fit to read. Since I had no guide on this journey, I read many books which I now know were inappropriate (i.e., soft-core porn or overly adult subject matter. *Of Human Bondage* and the complete Erskine Caldwell, which I read in the sixth grade, come to mind). My hunger for the printed word was so intense in those years that I finished every book I began no matter how indigestible, no matter how much went over my head. Eventually, since I read with such speed, sufficient length became my primary criterion. Books were my safe haven. Books made me happy. Looking at them. Touching them.

I read especially torturous passages from the strange archaic English of Dickens or Shakespeare aloud again and again just for the glory of it. Intuitively, I not only understood the outdated language, I reveled in it. I loved the rich feel of it, the sense of continuity, the seamlessness of human experience.

Older and more utilitarian, I'd recite the difficult passages aloud until I could do so flawlessly, without the sharecropper intonations. It was years before I mastered turning my sharecropper patois off and on like a faucet, but as with all my self-initiated extra credit projects, I persevered. I could never understand others' lack of interest in what I was reading. Their resistance to *Treasure Island* or *The Three Musketeers* was a mystery. But I persisted. I always figured I just wasn't making the benefits well enough understood. I was trying to help.

I'd thought I was helping when Wina had written me a letter from a weekend church trip. I had it waiting for her on her return, corrected and neatly rewritten. She came to me excited about a book I'd recommended, but I kept interrupting to correct her misinterpretations and mispronunciations, so she quit in tears.

Once when I was fourteen or so and all-knowing, I was bragging to a group of cousins that I wouldn't have been a slave, that I'd have fought back even unto death rather than be inventory.

Even at Wade, we had learned nothing about slavery, Reconstruction, or Jim Crow. We had simply learned that that there was a civil war which ended in 1865 and inspired the Gettysburg Address. Even so, I'd absorbed enough from my reading to know to be ashamed of my people for allowing ourselves to be enslaved. I didn't blame whites, I blamed us. We shouldn't have allowed ourselves to become chattel. I wouldn't have.

Out of nowhere, Paw Paw, the man who laughed at everything, was standing over me squeezing my arm to near uselessness.

"You wun't a done nothin," he sneered. "You'd a prayed and cried and begged Massa for nother morsel a food to keep body and soul together jes like erbody else."

At that moment, I wasn't thinking about his African slave grandmother—sold away, never to be heard of again—but I bet he was.

"Even had you a, all you'da done was git erbody whupped! sold! kilt!" He dropped my arm like it was diseased and snarled, "You wudn't a done nothin. The other slaves wudda kilt you theyselves."

All in all, there was just no talking to blacks.

In high school, which was majority white but predominantly working and lower middle class, I didn't join the black student organization. I always had a job, a great many responsibilities at home, and my school was so far away that I spent any free time I had reading. I used to wonder what SOBI (Students of Black Identity) was for—to sit around being black? If they had an agenda beyond shoring up their own social predominance and creating opportunities to pose for Polaroids with the principal, I never knew what it was. It wasn't lost on me that the leaders of SOBI were just the Negro subset of the same cruel snobs that ran everything else at school. In my experience, black student groups exist primarily to provide spotlights for the children of the black bourgeoisie.

Also, and more importantly, in the 1970s I had come to truly believe that we had "overcome" in the sixties and that the post–civil rights era required all good citizens to move beyond group identifications and forge a new collective identity as plain old Americans, not fill-in-the-blank ethnic Americans. Black student groups were counterproductive self-segregation.

I went my own neurotic way, but as I swam against both tides of underachievement and pseudomilitant posturing, the first layer of resentment and a budding conservatism was formed. Having no intercourse with whites other than my schoolmates—who never hassled me for failing the "paper bag" test or for not having "good hair"—I grew wary of blacks and stubbornly nurtured my disapproval of nearly everything and everyone around me.

GOING BACKWARDS

Gifted elementary students trapped in the St. Louis public schools were merely shunted to Southwest High School, labeled "Track 1A," and allowed to take whatever classes we chose. At Wade, in the eighth grade, I had the same books my high school sophomore sister did, so by the end of my sophomore year, there was nothing left to take. Not only that, the learning environment was one of warehousing and diminished expectation for the lower classes. As college neared, I careened between fraud syndrome and lofty contempt. Soon, I stopped trying to learn anything and took classes like "Rock and Rhyme," where we studied pop song lyrics for English credit. By junior year, I was begging my mother to let me drop out and take a GED. God knows we needed the extra income I could generate from switching to full-time work, and anyway, why forestall destiny?

We compromised: as long as I graduated, I only had to attend school when I chose. Given the low standards applied, I had no trouble with that and only made an appearance for exams. Most teachers lowered my grades because of my constant truancy. So what?

I educated myself through my reading reading reading. I was a junkie. I carried a heavy backpack everywhere for fear I'd finish one book (Wade taught us speed-reading) and not have another at the ready. Kurt Vonnegut kept me sane with his special brand of surreality as I grew more withdrawn from my own life. I spent more days than I can recall anesthetized under the spell he cast; the characters he created were every bit as flummoxed by life as I was. I could watch young men pass paper-bagged malt liquor between them at our early morning bus stop and blank out on it by mumbling passages from *Breakfast of Champions* and giggling to myself. I read *Slaughterhouse Five* and thought, for the first time, of writing. When the protagonist experienced a war movie from end to beginning ("mustard gas and roses"), I actually gasped aloud at the hopeless, loopy beauty of it. But Steinbeck and Dickens, those writers with calloused hands, were my most faithful companions. The denouement of *Of Mice and Men* literally bent me over double and punched me in the stomach.

Only when I was reading could I actually let myself feel things. My own life had to be muffled in heavy cloth, but on the printed page my emotions ranged freely. But I was twenty years from even attempting to fill a page; if people like me couldn't be lawyers, they certainly could not write.

I was more diligent about the other half of my schooling at vocational O'Fallon Tech. Part of most days I spent learning to type, file, take shorthand, and operate office machines there. I was quite good at it: I could type 100 words per minute and take dictation at over 200. I competed in secretarial Olympics against other teenage drones from different schools. I was the star of O'Fallon Tech, and calmly confident of my oft-foretold vo-tech abilities. No teacher or counselor ever asked me why a gifted student was planning to become a secretary. Indeed, until my thirties, I never asked myself that question either.

My junior year ended, my senior year began, and I was that much closer to the end of my own history. Other students spoke of college prep classes and the SAT. I wasn't sure what those things were, and so faked it when they came up. Lord knows my mother didn't know and the school counselors—well, I have no idea what they did with their time. I never got in trouble and so never got sent to them. They never sent for me.

One day, I was waiting in the administrative offices to get the signature which would allow me to continue working half the school day. There was a long queue of students signing up for something. I just kept reading and moving up in line. When it was my turn, the office lady handed me forms to fill out. I was perplexed.

"Aren't you here for the PSAT?" she asked.

Was I supposed to be? Was the PSAT a good thing . . . or had I missed some requirement through my infrequent appearances? I stood mute, so she pressed the forms on me.

I appeared obediently at the time and place I was ordered to by the card that came in the mail. I did no preparation. When my scores were returned, calls and letters from colleges came flooding in. I was miserable.

The score was just a number to me; I can't remember what it was. No one at Southwest called me in to interpret it for me or talk about my options. I had to learn from one of the recruiting letters that I'd scored in the ninety-fourth percentile for black students nationwide. So? I went to church with manual laborers who sang better than Aretha Franklin and danced better than Fred Astaire. We had an illiterate deacon who could calculate immense sums in the blink of an eye without pad or paper. Mama could take apart anything in our house and figure out how to repair it by tinkering with it. Ninety-fourth percentile was like being five foot seven and brown-eyed. Big deal.

I was tormented by the colleges' offers; I couldn't possibly accept. I wouldn't last a week at a university before I'd be found out as the unworthy upstart I was and thrown out. I saw no connection between my intellectual yearnings, my grades, and a college education. So what if I got good grades? I was blue collar. No one had to tell me I couldn't go to college because I was poor and black. I told myself.

That didn't stop me, however, from reading and rereading those wonderful, awful letters. My mother collected them, her eyes shining as she filled a small drawer with them. She thought them lovely non sequiturs, too. She'd talk about them to the white folks working late at the architecture firm I helped her clean when I wasn't at my own job. I was always rude to these people, all of whom went out of their way to be nice to the cleaning lady's kid. They tried to give me candy and things but I just rolled my eyes and continued vacuuming, refusing even to return their greetings.

When I failed to respond to their letters, the admissions officers began calling. I stuttered and stammered. Most calls, all I ever said was "yes ma'am" and "yes sir." I'll get the application in right away. By Monday, yes ma'am. You'll waive the application fee? Thank you. Yes, I'm real excited, too, I'd say as my stomach roiled and heaved. Sometimes, though, I was cocky and arrogant: Why should I come to your school? Lots of schools want me, you know. But usually I just made up fantastic excuses about why I couldn't talk right then. Or, I'd lay the phone on the table and stare at it until I heard them hang up. But they'd just call back.

Finally I had Wina talk to them. I couldn't even stand next to her. I'd fidget in the kitchen doorway with my hand over the extension mouthpiece and whisper questions for her to ask. What are the dorms like? Is there a choir? What's the weather like in New Hampshire, New York, D.C.?

By March, though, I'd run the gamut of emotions and landed smack-dab at bitterness. Enough foolishness. There was work to be done. But they called and called and called. They had students call, they had alums call. Annoyingly, their entreaties always included one from the president of the black students' organization; that always pissed me off. I wanted to be wanted only for my aptitude. But in the end, I didn't want to be wanted at all.

I resumed answering the phone and told each I'd accepted another. Only then did they stop trying. They wished me well and congratulated me on my bright future at Duke, at Washington University, at Bryn Mawr.

I'd sit at the kitchen table and stare at the phone, hoping that one canny recruiter would see through me. I prayed for the phone to ring now that I could be sure it wouldn't, and I didn't know what to think. No one before had ever asked me what I wanted to do, where I wanted to go, where I saw myself in ten years. The mistake they made, all those faceless white people who reached out to me, was assuming that I saw in myself the same things they did. So I made it all disappear. I hung up the phone on my future. I never filled out even one college application.

Instead, I continued working as a waitress and short-order cook instead of going to school. In between hamburgers one night on a double shift, the pay phone rang and I learned that Daddy was in the hospital. Dying. Lung cancer. The conscious part of my brain shut down and I simply sat, like a lump, with the gaggle of relatives at the hospital. The doctors performed lots of tests and exploratory surgery and gave us grim news.

It had never occurred to us not to fly to Daddy's side when the news came. Sharecroppers share. However present we may have been, though, we couldn't have been much comfort. As always, we had no idea how to reach out to one another. There was little conversation, most of that strained and painful. Yes sir. No sir. Do you want some more water, Da— . . . sir? We could only sit slumped in our private miseries, Dickersons to the end, without a word of comfort for each other. He may have talked to his wife about things that mattered, but to his children, he remained a blank wall. We all pretended we assumed he would be going home soon, saying blustery things like "Guess somebody'll have to mow the lawn for you for a while, won't they? Heh, heh." I thought I'd scream with the strain.

The doctors removed one lung, part of the other, and part of the lining around his heart. Soon, he was on a respirator, conscious but unable to talk. Then, he was in a coma. Then he was dead. Handy, that, I quipped: his dying just then saved me coming up with an excuse for not going to my prom. As if anyone had asked me.

So I watched my father's coffin lid close and made myself childish promises. His memory was not going to drag me down. He was not going to send me to therapy. He was the parent, I was the child; the onus had been on him to try to rectify the situation. That he never did, I sniffed, is his cross to bear. I was just going to get on with it. For years, I made people gasp at my jagged one-liners, like my prom crack, about what a jerk he was. That meant I was tough. That meant I wasn't repressed like the rest of my family.

I fought back my horror as I watched my father's coffin lid close—they were suffocating him!—and repeated my mantra. His mantra: What I don't have, I don't need.

Thank God for the printing press. I withdrew further and further from my own life. When I was neither working nor reading, I was sleeping. At first it was eight hours, then ten, then nearly every moment when I wasn't required to be doing something which required consciousness. I slept and slept and slept in the basement I shared with my sisters. Since childhood, I'd been an insomniac and fitful sleeper tormented by the least light, the lightest footfall. Now, I knew a blissful vacuum as my brother spitefully did his laundry ten feet from my head, boom box blaring. My sisters filled our basement with their chattering girlfriends or gossiped on the phone but I never knew they were there. Awake, I never thought farther ahead than the next order of fries, the next mess to be cleaned up after Bobby, the next book I could read.

By July, my mother pointed out to me that the only clothing of mine in the laundry pile was underwear, my work uniform, and my nightgown. I could only shrug. What else did I need? I even sent others to the library for me, that holy of holies, that place I used to wish to be locked in "accidentally" overnight the way other kids wished they could be locked in a candy store. I lived on chocolate cupcakes and Pepsi snarfed down in bed and gained back all the weight I'd lost from my fatty four-eyes girlhood.

Then, August began and I couldn't sleep a wink.

I prowled the house all night, book in hand, while everyone else slept. As in my childhood, I was again moving from window to window, staring into the predawn darkness without ever knowing what I was looking for, wishing I was dead. I used to think then about people in ancient times struggling with things they didn't understand but which we now have names and fixes for. Imagine being a slave with asthma, a manic-depressive medieval woodsman, an epileptic Russian serf. I knew there was something wrong with me and I knew it had a name. But because I was a coward and a conformist, I didn't think there was a cure.

With all the extra exhausted hours in my days, I spun out one Walter Mitty fantasy after another and prayed they'd be enough. I assumed I'd learn to tune out the way my mother did as she floated above the drudgery of her life with a thousand-miles-away smile on her face that had nothing to do with us. And then, one mid-August morning, one week before what should have been my freshman year was to begin, I looked out the window and saw my future gaining on me.

Outside, the neighborhood women were trudging off to their lives. They thronged the bus stops, pinched-faced and sullen, in their run-over shoes and cheap fabrics. A name tag pinned to every overflowing bosom. The old crones were difficult to distinguish from the young women. I could tell they'd all already been up for hours, preparing breakfasts and lunches, wrangling with their irresponsible kids' kids, arguing with their husbands and sons, perhaps late because the electricity had been turned off again during the night. After nine years riding city buses to school and work, that morning I noticed for the first time that no one speaks at a bus stop, not in the early morning. My own head was always buried in a book, unless it was winter and too dark to read. Most everyone else stood slumped in his or her own pre-Walkman misery, trying to catch a few fleeting moments' rest while standing, trying to enjoy these last few moments of freedom. I opened the window and pressed my face to the iron bars, unable to look away.

All at once my future spread out before me, an endless stream of letters to be typed and coffee to be fetched. I couldn't breathe. Literally, I could not breathe. Gasping for air, I ran downstairs to the basement, threw street clothes on for the first time in weeks, drove my mother to work, then used the car to speed back up West Florissant Avenue to Florissant Valley Community College. It wouldn't open for two hours, so I paced outside the Administration Building nearly hysterical with panic and fear that I was having a heart attack. Then, I begged the first person who arrived for work to admit me.

OUTED

"Miss Dickerson, what is this?" Mr. "Smith," my Philosophy 101 instructor. He had an oft-invoked M.A. from nationally prominent Washington University. I always got the impression that he was mentally holding his nose with us.

"A table." Used to his grandstanding, I wouldn't give him the gift of my resistance.

"What is a table, Miss Dickerson?"

I just looked at him.

"How do you know it's a table? Rather, what makes you think it's a table, whatever that is."

By the second month of the semester, he and I had developed an amiable lack of respect for each other that the rest of the class relaxed into and abetted; he routinely said things I thought ridiculous and I challenged him frequently. Usually reticent and cowed by authority figures, I found that the little popinjay's faux elitism and frequent racial and sexual insensitivity relieved me of my hesitancy.

"I know it's a table because of its shape, its construction, and its obvious function."

"'Shape,' Miss Dickerson? What's that?" Preening, he posed these questions as if they were of Talmudic obscurity and brilliance. "How do we know that what we perceive is actual reality? What if we're incapable of perceiving things as they actually are?"

Presumably, in the hands of a real thinker, this conversation might have been conducted on an intelligent level, but in Mr. Smith's hands, it was just another exercise in public masturbation.

"What's the significance of all this, Mr. Smith? Even if everything you pose were true, what difference would it make? So what if 'green' is really 'blue'? There is no sustained way to challenge or disprove our reality, so isn't this just a lot of fancy talk? Our world seems to function perfectly well for all this mass psychosis of haywire spatial perception and color blindness. We can't deal with what we call 'table' in any other way; so what if it's really a rhomboid, as long as my watermelon and fried chicken don't fall off?" I threw that in to goad him. "Couldn't it be that things really are as they appear to be?"

"There's a name for that kind of thinking, Miss Dickerson," Mr. Smith said ominously, and paused for dramatic effect. "Naive realism." He made it sound like "necrophiliac pedophile."

My classmates chuckled or gasped, depending on whose side they were on. But I had a moment of complete calm.

I knew, down at the bottom of my soul and forever, two things.

One: he was right.

I *am* a naive realist. For all the veneer of sophistication I have acquired since, I know that no matter how you camouflage reality with fancy talk, you can't escape it. Mr. Smith was living proof. He had a fancy-boy degree from a fancy-boy school, but he had little to teach me, either intellectually or in terms of character. He was his own worst enemy because, through his weakness, he taught me that I had power.

The second realization was this: he couldn't hurt me.

Over the semester, as I'd watched Mr. Smith cow my classmates and pat himself on the back, I'd become annoyed, angry, and disappointed; much to my surprise, these feelings combined to produce bravery. He had tried to silence and embarrass me, but instead his bullying gave me confidence. I was used to feeling unworthy and out of place. But somehow, by the time I was eighteen and in college, I had learned a thing or two. His disapproval meant nothing because I had no respect for him. He had substituted his unilaterally presupposed superiority for reasoned discourse. If he was so much better and smarter, why didn't he prove it by besting me in a debate instead of dismissing me?

All my life, I had been intimidated by my "betters"; I'd conveniently done all the work of cowing myself for them. Now, I understood one of the unacknowledged reasons underlying elites' insistence on keeping their social inferiors ignorant, their choices circumscribed—familiarity really does breed contempt. It was clear to me that prolonged exposure to my supposed betters could only bridge the gap between me and them. As time went on, they just seemed less and less superior. I was ready to accept that I was wrong, but if I was, Mr. Smith was going to have to do better than roll his eyes to convince me of it.

My first act of social rebellion was letting him have the last word. Watching him, I saw, so clearly that there might have been subtitles inscribed in the air over his head, that expensive schools and parchments inscribed with Latin are no guarantees of fitness. Because I no longer needed the approval of this designated superior, I saw in a flash that my time and attention were valuable commodities—he wasn't worth it. I sat silent and perfectly comfortable as Mr. Smith mocked me, and thought about how Daddy used to say: Never waste two seconds on a fool. This man is a fool, I thought, and felt no further need to engage him.

But a fool to whom I am indebted. Mr. Smith was fuel; he made me want to catch up.

While I was en route to class one day, a man ran a light, made a left in my path, and caused an accident that left me unconscious and another car damaged. The mark of Zorro on my forehead, I shook glass out of my hair for days. The driver left a fake name and address and was never heard from again. My '62 Valiant was totaled. State Farm, the damaged car's insurer, came after me. Even though it freely admitted I wasn't responsible for the accident, it claimed "that wasn't the point" and that it could make me pay for the damage to the third car since the person who'd caused it couldn't be found. Probably they were lying, having judged from my circumstances that I had no way of fighting. But after weeks of phone calls so threatening I'd start crying whenever the phone rang, we borrowed money to pay them off. I felt like a rag, like a shameful thing with no rights and no worth.

My image of lawyers as Atticus Finch replicas and the law as that noble body which had freed blacks was replaced by a loathing so deep I swore I'd rather die than be associated with it. After State Farm, I saw the law and lawyers as part of an abusive, exploitative system dedicated to keeping the rich rich and the poor poor. It was the intellectual shamelessness of it, the willingness to make any amoral argument in the name of winning, that I couldn't abide.

But that only made deciding what to do with myself, with my future, that much more difficult. Even through the worst periods of my low self-esteem, becoming a lawyer was always in the back of my mind. My grades were good, but they'd always been. It was just that I had no idea what I was doing or why. I didn't know how to think about a future. What was it that I was trying to be? I had no point of reference for anything other than manual labor; what could I do but clean offices or change diapers? Engineer, doctor, banker: these were mere words without content. I had no idea how to get there from here or whether I'd enjoy it once I arrived.

As well, I was alienated from everyone around me, the blacks especially. Even community college was an environment fraught with opportunities to be humiliated both socially and intellectually. In that majority-white environment, we blacks just seemed so loud and so backward. The day a black work-study coworker bragged about getting some class notes down "verbatim for verbatim," I thought I would die of shame. One invoked her "baby daddy" while warming up greens and cornbread in the office microwave. I had to leave. But I had a double standard: when a white paraded his ignorance, he was simply a stupid individual. A black who did so I elevated to a symbol of our race. No Klansman was as racist.

At home, overnight, puberty had hit and Bobby inherited his father's body—barrel chest, skinny legs—as well as his need to intimidate. He'd gone from fey to ferocious, from charming to churlish. His previously odd but fairly harmless behavior disappeared. His destructive tendencies came to mirror those all around us in the neighborhood—fighting, drunken carousing, misogyny. They obliterated his guilelessness and desire to amuse; it was hard to believe he'd ever made us laugh and even harder to believe we'd ever pitied him and desired to protect him.

For years after, he called me little other than "bitch." If I mopped a floor, he saw no reason why he should take the long way around it. If Mama left dinner on the stove for me or Wina for after work, he ate it. Left the empty plate and aluminum foil for us to clear away. He wouldn't use the napkins we'd set at his plate because he preferred using the dish towels or the curtains, whatever was most convenient for his highness. He'd come home at 2 A.M., make no attempt to walk lightly over our heads even though he knew how the uncarpeted floorboards amplified sounds, then turn on the basement lights and do laundry. Radio blasting.

Had he been trying to bedevil us intentionally, it wouldn't have been so bad. But we weren't that important; the sun doesn't try to give us mere humans skin cancer, it's just doing what it does, it's just being what it is, the center of the universe. We weren't even presumed to have any wants and needs. "Jes cook yourself some more, girl," he'd snarl impatiently after eating our meals, as if I'd demanded he urinate for me.

He drank my infant nephew Johnny's milk. His thuggish friends leered at us. He gave our possessions to women he was trying to woo and was annoyed by our protests. It was like living with Henry VIII. All housework was "bitch work," all his sisters old maids who needed to "kiss my ass." He never washed a dish, never dusted a stretch of wood, never made his own bed. Just like his father, he knew everything and proved his points by bellowing and insulting those who demurred. Disagreeing with him only proved our stupidity. But I wasn't afraid of him; I hated him with a passion that lived and breathed. Also, I was deep in the throes of a full-blown hatred for my father by my teens; I was determined never to live in fear of another man. No more cowering in terror. So I set Bobby up again and again to say and do stupid things, then laughed in his face.

Bobby could have handled his status as that holy of holies—a black male—completely differently. Had he been nice to us, or even merely indifferent, we would gladly have waited on him hand and foot. As it was, only our mother could bear to be around him. A true black man, he was an unrepentant mama's boy. Only with her was he gentle and kind.

Drunk, high, bloody, bruised, unheard-from for days, he'd drag himself home at 3 or 4 A.M., go sit on her bed, and wake her up to talk. Since he'd woken me as well banging along overhead, I had no choice but to lie in the dark listening to her giggle at his muffled stories. He and I barely spoke except to trade insults, yet with her, he was a human being.

I was her right hand, I brought home straight A's, I stayed home, I ran our house like an adjutant. I was taken for granted. Bobby contributed nothing, Bobby would have been left back repeatedly except that no teacher wanted to have him twice, Bobby fled our home as if it were on fire and used it as if it were a highway rest stop, Bobby couldn't be required to even flush after himself. He was her pride and joy.

One day, I came home carrying a black dress from the cleaners. I'd cleaned the house and cooked the family dinner beforehand. There was a trail of mud and grime from the front door to the kitchen, greasy car parts lay atop the kitchen counters. Bobby stood eating with his filthy fingers from the pots I'd prepared. If I'd had a gun I would have shot him.

"Fuck you, bitch," he snarled predictably. He dunked a greasy cuff in the pot and made big, innocent eyes at me. My silence made him think he'd won and he leered in triumph. But that wasn't why I was quiet.

Standing there watching him revel in his self-absorbed animality, I buried my brother. He wasn't going to make it, that much was clear to me. He was going to be another chalk outline in a gutter somewhere and I mourned him and his wasted life. For about a second. Then I let him go. I wasn't about to be one of those ghetto women caught in the undertow of a two-bit man who didn't know how good he had it. *You want to die, you want to be something less than human? All right. I give up on you.* I sent that forth to the cosmos like a graveside prayer in a prison cemetery. Watching his coffin lid close wasn't going to take the wind out of me the way Daddy's had. This time, I'd be ready.

I watched him curse me and act like a gorilla and felt very calm. Bored almost. He thought he was punishing me with his bestial antics—he was too stupid to see he was punishing himself for reasons he was too stupid to articulate. Would it be a long prison stretch? Homeless winehead? Or just a simple white casket? No matter. I'd be there to take care of Mama when the inevitable came. I'd seen this movie a thousand times. Now it was simply our turn. He was just like too many other black men I knew, determined to kill himself but not until he'd wrung the last drop of love, energy, and money out of every decent person around him. I watched his performance and swore two vows: he was not going to drag my mother down with him, and I was not going to help him self-destruct.

I thrust the black dress in his face. "I think I'll wear this one to your funeral."

The blood drained out of his face. He flung himself away from that dress like it was a severed head dripping gore on the linoleum. I laughed at him—I couldn't help it, he was such a weakling—and he ran out the front door. When he came home three days later, he was beaten and bloody, but victorious. He'd sent three other boys to the hospital.

With minor exceptions, I did not speak to him again for five years. To me, he was dead and there's little need to speak of spirits.

PINK-COLLAR GHETTO

I worked a raft of pointless clerical and food service jobs to help out at home while piling A atop pointless A at school. But why? Why was I born, why were any of us, just to toil in peonage at unfulfilling, unremunerative scut work? I never contemplated suicide but I often wished I would just die.

I used to scour the newspaper for stories of young people just like myself "tragically" killed in car wrecks or by freak, painless acts of nature. Why couldn't that happen to me? To help things along, I started smoking. I stopped using seat belts, started dressing inappropriately for the weather. Typically working class, I was too passive, too defeated to take even that bull by the horns. Plotting elaborate ways to place myself in the path of danger gave me many hours of grim amusement.

As the end of Flo Valley's two-year program neared, I panicked. Yes, again. Now what was I supposed to do? What would graduating mean for someone like me? I couldn't figure out what I was supposed to do once I had a diploma, so my 3.9 GPA and I dropped out six weeks before graduation.

I took several dead-end secretarial jobs. They were such horror shows of moronic, sexist bosses and brain-dead coworkers that after a few days at each, I simply stopped going. Some of them sent me checks for the few days I'd worked, some didn't.

I took a job at a bank that was mind-numbingly simplistic. I checked credit. The loan officers would give me a name and Social Security number, I'd put the information into a little computer and out would come a credit history. Before lunch each day, I had no work left to do.

I shared a big, open office with twelve or so catatonic people and I'd bother them for work to do. I learned to do a great many jobs that the bank would have been surprised (and fined by the federal government) to know about. The loan officers sat in the open in the middle of the ground floor, a creepy place to work. Bored nearly to tears on a very slow, very rainy Monday in August 1979, I stood talking with my favorite officer, Tony.

I was miserable. It was harder and harder to drag myself into the office every day. There were two blue-haired little ladies in the office.

They bragged about having been with the bank for twenty-five years. They kept worn house slippers in their bottom desk drawers that they padded around in all day. Through my in-house moonlighting, I'd learned how to read all sorts of computer files. I'd seen their paychecks—I knew exactly how much the bank cared about their devotion.

I bitched and bitched and bitched to Tony about the stupidity of the bank executives and the vacuousness of the job. I told him I didn't intend to be there long. That I was going to travel, I was going to finish college. Maybe write, maybe . . . maybe who knows what I might do. I blabbed on and on and he just let me. When I was finished, he said, "No you won't."

I was stunned. "Excuse me?"

"You won't do any of those things."

I could only stare.

"You'll never get out of here," he said. "Everybody says what you just said when they start here. Hell, I said it. But nobody gets out. First, you get an apartment you can barely afford. Then a car. Then you get married and the kids start coming. Before you know it, you can't quit. But don't worry. You'll get used to it. I have."

I know he was just describing the suburbs and the PTA and sex once a month, but it sounded like Kafka to me. I crawled back to my office and just sat there. I imagined myself a grandmother still dragging in to move twenty-five dollars from Mr. Smith's checking to his savings. The vision was no less a nightmare than the one I'd had of myself waiting at the bus stop with the other manual laborers.

What got me most about Tony's prediction was the calm way he'd consigned me to that living hell, the calm way he knew himself to be trapped. How could he recognize his own doom and not make a break for it? He made it all sound so inescapable, like he was putting a quiet little curse on me.

Five days later, I was in Columbia at the University of Missouri begging to be admitted. Classes began in just seven days. I was smart enough to have brought my transcripts with me. Once I produced them, the black admissions officer stopped sermonizing about the triflingness of black students and their constant lateness and started slavering to have me.

I'd been at Mizzou only about six weeks before St. Louis dragged me back. Bobby. Again. I lay in bed that morning trying to muster the energy to spend another day with the brother to whom I had not spoken since I settled on my wardrobe for his funeral. I'd only listened long enough to find out which jail this time and hung up on him. I wouldn't have bailed him out of the home he preferred, but I couldn't let Mama go there alone.

Sixteen years old, Bobby had been arrested for drunken brawling yet again and had spent the night in the tank. It was impossible to calibrate whether he was more drunk than high, but in those precrack days, the cops (it had taken six of them to control him) didn't expend much effort differentiating between Thunderbird and Mary Jane. This time, he'd led a twelve-person fight at school which involved dangling a freshman from a third-story window. Enough was enough; the school administration made good on its promise to expel him.

I caught Greyhound home. All too soon, we were bailing him out. Silent in the car, I dropped our sighing mother off at the vending machine factory to join her assembly line. Bobby and I tended the silence we'd cultivated like a rock garden for the past few years; no mimes were more adept at avoiding verbal communication. We drove to the worst neighborhood in black St. Louis, to Pruitt, the high school set aside as the last exit en route to jail. We could only stare in stunned silence at the concertina-wired teachers' parking lot, the squint-eyed security guards with real guns, high-voltage Tasers, and no patience left for their charges. Pruitt was much more about the guards than the teachers. This time, my brother the tough guy couldn't feign indifference; I saw his eyes widen. As we sat in the car, a group of male students accosted a female one. They had her back embedded in the chain links, her feet off the ground, her skirt yanked up over her hips. In no particular hurry, one annoyed guard ambled over to break it up. As the boys moved off, bored again, the guard yelled at the girl. He looked disgusted. I couldn't help myself. I had to speak to my brother.

"You happy now?!" I yelled, and spit rained down on the dashboard. "This is what you wanted, right? What you been aiming for all your miserable life. I guess now you can die happy in this toilet bowl, since you're bound and determined to die. Could you just do us a favor and die a little more quickly?"

I got out and slammed the door. We made our way through the many security checkpoints to the principal's office, where, with a weary wave of déjà vu, I formally handed authority over to Pruitt's principal. How many times had I done this—getting him back into school, finessing a gullible principal, humbling myself before the parents of a mauled child so they wouldn't press charges?

We maintained an uncomfortable silence while the principal reviewed Bobby's long history of trouble at Beaumont. Staring out over his bifocals, he read implacably over the more gruesome aspects of the fight which had brought Bobby to Pruitt. Bobby remained impassive throughout, but with that familiar stubborn jut of his chin. The physical resemblance to our father, dead now for two years, wasn't helping me feel any more charitable.

Embarrassed and ashamed, I tried to finesse the principal as I'd done so often in the past with landlords, utility companies, and the like. I tried to get him to agree to contact me before taking any drastic action since it was a foregone conclusion that Bobby would screw up. The principal cut me off with military briskness; he wasn't about to be "worked." I didn't doubt that he'd have no trouble handing Bobby over to city cops to face criminal charges if he caused trouble at Pruitt. For my mother's sake, I hoped Bobby believed him, too. Personally, I didn't give a damn.

Still silent, my brother walked me back to the car, his face smashed and purple from the fight he'd won, and I drove off. For once, he didn't call me a bitch, didn't tell me to shut up. He said nothing at all. In the rearview, I watched him watch me pull away. Guards yelled at him to get back behind the security barricades. His expression was unreadable.

Bobby survived Pruitt. Indeed, he spent most of his high school career there, too feared to face much opposition. Years passed before we spoke another word.

I took the bus back to Mizzou and my own problems. I had changed my major and classes so often that the administration required me to get an increased number of signatures authorizing any further changes. I was renting a cheap room in a slummy house with a bunch of drug-using women I hardly knew. Having shown up for admission only a week before the semester began, I'd had no shot at a dorm room. I had no friends, and my white boyfriend, the one who made the black students disown me, was cheating. With a white girl.

Sitting in the Student Union, I'd watch groups form, coalesce, break up, re-form, and have no idea how to break in. I felt both invisible and glaringly, indelibly stained with some mark of shortcoming. "Hanging out" was simply foreign to me because Daddy had never allowed it. You got time to lean, you got time to clean. Life is a struggle, them that work is them that get: I didn't know how to relax. Whenever I had a free moment, I lost myself in a book, the one pleasure I could always count on. Indeed, I took a bleak, Protestant pride in the featurelessness of my own life, little realizing how much that made me like the father I hated.

The blacks especially disturbed me, since I knew I was expected to bond with them. One part of me wanted to try to make friends, another stubbornly wanted to do so more in the course of things, through shared interests and classes. Also, it was obvious that the same social rules would pertain at Mizzou: if you light, you all right. If you black, get back. I was sickened by the pigment/hair follicle hierarchy, mostly because I could only lose at it. And I was embarrassed by blacks' pathetic aping of white Greek traditions. Whites had whole city blocks at Mizzou of gracious houses and sweeping lawns emblazoned with the Greek letters of unintegrated, hoary fraternities going back generations and lovingly supported by doting alumni. Blacks had fetid apartments crawling with dope-smoking near-dropouts that they insisted on calling "frat houses." The blatant wealth of so many around me choked me with shame and rage. Thank God I hadn't attempted Dartmouth or Bryn Mawr in that state of mind.

In the end, none of this mattered at all. I had no time to socialize because I had three part-time jobs and only slept in snatches. Chronically broke, I lived on canned soup and popcorn. There had been a spate of campus rapes; I was always alone so I was always afraid. My only comfort came from reading the newspaper searching for stories of quick deaths visited upon stupid people in bizarre situations. Again,

I used them to devise grandiose but passive fatal-accident schemes which all had in common painlessness and the element of surprise.

Worst of all, my stint at the bank had opened up a whole new source of confusion. There had been college-educated people there, filling their hours with work so unrewarding just watching them do it made me want to poke my eyes out with a sharp stick. I saw then that just as that vaunted sheepskin was no guarantee of the bearer's fitness, neither did it guarantee a life worth living.

Left to my own preferences, I would, of course, have majored in literature. Then what? Been a teacher, I guess. But I waited tables with literature Ph.D.'s. Most often, however, I was sure I'd never escape my working-class fate. I attempted to get some guidance from my guidance counselor but I merely annoyed him. "I sign study cards," he said gruffly. "When you know what you want, come back." So much for guidance. I just read and moped and attended the classes which, in the end, I'd chosen pretty much at random.

But there were a few signs of hope. They were perverse signs of hope, but they gave me what I needed. The most satisfying was being plagiarized by a professor.

Like Mr. Smith, he was a pompous windbag who chose teaching simply to have a captive audience. One of my many roommates took a different, though related, class from him. She asked me for help with a paper and showed me his instructions. Included in them, completely without attribution, was a large chunk from a paper I'd done for him; it was Xeroxed into his own writing so as to appear organic.

I was awed by my power over a man old enough to be my grandfather. He had a doctorate, he'd studied at prestigious universities, and yet he had to steal from me, a nobody. What else could he be saying but that I was a better thinker and writer than he? It gave me an enormous jolt of confidence. But it wasn't enough. All I had was options. What I needed was direction. All I knew for sure was, I had to get away from St. Louis and I had to have a job with meaning. If I'm to type, so be it, I thought. Just let me type in the name of something meaningful. I needed a reason to get up in the morning.

I got one.

PART II

THE POLITICAL

CHAPTER THREE

AIRMAN DICKERSON

BASIC TRAINING

March 10, 1980: my first day of basic training in San Antonio, a month shy of my twenty-first birthday. In my flight of fifty women, few had been to college, few were older than eighteen. We were almost entirely working class, almost entirely white except for four Hispanics and four blacks.

I stood at what I hoped was attention while a team of TIs performed a "health and welfare" inspection on our luggage. Ostensibly, they were looking for contraband before our bags were stowed for the duration of training. The real reason was to show us that we were at their mercy; contraband items (marijuana, candy, other people's belongings) were merely confiscated, no one got punished. All personal belongings were dramatically pawed through, lacy bras held up to the light with great seriousness to ascertain whether they were transparent. The female TIs hung at the edges, laughing at the males' jokes, letting us know whose side they were on. I felt confident, knowing my luggage contained nothing at all interesting. For once, being a bespectacled nerd was going to pay off. The sense of surreality was immense; nothing fully prepares you for the self-contained, Jabberwocky world of the military. The mob of TIs finally arrived at my bunk.

One stepped forward and came to stand nose to nose with me, hoping I'd squirm or try to see around him like the others had so he could dress me down. His highway-patrolman hat dug a trench in my forehead and cast both our faces into shadow. Combat boots crushing my feet, he stared me down. Looking away would only make him light into me—north St. Louis taught me that. Daddy had told us about boot camp on Parris Island when his drill sergeant had woken them all up at midnight in his skivvies, combat boots, and that designed-to-intimidate hat. He'd lined them up and gone down the row punching each one in the gut sans explanation. A sense of warm remembrance had permeated his tale.

All at once, I realized that the TI wasn't really crushing my feet; he was holding his mere millimeters above mine. I felt not pressure, not pain, but the simple nearness of another human. The hat brim was merely resting on my forehead; my imagination, my fear had dug that trench. All I had to be was brave. All I had to do was face this, the path I'd voluntarily chosen.

I tossed my head back and stood up to my full height. I felt powerful, knowing. I wasn't scared. The TI flashed me an almost imperceptible nod and backed off.

I could hear the ominous sound of the taps on the TIs' shoes ricocheting around the room. With my peripheral vision, I could see gangs of them roaming the room like wolves to bellow and attack people: fidgeters; that one girl who would cry for the entire six weeks; feisty "Rodriguez" from a little Texas border town, who would brag that her daughter was conceived in the front seat of a Pinto at McDonald's and who would never, in six weeks, wipe the kiss-my-ass smirk from her face.

Much to my surprise, I *was* berated for the contents of my luggage. My father's stories had not been lost on me; boot camp was something I had a feel for. Aside from a minimal number of necessaries, I'd brought only my favorite author (six Dickens novels—one for each week).

"Looky, looky, we got ourselves a college gal. You been to college, aint ya?" A second TI mugged like a simpleton. He handled my books with feigned awe. "Nick-o-las Nickel-, Nickel-, Nickle bye-bye? Is that how you edu-macated folk pronounce that?" He stopped and stared at me; he was enjoying himself. It was a test—was I supposed to acknowledge him or not?

"Say somethin telligent, college gal. Come on, teach us poor ignent folk somethin, purty pleez!"

The irony made me smile. I used to be berated by black people for putting on airs; now it was as much a class thing as a race thing. That smile was like blood on the water.

The TIs descended en masse. But I was still smiling—I was on Parris Island in the 1940s, the white man at my back, the Japs lurking in the shadows to ambush me. Impartial victory waited in the wings, preferring only the boldest, most dedicated contestant. The TIs were going to yell at me whether I responded or not, whether I smiled or not. But no one there was going to throw me off a troop ship mid-Pacific to make sure I could swim. No one there was going to punch me in the stomach. No one there could terrify me like my father could. No one there could endure what my father had endured. After each slur, I yelled "Sir! Yessir!" even though no one else had, and kept smiling. That must have come to me from my father. This was a kind of lunacy I intuitively understood, and, in a weird way, enjoyed. There was only so far these people, unlike my father, would go.

They could yell all they wanted, as long as they let me stay.

In many ways, basic training was a lark. When it was difficult, it was so because everything had to be done as a group, meaning that all progress occurred at the pace of the weakest link. When we went to the clinic for shots, the whole unwieldy flight had to be marched en masse across base for them. In full formation, a five-minute walk could take a half hour. When we ran, no one could be left behind; sometimes we'd end up "running" in comic slow motion while somebody puked alongside the track. No one was allowed to fail, no matter how mundane the task. I folded a thousand duffel bags for the fumble-fingered, hospital-cornered thousand beds.

Since I had no point of reference for the day-to-dayness of the military, no understanding of why they made us do the odd things they made us do (e.g., folding socks in a particular way or progressing through the chow hall according to a precise pattern of movement), I simply threw myself into each assigned task, however tedious or inexplicable, as if my life depended on it. I'd hit rock bottom as a civilian. I had to make the Air Force work.

When we were sent out on "weeds and seeds" detail (i.e., picking up litter), my neurotic competitiveness drove me to retrieve the most cigarette butts. When we buffed floors, mine had to be translucent. My life had to mean something, I needed to be able to feel my life, even if my life was picking up trash. Anyway, I couldn't help it; my parents did it to me. Sloth was a sin to us and I was no sinner. Also, I didn't want to get yelled at. Soon, however, I was addicted to the high of the TIs' approval. In the beginning, we were pushed no harder than manual labor, but soon we were all thrust into leadership situations to see how we would fare. Not that I realized that then. It was all about not having the TIs turn on me, not getting shipped back to St. Louis in disgrace.

Whether we were sent in twos and threes for weeds and seeds or twenty at a time to do KP, one of us was placed formally in charge and held responsible. That someone was usually me. That responsibility included everything from Airman Brown's rumpled uniform to Airman Waller's failure to salute, to Airman Cady's "flip" attitude and the floor that wasn't quite shiny enough. One of my troops burped during inspection and I was hauled onto the carpet. In the military, someone is always responsible. In the course of any given day, I went from begging my flight mates to behave to cajoling them to psychoanalyzing them to threatening to kick their asses after lights-out—but I got the job done. No one was more surprised than I.

Having grown up under two strict disciplinarians, one of whom thought he was still a marine, I had no trouble adapting. People around me got yelled at for having their hands in their pockets—my mother used to cut mine off or sew them shut to keep me from doing just that. My flight mates would unbutton their shirt cuffs in the Texas humidity; my mother cut my flapping cuffs off. My posture was already ramrod—Johnnie Florence would come up behind me and jerk me up straight when I went through my preteen slouching period. I never got yelled at for not saying "ma'am" and "sir"; I've addressed every elder, every person in a position of authority, that way since I could talk. To this day, my mother, my best friend, is still "ma'am." After her strict housekeeping and my role as Mama's adjutant, I was relieved to have only one bed to make, one area to keep tidy, one set of laundry to keep clean. Since my father subjected us to 6 A.M. Saturday morning white-glove inspections for as long as he was around, there was nothing new to me there. No water in the sinks, no trash in the trash cans—I'd always had to live like that. I was amazed by how difficult my flight mates found this. Did they have to do no work at home?

For a bookworm, the academics were a breeze. A true daughter of the Great Migration, I instinctively coupled my strict upbringing with my education and love of indiscriminate reading and grafted them onto the military's need to regulate the minutiae of everyday life. I learned a lesson in basic training that led me straight to the top of every pile I was in during those twelve years: the regulations are your friends.

The proper way to do everything, no matter how trivial, no matter how important, is written down somewhere. Whether it's the proper way to perform an about-face, the procedure for becoming an Air Force One pilot, or how to make three tons of oatmeal, there's a regulation. And NOTHING, but NOTHING, trumps a regulation. Terrified of making a misstep and comforted by reading and rereading the only printed material allowed us, I dove headfirst into the manuals we were given on wearing the uniform, military custom, and the like. I was the "answer girl," the one who could explain how a proper "to the rear, march" was executed and just how many inches away from the heart your decorations were supposed to be. Nerdiness, love of detail, and hyperorganization are valued traits in the service. They make you cool.

A few weeks into our six weeks of training, Sergeant Harris, our head TI, called me into his office and told me he was naming me dorm chief and that I was well on my way to distinguished graduate. Harris, who was also black, reminded me that I wasn't the first dorm chief; he'd already fired a couple of white girls. "You'll be highly visible," he said soberly, and we both knew what he meant.

A black TI designating one of the few blacks dorm chief would attract special attention and get us both fired if I botched things. Unless I shone like a star, he'd be accused of playing racial favorites and I'd be accused of getting over simply because I was black. We'd both be tainted. The Air Force is at once a huge, far-flung place and a tiny town—there are far fewer than six degrees of separation between any two members. In any event, our reputations, earned or unearned, would precede us. He was taking a chance with me, something military people do not do lightly.

It was the PSAT all over again. I begged to be passed over.

I didn't want to shine like a star. I didn't want to be "highly visible." I just wanted to be Air Force. I wanted a satisfying job I could wrap my arms and legs around and hold on to for twenty years until I could retire with a full pension and my memories of letters typed in exotic locales.

The look of quiet pride on his face changed to a sneer. He tossed the dorm chief badge at me and ordered me out of his office. I kept begging. He started assessing five demerits for each minute I spent disobeying a direct order. At the ten-demerit point, I about-faced in a fog and marched off. I wanted to die. There was no way I could pull this off. No way. North St. Louis, here I come.

I wept in the hallway for a while, then marched myself home (basic trainees can't just walk), my future passing in front of my red eyes. Hairnets and deep fryers. Welfare caseworkers and police investigators asking about relatives. Temporary restraining orders.

Hoo ya.

The black girls were ecstatic. "All right!" one crowed. "Now we can give all the shit jobs to the white girls."

My heart sank. On top of getting all our work done and making sure no one was left behind, I was also sitting atop a powder keg of interpersonal and intergroup chaos.

Then her choice of words hit me.

"What do you mean 'we,' Waters?"

Sergeant Harris wouldn't yell at "us" if something went wrong. "We" wouldn't be up all night with a flashlight checking wall lockers for conformity while evading marauding TIs.

"'We' aint dorm chief. I am." I wasn't happy about this. Couldn't they see that?

No, they couldn't. I saw it in their faces. Someone sucked her teeth in that way that says, I got your number, sister. I was on racial probation, presumed guilty. Now that I'd lucked up on a nickel more than the next black had, I had to consciously demonstrate the racial loyalty that had been presumed before or be damned for my success. But dammit, I had a job to do.

"Oh, it's like that, is it?" "Waters," the scariest human being I have ever been locked in a confined space with, stood to her full six feet. A Watts native, her voice was a cruel rasp and she had scars I was sure were from knife fights.

Even so, I was more afraid of Harris than of her. A beating I could recover from, but the loss of the Air Force and all its possibilities? All I wanted was a new life. The Air Force was going to give me that, so I was prepared to render unto Caesar by doing things the Air Force way. If I didn't run the flight efficiently, if things fell apart—well, that was an eventuality I wasn't prepared to face.

"Yeah. It's like that," I said, and stared them down. There was no going back for me and I knew what would come next. Since I wouldn't identify solely with the blacks, they wouldn't identify with me if I ever needed backup. If I black-identified preemptively, they'd back me up no matter what; any opposition would instantly become "racist." If I wouldn't, I would be on my own if I got into trouble. So be it.

The white girls, too, challenged my authority. Not so much on racial terms as on general principles. But as we moved along in the program, everyone adapted, became more confident. The TIs lightened up, too, since we were doing so well. We were all after new lives, all happy to lose ourselves in the program. Inevitably, I bumped heads with lazy girls, girls who felt they should be dorm chief, or girls who simply pulled something boneheaded, but I managed. It was then, the first time I got to make myself over, that I found out I was funny.

Desperate to graduate, I often relied on humor to keep the girls' cooperation. Also, the fact that I was a sharp airman (could Eddie Mack and Johnnie Florence's daughter not be?) won their deference. We were all being made over in the Air Force's hard-charging image, and our previous conceptions of what was cool and what wasn't mutated to the Air Force's version. Peer pressure, yes, but good peer pressure for once. I had to play ghetto girl off and on and talk tough—laughable since that was a role I couldn't play when actually in the ghetto—but they bought it.

The Hispanic girls, all from barrios, most definitely did not buy my badass routine, so I never pulled it on them. They found me amusing, though, and didn't fight me. Most of their hostility was intracommunal—New York Puerto Ricans versus southwestern and West Coast Mexican-Americans (I hadn't known there were other than the latter before basic). Though I was terrified, I was also determined and I let everyone know that beefs beyond a certain level would not be tolerated and that I'd call on Air Force resources to squash them. Not black, not midwestern, but hard-core, polyester blue Air Force backup. Had I relied on the black girls to back me up, I think things would have turned out much differently. I'd have won, since we easily terrified the white girls and knew instinctively to power-share with the Hispanics, but it would have left the white girls feeling like "niggers": powerless, ill used, and justified in their knee-jerk resentment. Once I let it be known that I'd be doing things by the book, no exceptions, even the black girls felt relieved. We all got to put our baggage down.

It was a heady experience. I could feel myself getting stronger and I liked it. There could be no fraud syndrome in a place which found a way to quantify each and every facet of everyday life. I had to accept that I was actually good at this.

The most difficult thing about being dorm chief was the way the TIs competed nonstop. When we marched to chow, there'd be ten formations lined up to eat. TIs would show off fancy march steps and sing out their flight's average test scores and squadron ranking. They'd denigrate the competitor's trainee with the rumpled uniform, slightly too long hair. No elementary school bus ever heard as many insults as were hurled by a gaggle of TIs. Just like us trainees, they were held responsible for the progress and conduct of their charges, however beyond their control. Their promotions and evaluations depended on how well their flights did; just a few marginal flights in a row could get a TI busted back to the job he'd come from. Harris wanted to win, and the only way to do that was through his trainees.

He informed me that I had to beat Sister Flight's dorm chief to the drill pad every morning for 5 A.M. reveille so he could make Sister Flight's TI squirm. So I slept in socks, bra, panties, and T-shirt. I pinned my hair to regulation at bedtime and slept in my shower cap, which I tore off at the first note of reveille. On the run to the bathroom, I leapt into the uniform I'd prepared the night before. While I was peeing, one hand buttoned my fatigue shirt while the other brushed my teeth with a preloaded-the-night-before toothbrush. I splashed my face at the sinks, raced back to retighten the blanket on the bed whose coverings we all slept atop. I grabbed my hat and raced downstairs. My personal area returned to regulation standards, it never took me more than a few minutes to hit the drill pad. As the race got tighter, I gave up peeing and brushing my teeth beyond one quick swipe. Better kidney disease, better trench mouth than failure. Then I hacked my hair off. Sister Flight's dorm chief never beat me. Not once.

Harris smoked in the darkness behind me. He was always the first TI there, too. He never spoke to me until the duty day had officially begun after this formation, but he didn't have to. As both his peers and mine straggled in to take their places, the places behind us, we both stood tall.

Standing at parade rest in the pitch black of a humid Texas predawn, uniform "strack" (not just militarily perfect but also with a dash of panache), wide awake and alert, the first person to report for duty, I couldn't help feeling a sense of accomplishment. I was winning. I didn't know what I was winning, but that was enough.

It was just reveille, but nonetheless I started each day with a victory. For the first time, I wasn't overthinking, I wasn't worrying myself to death. The Air Force kept me busy all day, made me too tired not to sleep at night, and gave me no time to worry about the future. It had big plans for me and I just let myself fall headfirst into them.

Eddie-like, I found it impossible to ask for help, so though I could have ordered them to, I never required my flight mates to police my area for me during my headlong flight downstairs. Soon, though, we were all caught up in the competitive atmosphere and the rush we got from winning. I'd sprint to remake my bed, realign my shoes, and check my wall locker—five trainees would be hard at work on them, shouting, "Go, go! Get down there before that cow!" Flight mates would shadow me to the door, picking lint out of my hair, stray strings off my uniform. My four squad leaders would be getting the rest of the flight moving. They honored me by chipping in unbidden; I honored them by ceasing to check that they'd done so. As long as I did my job, they'd do theirs. Somehow, I had learned to lead by example.

One day, just a few short of graduation, as I marched the flight somewhere, someone or something marched with me. I knew I wasn't alone. It told me in plain English that the hard times were over. "Everything's going to be all right now," it said clearly, a fortifying whisper in my ear. Some think this was a religious experience. I think it was me. For the first time, I let my own voice come through loud and clear. No second-guessing. No fraud syndrome. No self-effacement. No smart-ass quips. No feigned ennui. I couldn't identify it then because I had never really heard it before; I was simply unfamiliar with the unvarnished Debra Jean Dickerson. I didn't recognize her voice then, but I do now. Since then, I've been unsure about what I should do, but never about what I could do.

So much came into focus for me in my first few years in the military. Having always been a shrinking violet physically, I discovered that I was athletic. Though I'd dreaded the muck and physical torture of the obstacle course, I found myself perversely enjoying the madness of it. After twenty-one years of enforced ladylike behavior, I reveled in the brute physicality of swearing, sweating, and heaving myself from one torture to the next. Everyone did better than she'd thought she would.

TIs were stationed along the confidence course screaming themselves hoarse to keep us moving. I thought them sadists. Low-crawling beneath strands of low-slung barbed wire while a simulated firefight took place over our heads, I simply ran out of steam. I couldn't help feeling like an escaping slave, slithering through long rows of cotton with the "paddy-roller's" bloodhounds at my heels, my elbows and knees all scratched and gory. I lay with my face in the dirt, trying to clear my mind of that draining mental image, praying for a second wind. From nowhere, a TI was in my face screaming bloody murder.

I was covered with dirt. Ants were crawling down my T-shirt and I had a thousand nicks and scrapes. The person behind me was hissing curses and pushing at my feet to get me moving. I wanted to cry. But more than anything, I wanted to smack this TI. Then I noticed he was faking it. Round with concern, his eyes flicked over me from head to foot to see if I was injured. He couldn't motivate me in any other way except through fear and disapproval; a firefight is no time for a pep talk. I couldn't say I was tired—that would be whining. I couldn't say it was freaking me out—that would be worse than whining. What could I do? What would my father have done? Laugh, I guessed, so that's what I did.

"Airman! What is so goddamn funny?" The bewilderment on his face made me laugh again. I found my second wind.

Scrabbling forward with renewed vigor, I yelled at the top of my lungs, "JUST HAPPY TO BE HERE, SIR!"

As I ran along, I distracted myself thinking about why the name had been changed from the obstacle course to the confidence course. The point was not to needlessly burden us; it was to show us how to tap into those reserves of drive and competence we'd never learned the way to. Under no other set of circumstances would I have attempted such public humiliation; I was the girl in school who'd watched the baseball land at her feet instead of trying to catch it and failing. At Wade and Southwest, there were no repercussions for a girl not trying in gym; in the Air Force, it meant expulsion. But they didn't want us to fail. They wanted us to soar.

I'd never run before, yet I found that I was a natural. I aced the physical portions of the training and reveled in it. I was disgusted by the weakness of some of my flight mates. They would beg and mule for permission to go to the airmen's club, where they'd dance all night like whirling dervishes. But a simple half-mile jog would have a third of them faking convulsions. This caused problems for the whole flight because the institutional response was to slow the flight down to accommodate them. But we had to accomplish the run in the time allotted or we wouldn't graduate; it mattered not at all how fast we could run it as individuals. Also, it negatively affected our standing in the squadron competition for Honor Flight. So many were dropping out and fleeing to sick call with "exercise-induced" this and that, that Harris told me to handle it.

With the slackers, I was merciless. I gave onerous duties to people I considered to be faking or punking out. Also, a midnight conversation with Waters (who turned out to be a lovely person desperately trying to escape the ghetto) helped even the laziest tap into reserves of athleticism she never knew she'd had. Most, though, were like me and just needed a push to find out what they were made of. Those of us who ran well helped them one on one. We became Honor Flight. And just as had my father, I became a warrior who didn't know when to quit.

HOW THE AIR FORCE MADE ME A HUMORLESS FEMINIST

I became a 20834G: Korean linguist. Nobody knew me, so I reinvented myself as the carefree "D.J." and embarked on my new incarnation. D.J. smoked. D.J. cursed. D.J. said what she was thinking, even if what she was thinking was cruel, because D.J. was funny. D.J. threw herself at mean men who were just like her father. D.J. overcompensated.

Learning another language was glorious, especially one so exotic. I sailed through the program. I wouldn't even have taken my books home from the classroom except that it was against regulations to leave them there. After a week of doing so, I was officially counseled by an Army classmate who, having served a prior hitch, was our designated classroom leader. Rather than say "Don't leave your books here," he actually read the applicable reg to me in its entirety while I thought about how much he epitomized the weak-chinned, thinning-haired prototypical nerdy white guys I was now surrounded by. The kind of men who wore a huge tangle of keys on their belt and wore their military patent leather shoes with civvies. Guys like him thronged to the military because it was the one place where nerds ruled.

He was so nondescript I could barely remember his name. I used to snap my fingers in his face as I searched my memory, finally just settling for a bitchy "Uh, Sergeant Whoever." Then one day he wore the Army's soon-to-be-phased-out khaki uniform to class and I was smitten senseless. Out of Army polyester-puke green, he was an Adonis; broad shoulders, narrow waist, and a piercing need to humiliate any woman he couldn't terrorize into leaving him. But I had a high threshold for terror. Like me, he was a working-class refugee whose intellect was too big for his station in life but too untamed to lead him farther away from it than military transport could take him. It would take me four years to get this disturbed, desperate (and, underneath it all, wonderful) man out of my system. Another fifteen to trust myself to fall in love again.

After a year of language school in Monterey, there were six months of technical training in San Angelo, Texas. Both segments had very high washout rates; our language program was the equivalent of a four-year course crammed into one fast-paced year of constant testing and milestones. The tech training called for us fuzzy liberal-arts types to master sensitive monitoring and satellite equipment. It was a combination of skills that remain in short supply, especially given that it was nearly two years before we got to our first duty assignments. But it was so easy, so much fun for me, I had no sympathy for those who couldn't cut it. I wouldn't associate with anyone who was struggling because I was sure they just weren't working hard enough.

There was a girl in our class who'd already been set back once from the previous class. She wept quietly in the back of the room while the rest of us battled joyfully for the top spot. Within two weeks—she could barely even pronounce the Korean name we'd all been given—she was gone and I was glad. She'd been deflating our class average. Without her, our class was known as the Gang of 4.4—the highest score on the Department of Defense's language qualifying exam.

My year in Monterey, California (officially, the Defense Language Institute Foreign Language Center, or DLI-FLC), was extremely collegiate. Our duty was to attend class daily from 7 or 7:30 to about 3:00. My closest girlfriend, Martha from Nebraska, learned Russian as easily as I learned Korean, so we had our evenings free to trade books and see movies. There were desultory room and uniform inspections, a Monday morning formation, rotating shifts cleaning the barracks, and some PT. But mostly, the Air Force left us alone to learn our languages and to be initiated into the time-honored military traditions of binge drinking and promiscuous heterosexuality. Life was good.

Most of the other young enlisteds were either working class, like myself, or rural. Also like me, most were diamonds in the rough. While I'd only just begun to see it in myself, I was saddened by how many of these bright, inquisitive young people had no idea how smart they were. One woman on my squad was breezing through Serbo-Croatian during the day and teaching herself Polish at night with my roommate's materials, just for the joy of it. When I complimented her, her eyes went round. Then she burst into tears. No one had ever told her she was talented. I was surrounded by gifted, hardworking, self-sacrificing kids whom society was prepared to squander, but for the services.

Dave, another working-class kid, was so smart he was annoying; things were so easy for him, he drove the rest of us crazy with his excess energy and drive. Every time we smokers lit up, he'd drop to the floor and pound out ten push-ups. To torment him, we'd stagger our light-ups, but he'd just gut them out. We gave him an awesome physique. Not only was he acing our Korean class, he taught himself extra Chinese characters and Japanese to boot. At one of our Monday morning formations, we were presented with an airman who was going off to the Air Force Academy. I found Dave and told him he should do that, too. He was horrified at the suggestion. I had to nag him and search out his hiding places for a few weeks as he tried to avoid me. In short order, though, he was neck deep in the arduous process of winning admission to the United States Air Force Academy from the enlisted corps. Not only was he selected, he graduated with honors, won a graduate fellowship where he met his wife, and is now an F-16 pilot and a major in the United States Air Force. Civilian society would have wasted him because he was a trailer-park kid, just another community college dropout.

The class issues surrounding me were starting to bubble to the surface of my consciousness. Gender issues announced themselves from day one.

I was continually amazed by the contradiction in the women around me. Most were strong, sturdy women who'd been the unsung backbones of their own hardscrabble families before enlisting. Indeed, many enlisted to escape the drudgery and to have a chance to put themselves first. Most exhibited a ferocity and tenacity to gain control of their lives that surprised and nourished us all.

Since we all had to sink or swim together, our ladylike gloves had been off by the end of the first week of basic. Politeness and gentility went out the window as one sweet little eighty-five-pound girl, Huff, from a tiny speck of a little Tennessee town, told the hulking Waters to "move her carcass" out of the way so she could hussle the flight's garbage out. Waters moved her carcass. If she hadn't, we wouldn't have cooperated with her so she could get her own job done. By the end of basic, none of Huff's declarative sentences ended with rising inflections, as they all had on day one. She didn't blush when forced to speak. Indeed, she never stopped talking, whereas in the beginning, Harris had had to give her demerits for replying only with wide-eyed nods.

As soon as they cleared basic, though, many of these newly empowered women reverted to off-duty passivity and the learned helplessness I felt sure they'd enlisted to escape. As soon as a man entered the picture, they forgot everything they knew about thinking for themselves.

During my year in Monterey from 1980 to 1981, we had to help recarpet the barracks. Workers were coming to do the actual installation, but we were required to move the ten-foot carpet rolls to their proper locations. As soon as we were told which rolls were ours on the loading dock, my floor mates started planning which guys to ask to carry ours and which of us women would run out for beer and pizza for them. I was appalled. Is that what we were going to do in wartime, wait for a big, strong man to carry our greasy old M-16s?

"Why don't we see if we can manage it ourselves?" I asked.

There were thirty of us, what was the big deal? My mother, sisters, and I would have starved to death had we waited for men to do things for us. When I was just a little kid, I'd helped move refrigerators, rehung doors, painted whole houses. Whatever needed doing, we women had just done it; it wasn't feminism, it wasn't politics, it was just our lot in life to have no help. My mother never put it to us in feminist terms—"The Lord helps those who help themselves" was all she ever said on the subject. We had uncles and male cousins we might have called, but that wasn't our way. What we couldn't do ourselves, what some man didn't just show up and do for us without our asking, we either paid a professional to do or, more often, lived without. What on earth were we waiting for with a few carpet rolls?

In the end, there were two camps. About a third wiggled their way over to the male barracks to tell them about the dykes they had to live with and to pout prettily for help. Two thirds joined me and we finished hours ahead of the little girls who had to wait for assistance.

Even so, I was consciously antifeminist then. In the sixth or seventh grade, I'd given a substanceless "I enjoy being a girl" denunciation of feminism in a classroom debate and gotten a standing ovation from the teachers (all female except for the science teacher). They marched me all over the school to repeat it. I used to remember this incident because of all the approval. Now I remember it as a political event. Had I made such unsubstantiated arguments on any other topic, Miss Enright would have stopped me mid-sentence, sent me back to my seat in disgrace, and failed me on the project, but they were all middle-aged women appalled by women's lib. That same school year, though, when my all-girl team was presenting our science project, they wanted to ask for special permission to wear pants and ties "so we'll seem serious."

"Why don't we seem serious now?" I asked.

They rolled their eyes. Everyone but me dressed like a boy. I didn't get it. Even so, I was a good girl then and I thought the bra-burners silly because that's what was said about them at home on the rare occasions when the subject came up. From the very beginning of my service, though, I had to think constantly about gender.

There were a spate of rapes in our barracks, mostly because the building's many entrances had no locks. After they began, the Air Force did two things: first, it conducted surprise "health and welfare" inspections to make sure we targets had no weapons. Second, it bought locking doors. But the Language Institute was on Army property and, we were told, the Army wouldn't allow them to put up the doors. So we sprinted into the building and into our rooms after dark, locked ourselves in our rooms, peed in containers, and came to fear our big communal bathroom where many of the attacks took place.

In addition to the general air of danger, there was the murkiness of our first forays into adult relationships. During my first four years in the military, I couldn't keep track of all the strong, together, brave women I knew who were getting pushed around by their boyfriends and blaming themselves. Date rape was rampant but rarely reported. When it was, women usually joined in the general denunciation of the victim.

There's a lot of off-duty drinking in the military; most discipline and personnel problems stem from that. I learned in Texas that what usually happened with GI date rape was, some woman would come tottering back into the dorms at 3 A.M., dress torn, eyes bloodshot, hysterical. Her friends would bustle her off and hide her away for a few days. Then, if she had a particularly bold friend, that woman would march up to the guy and be very, very rude to him. He'd become indignant. She'd march back to her friend and tell him she'd given him a good talking-to—but . . . *why'd you go into his room? You didn't tell me you'd had three beers. You kissed him. I mean, what was he supposed to think?*

In any case, most women had no such bold friends.

These women did their men's laundry, they shopped for them, they took their orders. Their men told them whom they could and couldn't befriend, what they could and couldn't wear, makeup or not. Given the volatility of military life and the mawkish sentimentality and immature notions of romantic love the lower classes are weaned on, GIs, especially young GIs, often marry hastily, to people they barely know. Though we were largely kept under lock and key in basic, by its end, three flight mates were desperately trying to marry male trainees they'd only been able to chat with briefly at chapel or our rare nights at the airmen's club. Disaster often followed. "Susie," for example, hurriedly married another linguist one month into their relationship (Assignments won't try to place couples together unless they're married). To complete the fairy tale, she got pregnant immediately, but by her second trimester she was reporting for duty red-eyed and compulsively chugging Listerine. She hated her new husband, now that she knew him. He was forcing her to send him off to work each morning with a kitchen-table blow job, since her increasing girth "made sex suck and [you] owe me." He'd come up behind her at chow, grab her head, and push it backward and forward while laughing, "That was you this morning, am I right?"

It baffled me. Not that he was a horrible human being, but that such a smart, capable woman had made such foolish choices. Worse, other women disapproved more of her giving her husband custody of the child when she finally left him than they did his public cruelty toward her. I allowed my boyfriend to be very mean to me—but do his laundry, take his slaps, let him control my life on such a mundane and overt level?

Nothing did more to make me rethink feminism and female low self-esteem than the two-track personalities I saw then. Women who ran their sections like Patton would turn into kindergartners in the presence of their boyfriends. Women took dives on their language exams so as not to outdo their boyfriends; women refused to test for promotion early, though they'd earned it, for fear of their men's reactions. I saw women not only downplay their accomplishments but also swear others to silence so their men wouldn't have to deal with their prowess. Later, with some of my male office mates, I literally couldn't tell whether they were talking to their wives or their small children on the phone. These women would deploy to Pakistan on twenty-four hours' notice with nothing but a lipstick and their ID card, but disagree publicly with their man? Not on a bet.

My nascent feminism was not a rebellion against my traditional upbringing; it was the logical conclusion of it. True, women in my world back home took a back seat to men, but they did so stridently; their strength and talent was never questioned and rarely held in abeyance. It's our love for our children and desire for familial stability that keeps us in check, not our men.

My mother was never anything but a tower of strength—my father never made her crawl, nor could he have if he'd tried. She never feared him and she never hated him; she pitied him and mourned the happiness they could have had. She backed him up and never spoke ill of him or tolerated those who did, but only because she chose to, because that was the kind of family she wanted to live in. She was always a rock. She never wavered about anything.

My aunts, my female cousins—not a weakling in the bunch. At the very least, the man who berated one of them for taking her job too seriously or for being too decisive would be ridiculed. He still wouldn't have to cook, clean, or tend children, but he would keep his paws off her psyche. Few men voluntarily ran afoul of the sharp-tongued females in my family. Women in my world fulfilled traditional roles for their children's sake, but they did it standing up. No cringing, no apologizing, no swooning. No schizophrenia. Very early on, I realized that being female in the military was going to be much more difficult than being black.

HOW THE AIR FORCE MADE ME A CONSCIOUS CONSERVATIVE

While the military takes a radical, "sky's the limit" approach to its human capital, it couldn't be more hidebound about politics if it forced its members to deny that the earth revolves around the sun. The institution is conservative because its members are, and vice versa; there aren't a lot of Upper West Side paleoliberals keen to take the oath of military office. Professionalism, competitiveness, and presumed success are in the air in the military; slackers are summarily dealt with. The good thing about such an atmosphere is that it fosters high expectations and pulls forth the best from its people; the bad is that it fosters an unsympathetic, "blame the victim" ethos.

In uniform, someone is always at fault, no matter how complicated the situation. In Korea in 1982, I knew an exemplary airman who, while drunk, accidentally dropped and killed his baby—forty years at hard labor. When I was an officer in Texas in 1986, we had an airman of whom we all thought highly. She tested positive for trace amounts of marijuana; her court-martial panel believed our character references, believed she'd only tried it once—six months' confinement, reduction in grade, forfeiture of pay, and a bad-conduct discharge. Had I been on the panel, I would have to had to concur given the structure of the Uniform Code of Military Justice.

Imagine how little patience we had for the complaints of the unemployed, the poorly educated, the structurally disadvantaged: they just need to work harder, they just need to tighten their belts, and most of all, they need to stop expecting something for nothing. The fact that such comments often came from fat, unfireable master sergeants with their feet up on a desk reading the newspaper all day was lost on me.

Most of us enlisted were intimately associated with the unemployed, the poorly educated, the structurally disadvantaged: unlike the bleeding hearts, we knew who cleaned up their messes, and it wasn't the Brahmins in D.C. or the ivory-tower patricians. We knew who'd disrupted our high school classes with their disrespectful behavior, we knew who'd been experimenting with drugs and irresponsible sex when we'd been experimenting with after-school jobs and trade schools. We knew who'd made fun of us for working hard and we knew who it was who now expected us to save them from themselves. No one's harder on the poor than the poor.

I was in Korea during our invasion of Grenada. We cheered Reagan and got drunk in his honor, but I couldn't have explained why it was necessary to pulverize Club Med. What I could have done, though, was describe having watched President Carter's ill-fated Iranian hostage rescue attempt on TV with a group of senior NCOs and officers the previous year. Many of them had served during Viet Nam and they were sick with grief and rage. Doors slammed, phones got thrown, and chairs toppled all that day as GIs, overcome with emotion, flung themselves about trying to find some way to be useful. Winning was better. I was still in Korea for the 1982 elections and tried desperately to register so I could vote for Reagan's minions. Thank God the antidemocratic voter registration regime he presided over made it impossible for me to do so.

My new life and my new career were going splendidly. I breezed through my operational training at Osan Air Base, South Korea, and was designated the evaluator for my specialty. I was good and I knew it. I worked hard and I got results. That meant anyone could; assertions to the contrary were merely excuses. By the time I'd completed my nearly two years of training, I was utterly confident, totally propagandized, and fiercely "incog-Negro."

HOW I MADE MYSELF A RACIST

While the military breeds for confidence and conservative politics, being antiblack was my own innovation. Indeed, the military is the most race-neutral place I've ever been because in uniform, nothing matters but success. Unless the base burns down, there's no excuse for not getting your mission accomplished, be that mission mail-sorting or bomb-detecting. If you've got only black troops to detect bombs with, you damn well better get over any problems with blacks you may have.

One of the reasons the military succeeds where society fails racially is that hiring, training, assignments, and the final work site are all firewalled from each other and operating in a very competitive environment. Recruiters have quotas of qualified hirees to meet—they are in no position to sabotage applicants. Trainers who shortchange trainees will suffer the consequences on their own evaluations; units in the field will promptly let it be known that they've received poorly trained personnel. All a unit can do is request bodies to fill certain positions, and until those bodies show up—in my case two years after being hired—you have no idea whether they'll be Jews, chicks, Georgia good ol' boys, or whoever else it is that sets your jaw. You have no choice but to get over it. In the military, the only way to "win" is through your people; the better they do, the better you do, because it's entirely legitimate to take credit for your people's work. In such an environment, you sniff out talent and nurture it, just as Harris did me, and together we made our flight Honor Flight; without a doubt, that was in his next Airman Performance Report. In the civilian world, it's not self-destructive to discriminate; in the military it is.

But the military is its own little world; blacks are a big, visible part of that world, and I could no longer avoid close proximity to "them" as I'd always been able to do before. The military transcends race by creating a highly defined, societally valued persona for all to cleave to. If you jettison any aspects of your personality or culture that conflict with the military persona, you're in. If you can't, you'll be shunned and forced out. When society talks about "transcending race," it really means "transcending nonwhiteness." In the military, you really do have to transcend race, including the white one. Boston Southie, Valley girl, or ghetto boy—you can rise to the top in the military or just have a fulfilling four years and move on. You don't have to give up your culture; you just have to stow it for the duration of the duty day if it's going to cause a conflict. If not, no one cares about your collard greens and cornbread for lunch because it has nothing to do with anything relevant to the job and the job is all that matters.

In such a demilitarized atmosphere, people take chances. On flight in Korea once, we were passing time talking about the upcoming unit Halloween party and what costumes we'd wear. Apropos of nothing, our Hispanic flight commander suggested I tie a rag around my head and come as Aunt Jemima. A stunned silence reigned. Little by little, the silence was rent by my white flight mates' escaping giggles. But I lived and worked with these people; I knew they weren't racists.

So I said to Lieutenant Salas, "OK. I'll wear a head rag and come as Aunt Jemima if you'll dry your back off and come as an American." The white folks nearly died laughing. Lieutenant Salas and I shook on it and moved on. Later, he taught me to two-step, a civilized dance I much preferred to the near rape perpetrated by many black men on the dance floor.

For all my interracial enlightenment, intraracially, I was a mess. I could never forgive the "hood rats" for embarrassing me. No one would blink when some black airman mangled his verbs and said "I be" while demonstrating his job for the general. No one but me. The fact that he'd been chosen by his superiors as the best (otherwise he wouldn't be doing the demo) was lost on me. All I heard was the sharecropper speech patterns. All I saw was the gold teeth.

There were few specific instances that led to my distaste for and disapproval of blacks; there was just the self-hatred I did not yet recognize which made me want them to disappear. Unless, of course, they acted just like me. Blacks were hypervisible, or at least they were to me, and I was constantly vigilant for signs of our group failure. Like a member of the white citizens' councils opposing the civil rights movement, I kept close tabs on our dangerous activities.

It was clear to me that black people chose not to work very hard in the military. Why else would so few number among the linguists, the commandos, the pilots, the officers, the academy grads? You couldn't enter a military administrative office without finding enough Negroes working there to make a Tarzan movie and it always embarrassed me. I expressed my embarrassment as annoyance. That's their choice, I thought; they might just as easily have chosen a more challenging field, but they'd rather simply take up space.

I was embarrassed to be one of so few linguists and I was embarrassed by the sharecropper intonations and low-class lack of home training I so frequently encountered among these "typing Negroes." I hated entering admin offices when I was junior enlisted because the blacks there tended to be my peers, by rank and age group, and there was an assumption of familiarity that made me uncomfortable. I was sure they'd want to "talk black," make fun of whites, scoff at the Air Force. Then there were the liberties black males felt free to take with me. Sotto voce, they called me "baby" and wanted to know when they were going to get "some of that sugar." When I refused to respond to their vulgarities, I was menacingly called "sister," a word often used to extract behavioral concessions from someone you hope will be too afraid of group disapproval not to back down. It means: "Don't forget you're black; act right or I'll call you a Tom." I got called "Tom" a lot.

As few as we were, the "Head Negroes" (self-designated arbiters of all things sufficiently or insufficiently black) tried every form of negative reinforcement to make us behave. There's a Head Negro anywhere there are African-Americans. At the Defense Language Institute in 1980, she and I began as close friends. How could we not have been? We were both working-class black girls from north St. Louis. She was much harder-edged than me and came from a much less stable home, but still, we knew the same schools, same neighborhoods, same churches, same rib joints. We'd even graduated basic on the same day. Later Martha, who was white and one of eight children of very religious Catholics, came along and we three were inseparable. But as Martha and I grew closer (through our shared love of books and traditional upbringings) and the two of us began to spend more time together, the Head Negro expressed her hurt as racial pride. Black people weren't good enough for me. Ironically, that was true except that she was smart enough, as a Romanian linguist, to make my grade. She just wanted to act so black: she wasn't shooting for DG, she mocked me for shooting for it and she was blasé about the Air Force. She went out of her way to cultivate every black she could find at DLI. She thought she'd hit the Negro mother lode when she networked her way into Fort Ord, the Army base not so far away (not far enough away for me). The Army is a third black, and on top of that, Fort Ord is an infantry base, i.e., full of ghetto blacks. Head Negro homed in on every one she could find who was just marking time, lugging a rifle and a fifty-pound rucksack. Unless the Mafia starts hiring, I used to sneer, what were they going to do next? She was trying to re-create north St. Louis and I was trying to exorcise it. She was determined to remain the ghetto girl I was desperate to bury.

She spent all her free time with those Army grunts and expected me to as well. These were the philistines who came back from three years in Germany with only a monstrous stereo, VD, and abandoned children to show for it. No travel, no savings, no college classes, no studying for promotion, no bucking for a commission. "Barracks rats" who go overseas and never stray more than two hundred yards from the main gate, whining the whole time about how "Coke just don't taste right over here." There wasn't a winner in the bunch. I could have stayed in north St. Louis if I wanted to hang out with trash-talking dishwashers and manual laborers, I thought as I made excuses to wriggle out of her ghetto clique.

Then there was my white boyfriend: I only wanted him because he's white, she said. You really need to leave him alone, Debra, she'd say. Why won't you go out with Derrick? Just because he's the linen supply NCO, you think you're too good. Pretending such an accusation to be beneath me, I refused to defend myself on racial grounds and I refused to modify my behavior to suit her, that ghost of the ghetto. I just didn't like the crowd she ran with—exclusively black and not interested enough in advancement.

Just like with my relatives, I was always tripping someone up. Someone would be griping about their racist commander and an undeserved reprimand. I'd ask a question like, "Well, how many times *were* you late?" Silence. They'd mention how long they'd been in and I'd ask if they were on the promotions list that had just come out. Glares. What else were we supposed to talk about? Their all-black gatherings made me nervous—it was sixth grade all over again and I knew my mannerisms would get me rejected.

She'd spring blind dates on me, knowing I'd never agree beforehand, then watch me squirm while some hood rat flashed his "grill" (multiple gold teeth) at me. She was evil to my boyfriend whenever he was around, so, just as she'd planned, I had to choose. I chose him. Even my white roommate was held against me, though I'd had no say in the matter. We'd gotten off to a rocky start when she'd found me moving into her room; she'd run back out again in a fury. I'd thought it was because I was black. But when she returned, she apologized and started moving her belongings out of my half of the room. "It was nice having so much space to myself," she said wistfully. It was actually I who was the racist; I was relieved not to have a black roommate.

Nevertheless, I thought race was a nonissue for me. I disapproved of blacks because they deserved it, not because they were black. Or rather, it would have been a nonissue except that blacks like the Head Negro, who headed the language school contingent of the black politburo—the blackest of the black in any organization—were constantly giving me the evil eye. My unwillingness to show obeisance to them and their dictates of what could and could not be done robbed them of a courtier, which reduced their power. I was only just beginning to understand that most of the racial whip-cracking that goes on is actually just the expression of personal power disguised as something defensible. All I knew was that I felt manipulated and I didn't like it.

I remained on racial probation, also, because of my interest in all forms of music and my failure to show up at black-only parties. My roommate, a Polish truck-stop waitress from podunk Pennsylvania, introduced me to rock. Through that banged-up little radio I'd grown up listening to, I'd enjoyed some sporadically. Soon, though, AC/DC was blaring on our shared stereo. Another mutual friend from the South introduced us both to all those three-named performers like Jerry Jeff Walker and David Allan Coe—I discovered how clever, soulful, and romantic country music can be.

At military clubs, the different musical genres alternate—soul for an hour, country for an hour, rock the next—so I was glorying in all the new sensory input. I could have avoided on-base clubs like the "real" blacks did and secreted myself away in blacks-only settings to keep myself musically pure, but I was loving my education. I enjoyed all of it, if only for the newness of it—it was all part of those limitless horizons I'd fled St. Louis to find. My album collection was huge, eclectic, and damning.

One day, I was in my room with a few white girls. I had on some black music, and as a joke, I pimp-walked across the room. Before I knew it, three white girls were pimping across my room. The joke was over quickly for me and I wanted them to stop. I was moving to take the record off when they stopped dead in their tracks. I turned to find one of the Head Negro's deputies standing in the doorway, a "gotcha!" look on her face. For weeks, blacks slumped into pimp walks as I passed. By graduation from our one-year language school, I was Negro non grata. All my friends were white.

All-black chow hall tables, all-black rooming groups, all-black off-base parties, nonmainstream music—all this was somehow sinister, somehow wrong. I couldn't understand why they'd join something as all-consuming as the military and then work so hard to remain separate from it. I didn't think of all-white groups as separatist. Those were neutral, baseline. Blacks to me, as to most racists, were less invisible than hypervisible. Everything they did took on special meaning.

They talked and laughed too loud at their Jim Crow table in the chow hall, too.

ROCK BOTTOM

Once at Osan Air Base, about fifty miles southeast of Seoul, I was fully, happily ensconced in a white world. Our job at the 6903rd Electronic Security Group was to monitor the military situation on the peninsula.

For two years, from November 1981 to November 1983, I did shift work on Charlie Flight. That meant three "days" from 6 A.M. to 2 P.M., three "swings" from 2 P.M. to 10 P.M., three "mids" from 10 P.M. to 6 A.M., not quite two days off. Weekends had no meaning, there were no holidays. Day, night. Light, dark. Morning, evening. Whatever. The 6903rd issued us blackout curtains and ordered us to buy battery-powered alarm clocks. Power outages and temporal dislocation were frequent and no excuse for tardiness. Lateness was not only an Article 15 offense (a career-buster just one step from court-martial), it was also considered an immoral breach of duty. You'd be shunned.

Your flight was your world because no one else was on your schedule and "dedication to duty" was the motto of that world. I served at "Skivvy Nine" for two years. Most of my first year is a blur of hard work and even harder partying. I'd had five or six girly sloe gin fizzes or tequila sunrises since enlisting. Pepsi was my poison. By the end of my first month in Korea, I was drinking like a sailor.

It was the early eighties and alcohol had yet to be "deglamorized"; liquor flowed at every gathering, official or unofficial. Whenever we weren't working, we were drinking. We even had our own bar in our Squadron Orderly Room with our own credit system, movies, and a band. Condoms were kept in a box under the counter; we women used to ask for them just to watch the First Shirt's (a senior NCO responsible for all the enlisted troops) face turn red, then blow them up and play volleyball with them. When we were downtown drinking, we got them from the town patrol. Our commander conducted our quarterly commander's call drink in hand. We held them in the bar at the NCO club just to save time since every function became happy hour. Our base liquor store provided us with cigarettes and alcohol so cheap it would have been a crime not to imbibe.

Skivvy Niners bred an atmosphere wherein heavy drinkers who could still anchor a busy shift were the standard to meet. Showing up drunk would earn you a court-martial and complete ostracization. Showing up monstrously hungover but twice as productive as the next guy made you a king. Being able to drink all night, not be hungover, and do your job like a wizard made you a god. That's what most of us were aiming for and it took a lot of booze to get there. Nearly every story told at Skivvy Nine began with "I was so drunk that . . ." The deacon's daughter finally off her leash, I thought I was having the time of my life.

Any GI could live like a king in preboom Korea. We were unofficially required to employ the Korean civilians attached to our units as maids and laundresses. Twelve dollars a month. If you tried to fire yours or shop around for a better deal, the Shirt would "urge you to reconsider." The shops in Song Tan, the town just outside the gates (called "the ville" or "downtown" no matter where in the world we were), catered exclusively to us; Koreans were not allowed in these establishments unless they worked there. Restaurants, gold shops, brass junk, blankets, custom tailoring, sneakers, plaques—and, most of all, bars and prostitutes: whether you were buying dinner for ten, drinks for ten, or whores for ten, nothing cost enough to think twice about and we threw our paychecks around like Monopoly money. The big joke was how you "went broke saving money" in Korea, because everything was so cheap. When bored, we'd "combat shop." We'd compete to see who could assemble a complete outfit and get back to the rendezvous point first, their old clothes in a bag. When the duty day was over, we "ran the ville." To alleviate boredom, we organized themed "runs," e.g., a "punk run" to bars that played punk music, a "disco run" or a "green bean run" for someone new. A "bucket run" was raunchiest of all.

We had a beat-up brass bucket and dipper in the CQ's office that the seniormost person on the run would bang while the rest of us gaggled drunkenly behind bellowing Skivvy Nine's unofficial song. It included lyrics like "We're a bunch of dirty bastards" and "born in a whorehouse. . . ." At each bar, the leader would bang the bucket down on the counter, we'd all toss money in, and the Korean waitresses and bartenders would start pouring stuff into the bucket. Anything and everything.

The first time I saw that, I was disgusted and had a Coke. The second time, I helped pour indiscriminate bottles lying atop the table in as fast as I could. We couldn't leave the bar for the next one on our "frag list" until the bucket was empty. Bucket runs were the stuff of legends. Generals and Viet Nam aces have led them. So have various entertainers while in town through the USO for us. Once, we passed a battered sofa discarded on a Song Tan street. We carried it from bar to bar all night, plopping it down on the stage or the middle of the dance floor, making out on it, tossing hapless passersby onto it and shanghaiing them onto our run.

There were country-western bars, metal-head bars, disco bars, black bars. Eventually everyone developed favorites; my friends and I hung out at either the Stereo or the A-Frame—basic R&B, Top 40 bars. The Stereo was widely popular. It was a straight shot from the main gate: newbies and visitors always ended up there. They couldn't know that the rest rooms at the Stereo were coed: there were "bomb-sights" (porcelain holes in the floor) in stalls for the women, plastic bins for used toilet paper, and urinals along the wall for men. We'd send the new guy in, then follow him nonchalantly in and chat him up while his eyes bugged out and his urine dried up.

I'd been in Korea about two months when Christmas rolled around. I was riding high. I'd aced my rigorous training and finished operational training at Skivvy Nine in record time. I was an evaluator. As luck would have it, Charlie Flight had Christmas Day off. We began drinking as soon as we woke up and drank off and on all day and night. My poison then was Korean "Oscar"; it came in peach and grape and tasted like melted Popsicles.

As the day wound down, we settled in at our orderly room/night club to drink some more. I was playing liar's dice for drinks. There were lots of Skivvy Niners there whom I'd never seen before, given our incompatible shifts. One of them squeezed into my dice game. Greasy-haired, acned, scrawny, and vibrating with nervous tension, he was the type of sad-sack loser that the military attracts in droves. He kept trying to make witty asides but they came out garbled and pathetic. He advised me grandiosely at the dice game, but only made me lose with plays a child could see were wrongheaded. I was the only woman in the game; the men abused him terribly, laughing at the geek, telling him to shut up, and finally ordering him to go away. It was his baby-puke yellow Sears polyester suit they found most hilarious and which most broke my heart; he'd tried so hard to cut a dashing figure. I defended him.

Pathetically grateful and needy, he dogged my footsteps for the rest of Christmas Day. He waited outside the ladies' room when I ducked in there to escape. He waited even through the taunts of my coworkers, who laughed in his face, made whip-cracking sounds, and called him my little puppy dog. But he kept his vigil by the bathroom door. Obviously no one had been nice to him in a long time and he wasn't going to miss this opportunity to . . . what exactly? I often wonder what he told himself he was planning for me. I felt sorry for him, but by evening's end, I'd had enough of this gum sticking to my shoe.

I gave him obvious hints like, "I'd really like to spend some time with my roommate now if you don't mind." He just took two small steps backward from us, his eyes pinioned to me like harpoons. My roommate rolled her eyes at him and wandered off. He took two large and undignified steps forward, releasing his breath in a grateful, relieved whoosh.

At about 1:30 A.M., I knew I wasn't going to lose him and I just wanted to go to bed. Roommate and her boyfriend wandered over and I saw my last chance to lose this strange, unhappy man. I turned my back on him as pointedly as I could and babbled about nothing. I mouthed to her, "Is he still there?" She giggled and nodded. Desperate for enough time to pass to make even him too uncomfortable to stay, I told my drunk and unsteady roommate I'd leave the door unlocked for her.

Then I gave up. I let him walk me home while he tried to toss off pickup lines that were supposed to be Cary Grantish but were, on his cracked and quivering lips, merely Elmer Fuddish.

A few hours later, I woke up with him on top of me. Inside of me.

But it was just a dream, a very bad dream. It wasn't really happening. It couldn't be because it didn't make any sense. The last thing I wanted was a pathetic little piece of a man like him. Inside of me. I'd gone to bed alone, I reasoned while he held me down and moved atop me, so this could. not. be. happening. So it wasn't. But just to tie up all the loose ends, to make sense of what wasn't happening, I kept asking him who he was.

Mama? That couldn't be right.

Roommate? Probably not.

Boyfriend? But it couldn't be him, the man I'd be happy to have inside of . . . he was on the DMZ.

John, the guy I slept with to hurt my boyfriend? No, not him either, I somehow knew even in the absolute darkness of the blackout curtains.

It seemed terribly important at the time to know exactly who this was on top of me. Inside. To each name, he answered "Yeah," annoyed. No hesitation, no stuttering. I guess I was distracting him from the one task he felt proficient in. Finally, he said with force, "You know who this is." It wasn't until then that I got scared, that I began to consider that "this" was actually happening. Mostly, I was afraid because I certainly did not know who this was. Inside of me? Not knowing who was fucking me was very upsetting.

I didn't know who it was until he'd finished repaying my kindness with rape and was rearranging his clothes. His baby-puke yellow polyester Sears suit took on a radioactive light in the slit between the blackout curtains there at ground level. Ten years later when I'd get the official file, I'd learn that he'd stood outside my door, the door he knew to be unlocked, for a long time weighing the pros and cons of raping me. I'd also learn that, annoyed at being semiwakened, I pushed him out of my top bunk. Undaunted, however, he'd climbed back up. On. In. Good old Air Force can-do spirit. Lucky for him, I slept naked back then, a habit he single-handedly broke me of. I sort of bitched at him afterward as he dressed. He was vaguely apologetic, as if he'd used up all the hot water.

I never screamed. I didn't call the cops or wake my neighbors through the also unlocked connecting bathroom door. I went back to sleep.

I woke very early, dressed, curled my bangs, and left. I wandered the base all day. Thinking.

I spent hours convincing myself that it hadn't happened. How could it have? There had to be another explanation.

But there wasn't.

So, I spent the next few hours telling myself that, OK, it had happened, but so what? I'm a big girl. A little unwanted sex wasn't going to kill me, not in a place like Osan where everybody was fucking everybody all the time and nobody was remembering it very well because of all the booze.

But . . .

OK, but he hadn't hit me, he'd had no weapon. I'm my father's daughter, I'm tough. Daddy never went to doctors and I'll never go to lawyers.

That actually worked for about an hour. Then I got mad. So mad, my vision went white around the edges. I saw things very clearly: after ruining my holiday with his boring, pathetic uselessness, that son-of-a-bitching bastard had raped me! He raped me! Those were the only words my mind could hold. He raped me! He raped me! It was as if a door in my mind had been flung open and a complete newsreel of what had happened poured through it. It was maddening. I barricaded the ladies' room door at the NCO club behind me and pounded on the walls, growling.

I wanted blood. I spent hours concocting schemes whereby I could get my brother, my uncles, and some cousins to Korea to beat the spineless worm to a bloody pulp. Angry as I was, if I'd been stateside, I know I would have told my family and not the authorities. But I wasn't stateside. I was on my own.

Running, snarling, snotting, I headed back to Skivvy Nine carrying a big stick I didn't remember picking up. I was going to kill him.

Unfortunately, some senior NCOs saw me brandishing a war club. I informed them that Spineless Worm had raped me in my own bed. On Christmas Day. I was going to kill him if they could please let go of my arms.

The Air Force dispatched two male investigators. The last thing I wanted was the scrutinizing company of men. I was never asked if I wanted a woman present and I was far from making demands in those days; I was forceful with my peers, but not with authority, especially in the state I was in.

In a room full of men—my squadron hierarchy and the OSI agents—I had to tell the story and answer a raft of horrible questions (e.g., "Did he ejaculate? How do you know?"). I was the only woman in the room and, at twenty-two, the only person under forty. I felt like dirt.

The agents took me to the base hospital. The doctor was a bungler. I was required to strip naked and wait while Dr. Kim searched high and low for the "rape kit." It was actually marked that way. The box was red, blood fucking red. Looking at it made me want to curl up in a fetal position.

Then, Dr. Kim stood muttering to himself with the rape kit instructions in one hand, the little comb he dragged through my pubic hair in the other. Then, there was the pelvic exam. It was like being raped by a stranger all over again. Repeatedly, I had to sit naked and pathetic while he searched for supplies or left the room to do God knows what. I was never offered a covering, never offered a counselor or a Kleenex.

A young male airman pushed the exam room door open with his

mop and bucket as I sat there, and took long moments to stop staring at me and leave. He wasn't embarrassed, he wasn't turned on, he wasn't curious about the rape girl. He was merely debating whether or not he could mop the room. Dr. Kim said nothing. I draped my arms over my face and stopped paying attention to anything after that. The doctor had to prod me with his stethoscope to get me to respond.

Had I known what the rape exam would be like, I would not have pressed charges.

In any event, I'd never decided to press charges; I had decided to kill the bastard. Once the situation was taken out of my hands, however, it never occurred to me not to see it through. I'd been raped and rape is wrong. I never contemplated what lay ahead for me. Given that both I and my rapist knew he'd raped me, what could I do but press charges? What could he do but go to jail? What could our coworkers do but support me? But as I lay spread-eagled while a strange, silent man prodded me with cold implements, all I wanted to do was go home and pretend it never happened some more.

Finally, the doctor let me go, after pressuring me to take sedatives and a "morning after" pill, both of which I refused. Word had, of course, preceded me back to the dorm. Roommate was waiting for me. I told her the story and got the only sympathy I was ever to get from a Skivvy Niner, with two exceptions. I didn't know what else to do but press on.

That first night was agony. I wouldn't allow myself not to sleep in my bed, though it seemed to glow with a malevolent phosphorescence. I said yes, though, when Roommate's boyfriend offered to spend the night. So there we lay—me in the top bunk, Roommate in the bottom, Boyfriend stretched out in the chair. All fully dressed, all miserable, all leaping back into wakefulness every few minutes when I woke up panting and struggling and destabilizing the bunks. Too bad I hadn't thought of that the night before. We looked like we'd been tortured the next morning as we chain-smoked outside the chow hall hours early, waiting for it to open. I couldn't let myself sleep. The thought of being unconscious made me fear I'd lose my mind.

Simply walking down the street after my rape required a kind of courage that let me know perversely, even then, that I could face anything. Passing men, I felt as if I had a bull's-eye drawn in blood red on my pelvis. I had a vivid new image of myself, of all women, as walking targets. In a flash, I understood what feminists had been preaching about the true nature of rape: it has nothing to do with sex. I realized that any innocuous man waiting for the bus with me could be a cesspool of raging anger and self-loathing looking for an outlet.

I felt naked and vulnerable and dirty with shame, but it was the loss of dignity I felt most acutely. To have been violated by such a poor excuse for a man in such ignominious circumstances . . . it's a heartache. I hated myself for second-guessing in the midst of the rape. How could I tell myself it wasn't happening? Why didn't I fight then instead of later? Why had I even felt it was my job to protect and defend the cringing lowlife in the first place, like some cosmic party hostess? God forbid anyone should be unhappy, not when there's a woman in the vicinity to smooth everything over.

I focused on making it through the nights. Having to sleep filled me with dread. Shift work was a godsend because I could often sleep during the day. I could sleep if I knew the sun was shining. No one gets raped in the sunlight, do they? But that only took care of a few days a week. For the unavoidable dark hours, I tried everything—sleeping fully dressed, sleeping with the lights on, sleeping with a baseball bat, setting elaborate traps. It went without saying that the bedroom door—not just the front door of the building but the door of the room I was actually in—had to be locked. I wouldn't even lie on a bed in a room without a locking door.

What finally made it possible for me to sleep, if only fitfully, was furniture. I could sleep for long snatches if the door was barricaded, the windows blocked. If they could not be, in an inconveniently outfitted hotel room, for instance, I'd stock up on cigarettes and stare at the door and windows all night. Or, I'd sleep fitfully in a chair. But not in an unprotected bed—never. I knew this was unhealthy but what was I to do? I'm not a baby boomer and I'm not a yuppie's kid—I don't expect there to be a cure for my every bedevilment. Some pains just have to be borne, outlasted. So I carved out my own numbed and Dickersonian way. I limped, but I kept walking.

A few shaky days later, during a long shift, I was near breaking. All I had to do was make it back to the barracks and collapse. It was still daylight, so I would be able to sleep. But no. The first sergeant was sitting in a car waiting for me outside the barracks. Lieutenant Colonel "Davis," the 6903rd commander, wanted to see me.

Davis was a cold fish. It was well known that he referred to us enlisted derisively as "the help" and looked at us with a cold mix of puritan disdain and superiority. We thought him a bastard. The Blues Brothers movie was a big hit in the military then; we put up a sign that said "We're on a Mission from GOD." Good old Davis, we'd snicker behind his back.

Inside his office, I was taken aback by the look of pained disgust on his face. He didn't ask me how I was feeling. He didn't express his sympathy or offer his assistance in any way. He didn't offer me a day off, or to let me go home on leave, or to use the direct stateside line to call home that he controlled. Instead, he left me standing at attention. That's how I knew I was in trouble. When you report to your commander, you do so formally by marching in, standing at attention, saluting, and announcing, "Airman Dickerson reporting as ordered, sir." Normally, a superior officer would immediately put you "at ease" in such a situation and offer you a seat. Davis meant for me to know that this was not to be a pleasant visit. The First Shirt looked like he was trying to pass a kidney stone.

Davis told me that he had reviewed the facts "of the case [I'd] brought" and decided that I was an alcoholic. I was to report for a complete evaluation.

Clichés are clichés for a reason: I literally could not believe my ears. I looked to the Shirt but he couldn't look at me. Davis was still talking, so I looked back at him, my eyes and mouth so wide I thought my face was going to crack.

True, I'd been drinking off and on all day and well into the night, but so had most of his entire squadron. He bloody well knew we'd only drunk slightly more than we normally did on any given day and that most of it was drunk right across the hall from his squadron headquarters in the bar we built with unit funds and kept stocked with the nearly free alcohol the government flew in to the base liquor store.

I was simply unable to process what was happening except that I knew I was being assaulted. Again. I felt dizzy. I aimed myself at a chair as best I could. I almost made it. The Shirt sprang forward to help me but Davis just kept talking. He reminded me that national security was at stake given my access to classified information. He talked and talked and talked.

It's all over, I thought as Davis beat me up. I can't hold it together. His words were actually painful. And the way he was looking at me, like I was a garden slug in his salad . . . I had to cover my face.

In the end, I had to wait in his anteroom, tacky with snot and dry heaving (I was barely eating), while his secretary made the appointment for my alcoholism evaluation. The Shirt waited with me, clearing his throat and crushing his cap in his hands. He half carried me back to his car, drove behind a building in a deserted area, and waited.

"I hate him! I hate him! I hate him!" I screamed for so long I could barely speak the next day. I meant Davis, not the Spineless Worm who raped me. Spittle flying, I spewed the vilest things I could think up. God bless the Shirt, he just kept nodding and dabbing his eyes and saying, I know, I know, I know. He must have given me some advice or encouragement, but all I remember now is his quiet decency. If someone hadn't been nice to me just then, I don't think I would have made it.

In all the hours that I wasn't sleeping, I had lots of time to consider my situation. A peasant at heart, I never spent much time pondering Davis's attitude; I didn't question the power of my feudal overlords. Instead, I spent my time figuring out what it meant for me. Finally, it came to me in a flash that made me jump up and spend the rest of the night chain-smoking. He meant to ruin my career and force me out.

Simply to be suspected of being an alcoholic, God forbid be adjudged one, was to seal your doom in intelligence. The reality, of course, is that in the 1980s, before "deglamorization," irresponsible drinking and alcoholism (like fornication and adultery) were rife throughout the military, especially in third world countries, especially in high-stress fields. You had to be nonfunctional for your drinking to matter; there were plenty of functional alcoholics and problem drinkers at the very pinnacle of military achievement. If you could confine your drinking to off-duty hours and stay out of official trouble, your drinking was your business. But commanders are gods. If he made an issue of it, you were toast. The bastard intended to cost me my clearance, and with it my career. At a minimum, he meant to have my clearance pulled and put me in limbo while my case wound its laborious way through the system.

As soon as the OSI agents knocked on his door, that Spineless

Worm confessed. Given that, I didn't know why Davis was after me, but he knew what an accusation of this type meant to a career, a life. The Air Force is a people-oriented place. The custom was an off-the-record tête-à-tête and tough-love-type oversight. I'd only been in the unit six weeks. I'd only been drinking for six weeks. I had an exemplary record. I doubt he'd ever even heard of me before. So why did he try to ruin me?

I didn't know, but I certainly knew what I had to do next: fight. So I turned my hatred of Davis into fuel. He was my focal point for pulling myself together, a seething socket deep within me that I plugged into for energy and drive. I was going to beat that bastard. If I fell apart, he won, so I decided not to fall apart.

Humiliated but too ornery to show it, I presented in crisp uniform ten minutes early for my drunkard's evaluation. The organization which provided what passed for mental health services in the Air Force was inexplicably called Social Actions. Going there was the kiss of death for anyone with a clearance—you were automatically considered to be a security risk and assigned "casual" duty, like handing out clean linen or answering phones. So people just fell quietly, or noisily, apart while the rest of us measured our behavior against theirs and took stock.

I sat there, focused on my hatred of Davis, and briskly refused the refreshments the two nice, white, scrubbed officers pressed on me. They smiled, they offered to put on music, they tried to chat. They looked uncertainly back and forth. I responded appropriately, formally. Finally, one couldn't stand it anymore.

"Why are you here?" he asked me.

My composure was momentarily rocked. That lousy bastard. They had no idea why I was there, knew nothing about either the rape or the drunkard's evaluation. Son of a vermin-infested bitch.

I was cornered. Nothing to do but be a Dickerson. I sat up straight and tall.

"I'm here because I was raped by a coworker in my own bed on Christmas Day, which proves to my commander that I'm an alcoholic. I'm here so you can take away my security clearance and short-circuit my career."

The look of horror on those men's faces was gratifying but I was still furious. I hadn't even told my family but here I was forced to tell two male strangers. I pictured Davis crushed under the burning wheels of a locomotive.

Finally, one stammered, "Have you talked to someone about the . . . incident? Why on earth were you sent here?"

The morbidity of it was irresistible. "Rape is a social action, I guess, so . . ."

To their credit, they made a few halfhearted attempts to counsel me. I responded with more sulfurous one-liners. They let me go. They assured me they'd take no action on the drunkard evaluation, and I left, standing tall and striding purposefully.

Up yours, Davis.

Even in the midst of my inch-deep militancy, I knew I needed help. Since the Air Force wasn't going to be proactive with me (they scheduled my mandatory pap smears, flu shots, and dental checkups but left me to handle rape on my own), I did try once to reach out. I waited weeks for an appointment with Osan's single nurse-practitioner.

I prayed that someone would have told her who I was. But no. And when push came to shove, I couldn't say it. D.J. the Badass just sat there while the major pursed her lips and looked pointedly at the clock. I willed myself to say the words "I was raped" again and again, promising myself that this time when I counted to ten I was going to blurt it out.

The major was annoyed. She was in the midst of some religious observance and she had to get to a special Mass. I was making her late but she was making me want to scream. Why couldn't she be a Christian in her own office? Snot bubbled in my nose but I fought back the tears, terrified that if I started crying I would lose it altogether. But this major, the only woman ever involved with my case, was a block of wood. I might have been unaware of my cultural aloneness, but I was acutely aware of how personally alone I was just then. I was in hell and no one, literally no one, gave a damn. There was no help. My problems mattered to no one but me. The major's stone face made that very clear.

Five minutes into the silence now, the major was very annoyed. I told her I'd made a mistake and left.

She sent a formal reprimand to my orderly room and noted in my medical record, right under the rape exam, that I had been uncooperative and wasted valuable appointment time. She hinted that I was unstable.

I gave myself a stern talking-to as I marched myself home from the clinic. You are on your own, Debra. No one is going to help you, Debra. Pull yourself together, Debra. You aint dead yet, Debra, so this shit can't kill you.

Those four sentences, my mantra, got me through my two years in Korea. Outside of Davis's assault, I never shed even one tear about my rape.

Davis never gave me a day off work, fine! I worked harder and was considered among the best of his "help." I won awards, I set records. I came in early, I stayed late. I continued to sleep around and drink way too much, just like everyone else. I had leave approved months in advance only to have it snatched away the day before. Fine! I volunteered to stay an extra year and didn't go home again until February 1983, a full fourteen months after I came to Korea. Die, Davis! Even I saw through the paper-thin psychology at work there, but so what? I didn't need fancy.

Nonetheless, the hard living, the high professional pressure, and the aftereffects of the rape all combined to wear me down. The unit disowned me (even though the Worm confessed). A group of females petitioned to testify as character witnesses for him. (He confessed!) They felt sure I must have provoked him. (He confessed!) Few in the unit would speak to me. (He confessed!)

But what could I do? I couldn't change jobs, I couldn't move; all I could do was brazen it out. I just put one foot in front of the other. I was the eye of the storm. It was quiet there, but all around me, conversations would stop when I entered a room. People would leave tables I joined. At the same time, a well-liked guy in our unit was being prosecuted for killing his baby while drunk. He was the unit darling. Everyone visited him, sent him cards and gifts, and filled the benches at his trial. His name was on their lips every day. Even Davis supported him, visiting and mentioning him at commander's call. I was a pariah.

It is customary for commanders to attend any court proceedings involving their subordinates; their presence communicates support both for the accused and for the military process. The commander usually acts as the accused's family's source of information and as their advocate. As in the case of my coworker accused of killing his child, Davis did so, as did others from the chain of command. I, on the other hand, went to court alone (except for one kind major who wasn't even in my chain of command). Women wept openly when my coworker was found guilty; those same bitches wouldn't speak to me. I received no encouragement or support from my command structure. I even had to beg the prosecutor to make sure the trial didn't conflict with my work schedule; the powers that be hemmed and hawed when I alerted them to the possible conflict, reminding me that if "we let one person off . . ." Buggerers. I would miss my own trial before I'd ask Davis for time off.

Since the loser confessed, there wasn't much of a trial. The defense had been planning to argue that I consented to sex and only claimed rape afterward to hide it from my boyfriend. That made me laugh for the first time since the rape. My boyfriend did exactly what I'd known he would when I told him; he flinched but said nothing.

The Worm had opted for a bench trial, so the court reporter, the two lawyers, and I waited for the judge's decision together in a small antechamber. Worm's lawyer bummed cigarettes from me and bemoaned his client's having confessed, a course to which he'd strenuously objected. The three then placed desultory lunch bets on the number of months Worm would probably get. They compared rape cases: never more than six without "violence," probably only four because she'd been drinking, maybe as few as two because he'd conf— . . . Finally, the prosecutor looked at me, turned red, and changed the subject. The stenographer, who never looked directly at me, said lazily, "I guess you think we're heartless, huh?"

No. Not at all.

The Worm read a statement apologizing to the court and to the Air Force. I suppose I was covered by his "any other person or persons who may have been hurt, if any" clause. He lost his clearance and was sentenced to six months in military prison in Denver. I've since seen the place; sad-faced airmen play volleyball in the cold and shine shoes a lot. If he'd falsified an expense voucher and stolen a few hundred bucks from the government, if he'd boosted tools from the flight line, if he'd smoked a single joint in a stellar fifteen-year career, he'd have gotten years, not months, and in a real prison. But raping a fellow soldier's not so bad. Still good enough for the uniform of the United States of America. It's not like he hit me or anything.

But even that, six months' confinement, was not to be. He only served two. Good behavior and all that. He was at a new duty assignment before I was. As late as 1989, he was still on active duty in Alaska, bragging that his family never even knew what had happened. He's married now and has children. Daughters?

Yes, I'm bitter, but I never blamed the Air Force. I blame Davis. I shared an elevator with him at the National Security Agency the next year and he wouldn't even acknowledge my presence.

Every now and then, someone would mention the rape, like the guy I asked to a function. "No thanks," he said politely. "I don't want to end up in jail." Another time, a new flight commander introduced himself to me this way: "Hello. I'm Lieutenant Big Fat Stupid Idiot. I hear you were raped." I came to understand that Worm's confession meant nothing to anyone but me.

There was no unit education on acquaintance rape or irresponsible drinking or sexual harassment. At one point, we'd had a rash of people getting bad sunburns that kept them from working—next commander's call, we got lectured on sunburns. The fair-skinned who got more than one work-preventing sunburn were punished. A couple of women got pregnant, and so had to return stateside; boom, we got lectured on not getting pregnant. If promotion rates dropped a percentage point, if people were making too much noise in the barracks—major lecture. But rape? Not a word. I got the message loud and clear.

You are on your own, Debra. No one is going to help you, Debra. Pull yourself together, Debra. You aint dead yet, Debra, so this shit can't kill you.

A NEW ATTITUDE

Korea was a turning point. All the disparate parts of my makeup collided as I consciously tried to make some sense of my life. The rape stripped away the last of the backwoods principles I'd been raised on. I realized then, as I endured the pointless, even impersonal mistreatment routine in daily life outside the cloister of my parents' home, that I had not been ready for the world.

I reviewed it all—my father, my bleak childhood, the constant maltreatment from men that my low self-esteem drove me to expect and accept, the existing social order—and dove headfirst into a boiling, bottomless anger. The world was a shitty, unlovely place filled with people who'd stab you in the back for no reason at all. I was disgusted by my own good-girliness and shrugged it off like a pair of Dr. Denton's.

I lived on black coffee, cigarettes, and alcohol. Sans effort or intent, I lost twenty-five pounds.

Then I became a serious jock. I pounded out hundreds of sit-ups each day, did hours of aerobics. I ran the six miles from Osan to Pyong Taek, the next town, twice, sometimes three times. I ran through rice paddies with local children dogging my heels. I ran through monsoons, snowdrifts, scorching heat. I ferreted out the best hills. I couldn't make things difficult enough for myself. I kept studious track of my times and distances, always trying to outdo myself. Black men called out rude taunts as I ran around base, but I'd have been disappointed had they not.

My makeover also included the beauty-magazine variety. I chose that moment to become a glamour queen. I stopped wearing fatigues and started wearing tailored "blues" (with skirts, not pants) every day. Heels and sheer hose. I stopped biting my nails, and when they grew long began a regimen of manicures and vampish nail polish; I wore every bit of jewelry allowed by regulation. I stopped swigging my beer from the bottle and stopped cursing like a sailor—phrases like "cluster fuck" evaporated from my vocabulary. I stopped carting things around in my fatigue breast pocket and bought a purse. I haunted the cosmetics aisle in the BX. I spent so much time and money there that the saleswoman pulled me close and said, "Don't you think you've spent enough?"

I took a tiny apartment alone in the Korean community and discovered the blues and jazz records at the base hobby shop.

I spent whole days listening to Bessie Smith, Billie Holiday, Ethel Waters, Nat King Cole, Dinah Washington, Louis Armstrong, Sarah Vaughan, Billy Eckstine, and the queen, Ella Fitzgerald.

At the base library I joined the twentieth century. I discovered Philip Roth, Anne Tyler, Solzhenitsyn, Eudora Welty, Norman Mailer, John Irving. I read Kurt Vonnegut in his loopy entirety. Then I discovered Ayn Rand. I would have carved her name on my forehead if that wouldn't have been a violation of the dress code. I read all her fiction, then special-ordered her nonfiction. Where had she been all my life?

With her as my spiritual guru, I took my reevaluation of myself to the next level. While for the first time in my life I felt powerful and confident through my job, my personal life was a mess. I had an on-again, off-again boyfriend whom I allowed to make me miserable for years. I was intimidated by black people. Rand completed my conversion to far right conservatism and firebrand feminism. No more profligate drinking and smoking, no more unhappy sex, no more loser men, and, most of all, no more fear of blacks and their disapproval. I entered a take-no-prisoners phase that lasted nearly five years. At the time, I thought it was simply a focus phase. It was that, too, but most of all it was about anger.

I wrapped myself in my anger at blacks and lashed out whenever possible. Before Rand, I'd always taken the long way past known trouble spots, like the Red Horse barracks (civil engineering; many black men perform manual labor there). Not anymore. I walked past Red Horse, through the black men's catcalls and requests for dollar blow jobs since I wasn't "nothin but a 'ho anyway." I was in uniform. Officers came and went through the main doors just below the windows where the black men howled at me, yet they said nothing. Had I or one of those men failed to salute them, they'd have taken our heads off.

I didn't falter. I didn't flinch. I wanted them to see how unfazed I was, I wanted to prove to myself that they were too pitiful to fear, and I wanted to store up on their abuse. Just like with Davis, I used them for fuel. They justified my distance from blacks. Just look at how they acted.

The defining moment of my new, confrontational attitude toward blacks and their nonsense came as I stood at a food cart off-base with four white male flight mates to buy greasy fried squid and newspaper-wrapped "yaki man do." Two black guys ambled over, eyed me. They eyed my friends a few paces away waiting for me to finish the transaction. My mistake was conducting my business with the cart guy in Korean.

"Look at this Oreo bitch," one said evilly to the other.

"I know, man. Think she the shit."

I said nothing. The pre-Randian me would have shriveled up and fled. The new me would have liked nothing better than a showdown with these deficients, but not with white folk present. I didn't want them to see how typical blacks acted.

"Bitch think she aint black no mo. Done forgot she a nigger, too."

"Bitch."

I never acknowledged them, just kept up a running conversation with the Korean man, knowing that that's what was really infuriating them. The black men kept their voices low, horribly intimate. No one overheard us.

"Bitch might need her ass kicked."

"Might."

They never stopped their evil commentary and I wouldn't let myself walk away while it continued. That would be running and that I refused to do. Just for something to do with my hands, I pulled out my Benson & Hedges and we reached a new low in intraracial comedy.

"Look at this bitch, man. She caint even smoke black. She caint smoke Kools or Newports. She got to smoke some goddamn white shit."

I stopped with my lighter halfway to my lips. My *cigarettes* weren't even black enough? I laughed so hard I dropped the lighter.

"I funny, bitch?" He snarled but I couldn't have been less afraid.

"Oops, careful, genius—lost your verb there."

It was just like playing the dozens again. I enjoyed their humiliation very, very much.

"By the way, just how low is your IQ?" I asked the first one. "Is it even double digits? Because I know it couldn't possibly be triple."

Their mouths snapped shut as if hinged but their eyes spoke volumes of violence. Only the power of a court-martial kept them from hitting me.

"Why don't you do yourselves a favor? Instead of harassing people who have what you want, why don't you just work on getting it for yourselves? The words 'black' and 'loser' don't have to be synonymous."

I was very, very proud of myself. Those words may look like tough love in print, but I meant them to crush. I had boiled blacks' problems down to the comments I made to those two men that night. A busy Randian with no time to waste, I used these formulations repeatedly to shrug off blacks' underachievement and self-defeating behaviors. I must have said them a thousand times in those years to bleeding-heart liberals and other assorted black apologists. I had it all figured out. I knew what their secret fear was—I'm a loser by birth—and I rubbed their faces in it.

Content, I walked away to join my oblivious white friends. I could feel the black men's eyes boring into my back, but I knew they wouldn't dare touch me now, not if there was the least chance I might get to speak again before they could choke me into silence.

UP BY MY BOOTSTRAPS

When I rotated home to the National Security Agency, Fort Meade, Maryland, in late 1983, I did so with a plan. I applied for, and won, a Bootstrap fellowship which allowed me to go to school full-time in lieu of work. I desperately wanted to become an officer. That was my big plan. Get a degree, any degree, and become the first Dickerson officer in a long line of cannon fodder. Davis was an aberration that I never held against the Air Force. I saw myself in Air Force blue for the rest of my life, and as a highly decorated officer to boot.

My up-close and personal experiences with officers, after two years in the trenches, had had the same effect on me as had that with my well-educated teachers at Flo Valley: none seemed to me to have accomplished anything that was beyond me. I watched them do their jobs and there was no magic there, just work. As always, negative reinforcement did more for me than positive; it was the sad-sack officers who most motivated me. If they can do it, I damn sure can, I thought.

Far from the timid second-guesser I'd once been, I was calmly sure I could have been a pilot, a commander, an airborne commando—but I didn't want those things. As a woman, I could never have maxed out in those testosteronic fields; I would always have been a bridesmaid, the one left behind to man the phones while the men won medals. I determined never to work in an organization I could never head. I could never lead an operational unit, regardless of what the posters say, but I could be Air Force chief of staff for intelligence someday. So, I wanted to be an intelligence officer working directly with flight crews in a hard-charging operational environment. I wanted to wear camouflage fatigues and combat boots all but a few weeks a year, I wanted to look down on headquarters "day whores," I wanted to lose track of time and spend years at a stretch overseas, and I was a committed Cold Warrior: I wanted to drop bombs on people who challenged the United States of America. Lots of them. I didn't want a degree. I wanted a commission and a jihad against my formerly meaningless existence.

Stateside, as my Bootstrap application was pending, I was working with a few of my competitors. The contestants were Air Force–wide; however, there were six or seven people in my unit who'd applied in the same cycle. A large percentage of linguists have at least two years of college, so it was unsurprising that so many of us bucked for a commission. All my competitors were white men, which I found unsurprising. At office parties and the like, we tended to drift together and update each other on any scuttlebutt we'd heard about the selection process. As announcement day loomed, one of them said to me with patronizing magnanimity, "You'll win since you're black and female, D.J., and that's as it should be, I guess." Oh! the look of noble suffering on his face.

"I'll win because I'm better than you!" I shouted. "Right now, we compare GPAs, evaluations, test scores, letters of rec, awards and decs. I'll be back with my file in five minutes and I better find you standing right here with yours."

I left him standing there red-faced while I ran back to my desk, where I kept a complete copy of all pertinent records, probably in triplicate and cross-referenced. Needless to say, he wasn't there when I got back.

For far too many white people, the existence of affirmative action means never having to consider that you're just not good enough. Worse, I got it from both directions: successful military women are routinely believed to have slept their way to the top.

Concomitant with my Bootstrap application, I applied for a spot at Officers' Training School and won it. I couldn't sleep at night with all my planning. I went home on leave then and ran into all my cousins and neighbors who weren't living their lives as they should. *That* started keeping me up at night. I was so tired of black people who wouldn't face reality and take control of their lives. There were lots of black admin personnel at Fort Meade and I was constantly trying to motivate the bright ones to take advantage of degree and commissioning programs. Enlisted then could get 75 or 90 percent tuition assistance, yet all I ever got were excuses. They never missed a party, but they never made it to class.

CHAPTER FOUR

BEGINNING AGAIN

I was accepted at the University of Maryland, College Park. It never occurred to me to apply to Georgetown or American, or one of the Ivys. There, I evaluated my credits with a guidance counselor whom I would not allow to wiggle out of doing his job like his Mizzou predecessor. I was closest to a degree in government and politics. I had no interest in government and politics, but no matter. I knew by then that whatever formal education I got, I had always been and would always be an autodidact. No one at College Park was going to work me harder than I'd work myself.

My existence was spartan. For the six months while I waited to be relieved of duty, I rose at 4:30 A.M. each morning, worked at the NSA from 6 A.M. to 2 P.M., worked out from 2:30 P.M. to 5 P.M., carried a full load of night classes at College Park, and was in bed by 9 or 9:30 P.M. I spent the weekends studying, doing research, writing papers, and doubling my workouts. I wouldn't allow a TV into the apartment. To my running regime, I'd added hard-core bodybuilding.

I immersed myself in nutrition, supplementation, and metabolic studies and evaluated every morsel that entered my body. I scoffed at those who ate for pleasure, and took carefully coordinated doses of vitamins and supplements throughout the day. I must have inherited my father's propensity for muscles, because I got results. My biceps were so big and my waist so small I had to have my uniforms tailored. I couldn't get strong enough, couldn't run fast enough, couldn't get high enough grades. I took a tumble down a gravelly hill one day and finished my untruncated run exultant, arms and legs bloody.

Aside from my baffled roommate, I saw no one. Finally, I broke things off with my hapless boyfriend and sautéed my soul with a very conscious hatred of men; I took a vow of celibacy that lasted years. My youngest sister was deputized to ask me if I was a lesbian.

One day at the height of a humid Maryland summer, I was walking down the street wearing as little as possible—miniskirt, halter top, sandals. From the corner of my eye, I caught sight of a guy with a great body. My anger at men notwithstanding, I couldn't help stopping to check him out. But it was me. I was looking into a plate-glass window and I was the guy with the great body.

MY LEFT TURN

At that point, I'd rarely read a magazine, a newspaper, or a work of (non-Randian) nonfiction. The 1984 elections were coming up, so I assigned myself the task of following the election closely. A staunch Reagan supporter, I relished the notion of following his every move. I began reading the *Washington Times* and the *Washington Post* every day, very much looking forward to using the former to prove how duplicitous was the latter.

Reagan was the first president I was fully aware of, and his decision to bomb Grenada, instead of merely yelling at it, impressed me greatly. In my simplistic mind, the president came as a package deal with the military, the institution I lived and breathed, the institution that saved my life. His conservatism and blame-the-victim ethos resonated squarely with my GI world. Based solely on the word of mouth of those around me, I bought his whole tough-talking, lock-em-up, cut-em-off-welfare shtick. Or, I did before I paid anything like close attention to him. A month later I was reeling with confusion. A month after that, I was howling with anger. Another month—I was laughing uncontrollably. The man was a moron. A sexist, a racist, and a howling elitist to boot, but by far his biggest crime was his imbecility. I was learning that my hero was neither honest nor bright.

I went out of my way to see him on television, the vaunted Great Communicator, hoping that would change things for me, but that actually made it worse. Though it would take more time before I gave up the ghost of my conservatism, I scoffed at the notion of his communicative genius. He talked to the nation like we were idiots or toddlers or toddling idiots. It was so obviously contrived, so obviously the grade B ham reciting the lines his controllers wrote for him.

The *Times* and the *Post* were not enough; I had to have more.

After I sucked all the knowledge I could out of my textbooks, I got recommendations from my professors for extracurricular nonfiction reading. Soon, I couldn't get enough news and analysis. I began reading newsmagazines. I was appalled by the state of the world. I'd had no idea.

Shielded by my parents, lost in books and my own misery as I grew up, overseas for two years, and insulated from the Reagan recession by my government job, I'd had no idea how bad things were for working people. With my new wide-focus perspective and all those pesky facts, as a college student in 1984 and finally thinking for myself, I began to see my relatives' layoffs and evictions differently. Maybe every detail of life was *not* completely within the control of the individual. Not that I gave in easily. There were spirited, even book-throwing arguments in my classes between us military conservatives and the civilian liberals. For the first time, none of the right-wing things I spouted went uncontested. My professors and classmates made points I had never considered before and could not easily dismiss. I had to fight for my rhetorical life in the classroom, and I argued the conservative cause far longer than I actually wanted to simply because I was still a bad loser. A prelaw course, especially, made it impossible to argue that individuals exercise anything like the unfettered freedom of will which justifies leaving every man for himself.

I began to view my relatives' struggles with more complexity. Every time I called home, another one of them would have been summarily let go from a job and be frantically scrabbling for a new one. They wanted to work, even though the jobs they were able to get barely afforded them a decent living. The long lines to apply for menial jobs that I saw on TV and in the papers told me that most people want to work. It maddened me that they wouldn't break the cycle with a degree, investments, or entrepreneurship, but for the first time, it occurred to me that some people just want jobs. You need money to live, so they work simply for money and look elsewhere to find the meaning that humans need to survive. They don't aspire to be CEOs, they don't aspire to work that fulfills or challenges—some people just want to exchange labor for money in a pleasant environment and get back home to their families.

One of the most arresting images I've ever seen was of those thousands of people shivering in a Chicago snowstorm as they waited to apply for hotel lackey jobs. Soon after, when the millionaire aristocrat Reagan thumbed through the want ads to prove that people could work if they really wanted to, I almost had an aneurysm. How could an honest person say such a thing? It was patently obvious that people were being buffeted by forces much larger than themselves, but I couldn't get my military friends to make that simple acknowledgment. We could disagree about what our societal response to that should be, I argued, but not about that basic reality.

But no, I had to sit through pious stories about their poor immigrant grandparents who came here with nothing, or about the guy from their hometown who sold tomatoes door to door from a little red wagon rather than accept government handouts. They posited a world wherein every individual was completely autonomous and in control of his environment. Their analysis was that some people just don't want to work or that people have to live with the consequences of their actions. It was Joe Six-pack's fault that Reagan ballooned the deficit, that he broke the unions, that he deregulated everything? Even if some people chose poorly and, for example, dropped out of high school or had an illegitimate child—should one teenage mistake doom them for the rest of their lives? Is that really what's best for America? I could never understand liberal opposition to workfare—there is no dignity in handouts, I've always believed. Also, people are rational; they'll factor the specifics of any given welfare regime into their choices. However, workfare, as usually espoused, is more punitive and humiliating than loving but strict. If a welfare mom has the brains to be an astrophysicist, are we really better off forcing her to pick up trash on the highway in exchange for her welfare pittance each month? Some will aspire no further than manual labor and every society needs manual laborers—but others pine for more. People from the lower socioeconomic classes need direction and support to aim high; they don't need the government to help them underachieve. Why not help as many citizens as possible maximize their potential and then require them to pay the cost of it back either monetarily (like my college loans) or through substantive community service (like working for low pay in underserved areas)? My conservative coworkers just rolled their eyes, called me a bleeding-heart liberal, and sermonized about giving people "something for nothing."

Even if your marginal existence is your own fault, I couldn't help wondering, is it really in our societal best interest to let people starve, to poorly educate them? Hopeless people commit crimes, so let's feed and educate them so they don't climb through our windows at night. Incarceration is so much more expensive and just about guarantees that the incarcerated will remain predators unable to support themselves legally: educated people commit white-collar crimes, the illiterate draw blood. What could be more conservative than crime prevention? But in response to my arguments about the relationship between lack of education and crime, all I'd get were sanctimonious non sequiturs like "Nobody ever gave me anything" and "Build more prisons." I couldn't even get them to concede the bare-bones notion that crime reduction and prevention were preferable to high prison occupancy. Some people belong in prison, they'd sniff. I actually had a four-against-one debate once wherein my coworkers argued that inmates should be offered only the Bible during their incarceration. No exercise, no classes, no TV, no work—just sitting on their beds reading the Bible from five to ten. The fact that prison guards would resist such a regime more than any goo-goo liberal fell on deaf ears. My continued reading of the right-wing press only hastened my looming defection. I was used to the intellectual dishonesty of the left and black apologists—they pushed me right. But then, the intellectual shamelessness and moral clay feet of conservatives pushed me left. The left annoys me but the right insults my intelligence.

I was in a constant state of intellectual and emotional turmoil. It was my college angst all over again: who am I? What's my relationship to other blacks, to America? How am I supposed to figure out what to do with my life? Why can't I stop thinking about politics? I felt strong and confident but . . . toward what end? All I had were questions; I needed answers. When my commander called to tell me I'd been accepted into Officers' Training School, all I could think was, Now what? My coworkers were cheering and clapping and tossing papers at me like oversized confetti. I was faking a smile and thinking, Now what do I shoot for? Why isn't this enough? I was happy, just not satisfied.

I lay in my bed one night all alone, my mind whirring with plans and counterstrategies, when a sudden thought imprinted itself on my brain. Apropos of nothing, I said aloud, "I feel like I've been mugged." I realized what my Osan malaise had truly been about. I was exhausted. Worn out by my own life. The effort of dragging myself from the working class to the middle class, though successful, had nearly killed me. Even my fixation on physical fitness had been just another way of simultaneously gaining control over my life and expressing a deep-seated anger. I never had to consciously decide between conventional attractiveness and the female bodybuilder's stylized look because once I started dealing with the root of my behaviors, I never again worked out with the same intensity. I couldn't.

Where I'd once had a "let them eat cake because it's their own fault they don't have bread" attitude about those I'd left behind, by the time I graduated in December 1984 I was feeling not so much vindicated as humble. No wonder so many people give up or never try at all; it shouldn't have to be this hard, I realized. But even if it has to be this hard, society should acknowledge the structural disadvantages so many face and ameliorate them as much as possible. What could be more conservative than abetting each citizen in maximizing her potential so she can contribute as much as possible? I tried and tried, but I just couldn't be satisfied with my own individual success. I knew I'd just been lucky.

DRIVEN TO ACTION

If a conservative is a liberal who's been mugged, a liberal is a conservative who realizes that she can't have what's being conserved. The final experience that changed my worldview was buying my first new car.

Military bases are full of concessions. As I planned to rotate back from Korea at the tail end of 1983, I bought, sight unseen, a Chrysler/Renault Alliance, the 1983 Car of the Year. That and the implicit military seal of approval were enough for me.

As I drove home from the dealership, the car died in the middle of the highway. It continued to die, for no discernible reason, for the rest of the time I owned it. The dealership tried repeatedly to locate the problem, but couldn't. Finally, they told me to have my car towed off their premises. The Chrysler representative laughed at me when I asked for a refund.

I was frantic. The car payment and insurance consumed most of one biweekly paycheck; I couldn't afford to buy another car, nor was Laurel, Maryland, an area well served by public transportation. How was I going to get to school?

I appealed to the military for assistance but was told it was none of their affair. I was, however, ordered to continue making the payments and reminded that I'd lose my security clearance for "financial irresponsibility."

Those were the days just before lemon laws; I was booted out of one lawyer's office after the other. Not only that, they did so in a manner which suggested personal disapproval of me. Just as had Lieutenant Colonel Davis when punishing me for having been raped, several of these lawyers failed to offer me a seat and snapped at me.

What was most remarkable to me about this experience was the vehemence with which everyone who refused to help me insisted that I keep up the car payments—not for my own good but because it was my duty. I was struck by everyone's deference to big business's interests, as if they were a proxy for morality; they could just as easily have been in my shoes. How brainwashed we all are, I thought.

It was January 1984. I'd been making payments since September. I'd only had the car a month. The last lawyer had just finished telling me I'd be better off buying another car. I couldn't take any more. What was I supposed to do, have someone "steal" the car or make four years of payments on a car that didn't run? I couldn't believe that these were my only options, I, who so believed in America. I felt like a rat in a maze with no outlet, like a speck of dust on a tabletop, like a thing unworthy of the least consideration. There was no way out of this situation, no matter how willing I was to work hard and play by the rules. This, I thought, is where outlaws come from.

I made for the door, blinded by tears and racked with sobs. Frantic for something to say, the lawyer sputtered about how his mother-in-law had gotten a couple hundred dollars' refund with a letter-writing campaign and maybe I should try that. I didn't even bother to respond, just dragged myself out to my friend's car and back to my one-sided responsibilities.

I was trapped. My only option was the letter-writing campaign. As I worried my situation around and around in my head, I stopped crying and started to get mad. Really mad. I hadn't done anything wrong, I always played by the rules, yet I was being abused.

I didn't just want out of my contract. I didn't just want my money back. I wanted acknowledgment of the wrong being done to me and I wanted revenge. So I took three days off from work and waged war on Chrysler.

At the base library, I explained my situation to the librarian. Unlike the lawyers, this lowly government worker was energized and outraged. We explored the government committee structure, which regulatory bodies did what, the structure of the automobile industry. I learned how to research corporate hierarchies and trace ownership.

In the end, I sent out a mass mailing of two hundred letters to everyone from Reagan and Bush (neither of whom responded with even so much as a form letter), Tip O'Neill, every female and/or black in Congress or the Senate, all the way down to my local Better Business Bureau. I swamped the federal government, the Missouri and Maryland governments, business, military, and women's groups.

I also mass-produced letters addressed to the chairman of Chrysler's board reading: "I am aware of the situation between you and Debra Dickerson regarding the car she bought from you which does not run and cannot be fixed but for which she must still pay. As a consumer, I will be following this situation closely and telling as many people as possible." They were to sign and include their city and state, then mail them to Chrysler's chairman in the pre-addressed envelopes I provided. I sent them to relatives all over the country and friends all over the world to disperse. Each letter I wrote made me feel less like crying and more like challenging the chairman of Chrysler to a duel. It's a dangerous thing to leave a person no way out.

Two weeks later, my office at the NSA had dedicated a phone line for me to answer all the calls I was getting. It was a populist uprising. People were furious on my behalf, which they saw, correctly, as theirs.

I had taken a scattershot approach, writing groups even only loosely related to my issue; many of the calls and letters I received began, "I can't help you with your problem, but I was just blown away by your letter. Have you tried this group or that senator?" Some of the callers were still shaking with indignation, my letter still in their hands. Many pleaded with me to keep them informed.

A lawyer with the Federal Trade Commission called to explain the warrant of merchantability and how any of the lawyers I'd seen could have gotten Chrysler to cave if they'd given it half a try, especially with lemon laws pending all across the country. But they just didn't give a damn about a mousy little black girl with no money, even though I went to all those meetings in uniform. Not one of them mentioned this concept of merchantability (that a thing sold will be fit for the purpose for which it was intended). Not one of them.

Shortly thereafter, I got a call from the Chrysler chairman's lackey. He apologized for the "mixup," made it my fault because "I hadn't sufficiently explained the situation before," and asked with feigned nonchalance how many miles were on the car. I said, "Twenty-seven. Mostly from towing." "Jeee-sus!" the man muttered. Again, with feigned nonchalance, he asked, "By the way, just how many people did you write?" That was when I knew I'd won.

Two weeks after that, in March, a very embarrassed Chrysler rep called and begged to know who else he should expect to hear from. You can actually hear an oppressor sweat when you turn the tables on him. We worked out the details of the buyback. Though my mother would have been able to, I couldn't help myself. My last words to him were, "Is it still funny?"

People from all over the NSA and the country asked for copies of the notebook I'd compiled or for me to act on their behalf. Unsurprisingly, a great many people had been victimized by car companies and had nowhere to turn. Had I been less well educated or had a less flexible job, I'd probably have been jailed for insurance fraud.

The magnitude of what I'd accomplished without lemon laws (or word processors) didn't really hit home until I was deferring to my insurance agent on the details of winding up the insurance, saying, "Just do what you normally do when a car company buys a car back."

"Debra," he said, "in twenty-five years, I've never seen a car company do this. We're in virgin territory." The Chrysler rep, as well, was at a loss as to how to proceed.

Including licensing fees, insurance costs, and payments on a car I couldn't drive, I lost nearly two thousand dollars and nine months' worth of peace on that deal, and with it, the last vestiges of my political innocence. Instead, I gained an appreciation of my own power as well as of the helplessness of the unsophisticated and uneducated.

That experience made it crystal clear to me whose side society was on and how much contempt the ruling class has for the masses. If a blameless person in uniform in the Reagan eighties couldn't get respect, who could?

I was appalled by the legal profession all over again when Chrysler refused to reimburse me for the money I'd lost on the deal (known legally as consequential damages). I saw the same lawyers again only to be subjected to their inexplicable fury. They accused me of trying to "steal from Chrysler," of "trying to get money I didn't deserve," of "trying to take advantage." None advised me calmly that it would cost me more to sue than I could hope to win. Instead, they lit into me. "You should be grateful instead of begging for more," one lectured. Where did we all learn to cringe before capitalism?

The last lawyer I spoke with was so vicious I hung up on her. Weren't they supposed to be technicians really, simply saying yea or nay to the facts laid out before them? Why the emotion? Why the identification with Chrysler and not the person they might wrest some money from? I think it made them uncomfortable that I was self-assured, well educated, and successful. I'd made them look foolish. I was uppity.

Perhaps because of the similarity, that distasteful memory of my long-forgotten run-in with State Farm resurfaced and I had another of those moments which reshaped my life.

Chrysler made me realize that I'd been wrong in my earlier dismissal of lawyers, after my Flo Valley accident. The vision I had for myself was this: to tackle the power structure head-on rather than to hold my nose and suffer nobly while it ravaged me and everyone else. I had to go to law school and perhaps to government office, though I still believed the law to be the tool of the ruling class, because ignorance comes with too high a price tag.

I stopped seeing these brutalizing experiences as particular to me. I could see now that all the little people got treated this way and would continue to be as long as we remained passive. It was clear to me that though with each passing year I became less vulnerable to exploitation, that was not true for most Americans. Few had the resources or personalities to engage in this type of work. The conviction grew in my mind that people like me have to fight for the masses who are unable to fight for themselves. It's just not enough that I, personally, got out of a car contract. It's not enough that I got a decent education, that I was able to haul myself up from the working class.

As my formal and informal education continued simultaneously in the most intellectually and politically pivotal year of my life, 1984, I began to see myself, my family, my neighborhood, my people in historico-social context. Some things were our fault, some things were not. Oppressed people have a duty to fight back, work hard, and retain their dignity, but society also has a duty to acknowledge disadvantage and work to end it. It was the second prong of that analysis that forced me to disavow conservatism. Liberals, with their condescension and lack of common sense, are wrong a lot, but at least they err while giving a damn about people.

Liberal concepts like "internalized oppression," "self-hatred," and "false consciousness" had always made me roll my eyes, but by 1984, I had to revisit them. I knew I suffered from all three, as do a great many blacks—from the overachievers to the troublemakers and the apologists for both groups. Self-hatred is the number one problem among black people; all our counterproductive behaviors stem from it.

I had a dream right about then. Really, it was a memory, but it came to me while I was sleeping. When I'd come back from Korea in November 1983, I'd been taken, as usual, to the same tacky, beer-sodden club in east St. Louis we'd always gone to. In my dream, I stood again in the back of the room on a riser, just looking at that room full of black people. Perhaps it was two years in Asia that made the sight of all that blackness swirling around me so arresting. I couldn't take my eyes off us. I watched us dance and flirt and drink and talk and cuss each other out, and for once, I hadn't felt afraid or annoyed. What I felt was wistfulness because I wasn't part of it. Even so, it was a soothing dream, one that filled me with hope and humility. I envied my oblivious brethren their places at the table and I wished I could move so unselfconsciously among them. For the first time, I also knew that anyone in that room who was wasting his time judging me and critiquing my every move wasn't worth worrying about. I even considered the possibility that nobody was paying me the least attention. How self-absorbed to carry on as if no one but me had mastered mainstream English or ever cracked the covers of serious literature. The weight of the community off my shoulders, I woke up smiling. It hit me like a thunderbolt. I was alone. Truly alone.

I didn't like it.

I wanted to be black.

I admitted to myself how ashamed I'd been of us and I simply let it go. I just walked away from it.

It was much easier than I would have imagined it would be. Once I stopped kidding myself about my true feelings, I just stepped out of that shell of self-hatred and felt a hundred pounds lighter. Once I did, my overwhelming emotion was—foolishness. I felt silly. How could I hate black people? That's like hating my elbows. If black people were no good, then I was no good. My mother, my sisters, strangers on the street. That couldn't be. I had a lot more thinking to do, but the more I lived, the more all my old assumptions were crumbling.

DIGGING DITCHES

It occurred to me that Bobby epitomized the false choice—sociopathology and active wrongdoing versus an upstanding but incredibly difficult life lived while society ignores you—that so many blacks face.

He was the only one left at home. While he'd calmed down from his wildest years, at twenty, he was still headed nowhere fast. Minimally literate, often either drunk or high, with a shoddy work history of gas station jobs held until he'd punched out the owner, he faced a future that did not look bright. The only ghetto folly he'd avoided was fathering bastards—I suspected a low sperm count rather than the use of birth control. I may have been reassessing my relationship to blacks at large, but I was feeling no more charitable toward my brother. Nobody was oppressing him; he was choosing to fail for no reason I could see.

Dorothy had just thrown him out of her place in Atlanta. I'll never know why I extended to my hated brother the invitation to come live with me at precisely that moment, January 1985. A tiny part of me wanted to help him, but it was a foregone conclusion that Mama's favorite would again fail ignominiously. In fact, I didn't even think he would accept, which was what I actually hoped would happen. Then, I could be the virtuous one without being inconvenienced. But he blindsided me: he jumped at my offer. No attitude, no questions asked.

I girded myself for six to eight weeks of his shenanigans. I figured that was all the time it would take for him to burn this bridge too. I planned to be merciless. It was one thing to mistreat me while we lived in our parents' home; I planned in advance to never forgive him for abusing me in my own. I just wondered exactly what it would be: pawning appliances, using my credit cards, peddling drugs from my living room, hoochie mamas coming and going at all hours? He hadn't been at Dorothy's long enough to reach his full negative potential, so I hid my valuables, braced for the worst, and looked forward to moving up a notch with our mother.

When I think of it now, I can't help thinking back to Emmanuel Missionary Baptist Church in north St. Louis where the old folks would cackle when we sang:

Dig one ditch
you better dig two
cause the trap you set
just might be for you.

So my brother came to Maryland and I greeted him with a long list of rules and "things I will not tolerate." It was basically the same spiel I used when my seven-year-old nephew visited. I was a benevolent prison warden; lots of rules, lot of low expectations. He just nodded and looked away.

He'd driven in at about 4:30 A.M. By 8 A.M. he was out job hunting, and by the end of the day, had not one but two.

It wouldn't last.

So I waited for him to fail. I waited for him to steal from my purse or tell me to kiss his ass so I could pass him on to the next sister in line. I waited for him to get arrested so I could *not* bail him out, as efficiently specified in my recitation of the house rules. But he never acknowledged or reacted to my disapproving scrutiny. He wouldn't play the Self-fulfilling Prophecy Game with me. He just took it.

He worked his two menial jobs, slipped off to smoke dope, and watched endless TV while I continued my bleak existence of studying, working out, and reading. It was as if he was waiting for his life to begin; it was as if I was training for some event that never took place. But I was watching him; I had no intention of letting him put anything over on me. As it turned out, he was watching me, too.

The first thing I noticed was that he broke things. He spent those first few weeks looking chagrined, apologizing for knocking over potted plants and knickknacks, upending drinks, dropping cups, burning pots.

"Everything's just so fragile here," he apologized.

He was the only man I ever had in my apartment. Of the few women who'd been there, none encountered the problems he did. This is what it's like, I thought—living with men. Or maybe that's what it's like to live with a man you make nervous. Cups that seemed normal size to me looked dwarfed in his man's paw, doors that swung easily on their hinges for me came off in his hand. He knew he was on trial; he'd call me sheepishly to the site of his latest crash, eyes big as a worried child's, and point in helpless apology at the pile of smashed crockery or scorch marks on the wall above the stove. His regret was new; it silenced the reproof forming on my lips. Growing up, he'd simply leave his messes for us to stumble upon and curse us for chiding him. Now, he had no more physical grace but he had acquired a newfound respect for others. As for me, while my initial response was the black woman's ever-ready, all-purpose anger and martyrdom, one look at his face, girded to endure my latest tongue-lashing, confused and shamed me.

His effort to change was unignorable, though he made no big speeches. I saw admiration in his eyes when I set off for the gym or to class with a fever, in a blizzard, in a deluge, or on a beautiful sunny day. I never cut a class or skipped a workout, a fact that used to make him sneer, yet one day I heard him yell at a new associate who called me a Tom as I drove off to school. In my rearview, I saw him grab his new friend by the collar and shake him. Later, his friend said to me nastily, "Humph. Your brother think you walk on water." I'd stopped being simply the schoolmarm to him and he stopped being an animalistic screwup to me. We became people to each other, not just two people involuntarily sharing DNA.

In a way that I cannot now re-create, my brother and I started over from scratch. Magically, we ended up at the kitchen table drinking beer and eating popcorn into the small hours. Talking, talking, talking, as my long-lost brother told me the story of his life. He introduced himself to me. We might have been two strangers chatting in a waiting room for all we'd known of each other. Two strangers who suddenly realize they are siblings, separated by tragedy long past, miraculously reunited by a twist of fate.

This is the story of his life:

A few months before my invitation, Bobby was just back from being kicked out of Dorothy's in Atlanta in near record time. Home on leave, I'd had to give him the money to get there; I'd tossed it at him and said, "Might as well be a bum there as here."

He hadn't been there a week before he interceded in an argument Dorothy was having with her boyfriend. Eddie Dickerson's true son, he took Carl's side and told her she was a poor excuse for a woman. He would never use the specific rhetoric of hell and damnation, but there was no real difference between his line of reasoning and his father's. No woman should be all the time loud-talking a man the way she did Carl. Bobby put forth his arguments with such drunken vehemence and broken crockery, Atlanta's finest came to give him his first look at the new Southern lockups he'd be patronizing. When he got out next morning, he found his things on the porch and his door key inoperable. I was the first one he called. That was good, because that meant I got to be the first to hang up on him. I refused to help, though I knew Mama would and that I'd just have to give her that much more money, but I wanted him to know I did it for her, not for him. Because I didn't care enough to ask, I had no idea of the specifics of how he managed to get home. Dorothy threw him out on a Monday. Mama didn't get paid until Friday. Bobby was homeless and nearly penniless in the interim. He lived in his car, refused admission by every family member in Atlanta, though one offered to let Bobby park out front so he could at least sleep close to kin. You can't blame them; every working-class family has to deal with some variation on this basic theme and every one has been burned. Somewhere, some family member is always between addresses and moving in with you "just for a few days." Then the squatter starts sleeping later and later, his or her lover starts staying over, and the phone bill reaches triple digits.

Bobby passed on the offer of the driveway and spent three days reviewing his life from behind the wheel of a car with a broken gas gauge.

Just like the protagonists in all the *It's a Wonderful Life* rip-offs, Bobby got to see what it would be like to get his wish. For years he'd brayed his frustration at being part of such a cloying family. For years he'd told his sisters he couldn't wait to be away from us, and now it had happened. For three days, he was all alone. No meals cooked to order, no handmaidens to right his messes, no well-kept home with corny family photos on the wall to smoke his dope in, no mama to baby him. As it turned out, however, there were still plenty of people to call him a bum.

Filthy, hungry, and scared of what he was becoming, Bobby picked up a day's work at a construction site by loitering where hard-nosed job bosses came to find men like him. By night, he loaded and unloaded crates at a dairy, supervised by permanent employees who made no effort to hide their contempt. "Bum" work, as it was called, at the dairy came with the perk of a shed to crash in while the cohort was finalized. Exhausted but too wary to sleep, Bobby watched as his comrades pilfered the belongings of a man who kept what was left of his life in the bag he used for a pillow. His pockets turned out, his head on bare earth, the man woke to rut in a hysterical rage about the shed. Bobby was ordered to help throw him out, the man's calls for justice met only with "Shut the fuck up, hobo!"

Ever Eddie Dickerson's son, he made a little extra giving dollar rides to shiftless coworkers. He refused to charge more. As he drove them about, a carful of fetid wretches sour with drink and failure, men sometimes old enough to be his grandfather, each would point out the homes of former friends and relatives they passed. Momentarily sobered or cackling with alcoholic glee, they'd tell the story of the final misdeed that closed that particular door to them forever. One somber junkie asked to be driven past the same house every day, slowly. After the first day, Bobby learned not to offer to stop and wait while they knocked. Instead, Bobby tried to get these men to pool their meager pay so they could buy cold cuts, bread, milk, soap, rent a room. But to no avail; their destination was always the drug dealer or the liquor store, which conveniently cashed their paychecks without ID. This time, he'd waited for them outside in the getaway car not wondering nihilistically whether the police would come and arrest them all, as he had in high school, but whether this life he saw passing before his eyes was inevitable.

The next day, there was no work to be had and the car ran out of gas, so Bobby and a newfound friend from the dairy pushed the car onto a lot and hoofed it all day. Bobby shared his remaining dope with his new friend as they walked, and my brother learned what it really meant to be a bum. The first stop was the blood bank.

"This just till my moms get paid Friday," he told the nurse. "It's just a big misunderstandin. See, my sister and I fell out . . ."

"Sure, honey," the nurse said, and patted his hand.

The second stop, a mission and free food. His stomach rumbling, his head aching from dehydration, nonetheless, he couldn't do it. The workers called out to his new friend by name but Bobby couldn't make himself eat. He says he couldn't eat because those around him looked so much worse off. I don't believe him. I think he couldn't eat because he's a Dickerson; it's better to starve than to take a handout. Instead, he helped unload donations.

It was hours before he could persuade his new friend to leave the mission to resume the quest for work. His friend chided him for his attitude. "All we need is some wine and a doorway," he said, "and we got the money from the blood." To Bobby's shock, he had no intention of working again until it was all gone. His friend was not even twenty-five and wanted nothing except a "big, fat woman with a lot of kids and a government job. Welfare aint enough." His friend had several such women whom he moved among, except, as now, when he preferred his "freedom." Bobby listened in fascinated horror, objecting only when his friend pushed him to demand payment from the mission staff for his labor.

Weaned in the tough but close-knit brotherhood of the St. Louis streets, Bobby wouldn't abandon his new friend. He fretted over the time as the day lengthened, but desertion was not an option. Finally, the staff required them all to leave, so Mr. X took Bobby to his favorite place to hang out, a nearby police station.

Mr. X's other ambition, it turned out, was jailhouse trustee. While Bobby washed his face in the jail's water fountain, Mr. X explained to him the crime he was designing to land him a protracted stay in the local jail but without sending him to prison to serve hard time. He knew how long it would take for the petty crime he envisioned to come to trial, and gambled that he'd get off with time served.

"Look at em," he said, pointing to the white-clad trustees. "They warm, they eat regular, they come and go and they get to talk to folks. They can even use the phone. Shit, man, that's a promotion!"

Mr. X called a trustee with a mop over to expound on his theories of life and Bobby couldn't help moving away across the room. When he turned back, his friend was out of sight. He found him in an alcove smoking a joint and rifling Bobby's wallet.

Too lazy even to be afraid, he handed the wallet back with a shrug.

At a loss for words, Bobby could only note peripherals. "Man, you been smoking my weed since I met you. Thought you aint had none."

Another shrug. "Give you a hit for fiddy cents," Mr. X offered.

Bobby walked away.

When he couldn't find paid work, he carried grocery bags and did yard work gratis wherever he saw women or old people. No matter what else he was doing, he thought about his life.

On Friday, Mom wired him one hundred dollars from her meager paycheck. Desperate to leave Atlanta, Bobby headed at top speed for the pawnshop to retrieve the TV he'd left there. The customer before him gathered his things and left while the store owner went to the back to bring the set.

"Twenty dollars," the pawnbroker said.

"I left it on the counter," Bobby said, fidgeting and tense with the need to be gone.

"Aint no money here," the man said.

In a flash, Bobby knew the previous customer had palmed his twenty dollars.

"Give me that motherfucker's address. Ima go to his house and Ima kill im. Then I be back for my TV." Bobby was cold with fury, the way he always felt before he pulverized someone, now multiplied by the accumulated frustration of the previous three days.

The man took one look at him and opened his cash drawer. "Here's twenty dollars. Just go. Please."

While fear flashed across the pawnbroker's face, my brother considered tracking the man down just on principle for treating him like a punk, just to make someone pay for the pass his life had come to. But the wiser Bobby took the cash, the TV, and left. At his first gas stop, he found the bill he thought he'd placed on the counter stuck to the others in his wallet. For the first time since Monday, he laughed. The beginnings of a new person reemerged from skid row and made its way back to St. Louis. Back to his family.

He spent the next few months quietly sponging off Mama, distancing himself from his old friends, confining himself to moderate amounts of beer and reefer smoked in his car. I wonder if he prowled the house as I had, peering out the windows, trying to force a life worth living to appear before his bleary eyes.

His cronies worked their way up to "whack," crack's virulent predecessor, but for the first time in his life, Bobby said no to the latest way to kill himself. He anchored the couch to the living room floor and made sure the TV would never be stolen. Now *he* was the Dickerson who never went outside, now he was the Dickerson who disapproved of his friends' activities.

He told me screamingly funny stories of taunting the cops, his misadventures with women, street-corner hoops. I was mesmerized. A good girl, I had never ever hung out on the streets, and this was a window onto a whole new world for me. Though I'd known there was trouble in the streets we'd grown up on, because I'd known, I'd made it my business not to know the specifics. Now, I howled with disbelief as Bobby told me which neighbor had been the pimp, which the five-dollar prostitute, which the cat burglar.

He also pointed out which of his "hoodlum friends" I'd so hated were beaten every payday by an alcoholic father with a baseball bat, which went to bed hungry every night in a house with no heat or electricity. Which friend's house was so filthy Bobby slipped out back to drink from the water hose when thirsty. Which friend's brother was such a thief Bobby put his wallet in his sock when he visited; the brother had two of everything in his bedroom and his parents never asked why.

He told me how he and Packy, the terrors of Pruitt High School, would come and go by way of the ground floor's huge windows. They'd weave in and out of classrooms that way, making the girls screech, the teachers clutch their hearts. Malt-liquored and high by 9 A.M., they held the sweating music teacher hostage, forcing him to play album after album for them long after the period ended, and the next class milled in the hallway, too afraid to enter, while they nodded out. How Packy brought a shotgun to school to saw off in shop when the teacher told them to bring a project that interested them. How the shotgun-toting thieves who robbed the crap game he and Packy were in took one look at their eyes and robbed everyone but them. He spent most of one evening trying to explain a scam they'd often pulled at the malls involving receipts and stolen designer jeans, but my bougie brain was never able to absorb it. He laughed so hard at my incomprehension, I thought I'd have to call 911. "Jesus, you straight!" he gasped, tears rolling down his face. Just like Daddy.

Bobby made me laugh until I thought I'd hyperventilate, but what I most remember are the heartbreaking stories he told completely devoid of self-pity or rationalization. He always made himself the patsy, no excuses. Listening, I laughed and cried at the same time. He is a natural storyteller. How can you grow up in the same house with someone and not know that?

Book-smart but woefully immature, it had never occurred to me that he had a different version of life in the Dickerson family. I'd assumed that everything was the same for him as for me. Until we lived together as adults, I had never factored in what it meant to be the only boy and the youngest in a house full of women. Fatherlessness, while devastating for us both, played itself out differently for him than it did for me.

At nine, just as he lost daily access to his father, he was also bused from our stable working-class area to a school in a much poorer, much tougher neighborhood. That much we knew. But we hadn't known that on his first day, as he got off the bus, local toughs punched him in his face, took his watch, took his lunch. These were his classmates. So the curly-haired pretty little boy with five older sisters and no father began a nightmarish initiation into street life.

Involuntarily, he ended up at one of the worst public schools in St. Louis, while I voluntarily attended one of the best. My school was white, his was black. Mine was safe, his dangerous. Mine provided a superior education, his merely careened along from day to day. From the very beginning, he was singled out for torture.

He told me innumerable stories of the violence and degradation he both witnessed and endured at Stowe Elementary School in the north St. Louis inner city. You would be shocked. But the one that encapsulates it for me is this one:

Once, Stowe played softball against another elementary school. In a rare moment of triumph, he hit a home run. The little girls cheered him; they loved the soft curly hair and pretty features he had inherited from our mother. He flew around the bases feeling like Babe Ruth, he said. But this was not allowed.

Randy, a boy who had developed a seething hatred for him, his neat clothes, and his neatly packed lunches, waited for him at home plate. Bobby slowed down, he said, praying to be thrown out and avoid having to face the boy who hated him and who wasn't even in the game. But no one dared throw my brother out and draw this hateful boy's fire. Instead, he ended up walking slowly, predefeated, to claim the home run he no longer wanted.

One pace short of home plate, this boy who hated him so much smacked him in the face with a baseball mitt with all his might. Bobby's eyes were blacked and his nose poured blood while the principals, teachers, and students of both schools watched the tableau from the bleachers. Randy then made him go all the way back to first base and off the field. Not directly from home plate. No. Bobby was made to completely retrace his steps and undo, base by base, the one good thing that he had accomplished at that horrible school.

My brother gave the story his best comedic spin, but that time, I couldn't laugh. Sitting at my kitchen table in Maryland years later, I learned to hate that school where baseballs came whizzing through open classroom doors to thwack him in the head and knock him semiconscious to the floor, where hysterical little girls were dragged into the boys' bathroom, where little boys ran screaming down the hall with lawn darts hanging from their backs.

Bizarrely, my nine-year-old brother chose that moment to emerge as the class clown. Every time he was beaten, he fought back with words. My verbal acuity gave me the gift of invisibility, which, while lonely, freed me from abuse. His jibes made him a star and highly visible. Unfortunately, he was still a pretty, roly-poly mama's boy who stuttered and had facial tics—every smart remark earned him another beating, but he wouldn't hold his tongue. His five sisters couldn't come to his aid because we were all spread out in different schools, different cities. In any event, he knew without having to think about it very hard that having girls run to fight for him would not only get him killed, it would make him want to die. If he told Daddy, he'd be forced to "fight like a man." In the end, none of us even knew what was happening. Just as he'd drawn our father's attention with inexplicable stabs at defiance and endured many self-inflicted whippings, he chose to employ the same fatalistic strategy at school. As a result, not only did all the tough boys he made laughingstocks of come to hate him, but so did the school administration; to them, any black boy not sitting quietly at his desk was a troublemaker. Bobby could just walk past a classroom and it would erupt in anticipatory laughter and head turns. He was sent to the principal's office more often than the boys who didn't even bother to beat him up out of sight.

He told no one about what his life was really like. He can't say why now.

The nightmare he lived through that year at Stowe ruined his life. It made him hate himself from every possible angle. The girls made much over his "good hair"; the boys beat him up every time they did so. On the day someone suggested a "good hair" contest, Bobby was sure he would be killed. His was the only head through which a comb passed without encountering a tangle, and his was the only head pounded against a desk at the contest's end. Three times in one day he was struck in the head with a softball every time he passed a particular part of the schoolyard. The third time he dragged himself to her office, the school nurse said gently, "Why don't you just spend the rest of the day here." She didn't call our parents, she didn't call the principal. She just gave him sanctuary. Randy and the boys renamed him "Wide-Ass," a sobriquet that even some teachers used.

Waiting for the school bus, Bobby watched as his classmates broke into neighboring houses. One neighborhood boy, Cookie, was a famed second-story man. Bobby watched one morning as he ascended a ladder propped against a neighbor's house. As he neared the top of the ladder, the homeowner leaned out with a sawed-off shotgun.

"Mornin, Cookie," the man said pleasantly.

"Mornin, Mr. Cole. How you?"

"Fine. And you, son?"

"Fine." They regarded each other for a moment.

"Guess I'll see you next time," Cookie said, and retreated down the ladder just in time to catch the school bus.

Bobby was far from their only victim. Another boy, Michael, was a special target of theirs because he wouldn't take his beatings like the punk they'd determined him to be. No matter how they beat him, no matter how outnumbered he was, no matter how exhausted, he fought back. They'd humiliate him and he'd tear into the nearest bully. Eventually, for sport, they'd make him run a gauntlet of thugs, fighting boy after boy until he'd sometimes have to be taken out on a stretcher. Finally, Michael's parents transferred him out. Bobby knew he should have been like Michael.

Instead, he was a punk among punks. He had a classmate who avoided most beatings by faking asthma attacks. Others coped by becoming one with the enemy. The punks turned on each other, each hoping to make himself seem less worthy of a beating than the next coward. Having lain down with dogs, Bobby began to develop fleas. Or tried to; not even that worked. When he called cross-eyed Rochelle by her cruel nickname ("Cross-eye"), she beat him up. Alvin, another punk who was often beaten up, beat Bobby every chance he got.

Soon, Bobby was going inside to join his school chums while they trashed the homes of decent people off at work. Once, Randy fell through a hole in the floor and cut his arm badly. Bobby helped him out and ripped off his own T-shirt to wrap his bleeding arm. He helped Randy back to school, giddy with relief now that he and Randy were buddies. When Randy got back from the nurse's office, he kicked Bobby as hard as he could in the groin with his shiny new brogans. Curled up in a fetal position, Bobby lay on the floor until the teacher who had witnessed the assault ordered him to his seat.

Their teacher went on maternity leave and Bobby's class went through fifteen substitutes seriatim—none lasted more than two days. The new teacher would turn her back to write her name on the board and the projectiles would fly at her head. Eventually, the principal had to move his office into Bobby's classroom.

Even though we didn't know exactly what was happening to him, Mama took Bobby out of Stowe after a year because he'd become a different person. We were always in the principal's office dealing with Bobby's disruptive high jinks, though he had almost completely lost his sense of humor at home. Where before he'd been mischievous and high-spirited, albeit odd, he'd become mean-spirited, snarling and eating everything in sight as if perpetually starved. Of course, he was, because his lunch and pocket money were always stolen, but we never knew this. We just knew that our lunches, our pocket money, our dinners began disappearing. He was withdrawn, moody, furious if he had to stay inside. He began throwing his manly weight around.

Mama transferred him to Catholic school. Things seemed to go well, but all too soon, Mama was in the principal's office. While Bobby was somewhat comically disruptive, they'd really called her in to tell her that they thought he should be in the gifted program. We relaxed even though my antipathy toward him was nourished by this latest act of favoritism. The good student was moldering at Southwest while the worst had a private school lavished upon him. Given our dire financial straits, it was a luxury we could ill afford, especially since, as I'd predicted, he was soon expelled.

Sure that he'd be safe among the ruler-wielding nuns, he was his old self for the first few weeks. Then one day, he was sliding down the sliding board on his belly like Superman. Ben, an older, troubled boy, stepped in his path at the last minute so that Bobby crashed into his legs, fell off, and landed on his head. In Bobby's mind, it was Stowe all over again.

Bobby said nothing, just checked himself over comically for broken bones while Ben and his boys laughed at the "fat f-f-f-faggot." Not knowing what else to do, Bobby went on to class, hoping someone would ask him what was wrong. No one did.

Two days later, in the cafeteria, Bobby became aware of himself tracking the people around him. As if he had radar, he knew where all the boys were, where all the girls were, where all the nuns were. His shoulders twitched when someone passed behind him. His breathing halted when footsteps fell silent an arm's reach away. He was a machine, mentally calculating his place in the "jive-ass" hierarchy and the likelihood of his being attacked. He couldn't help figuring the precise number of steps between himself and the door, the door he would never allow himself to run to.

All at once, he felt, rather than heard, wood snap. It felt, he thought, the way it did when we broke off switches from the trees out back so Daddy could whip us. He turned to the surprised, innocent boy next to him and beat him with his lunch tray. He had a fight nearly every day over the next few weeks. The final one culminated in his furious, incoherent attempt to box the nun trying to end the fight. So ended his Catholic school career.

Short of mind reading, there was no way the nuns could have understood that, to him, the sliding board incident (of which they were unaware) was like the sound of a car backfiring to a veteran with post-traumatic stress syndrome. Since his family didn't know what he'd endured at Stowe, the nuns didn't either. We had no idea how to help him because we had no idea what he'd been through. From that point on till he was expelled, Bobby saw no difference between Stowe and St. Engelbert. He didn't last even a full month at Corpus Christi, the second Catholic elementary school Mama sent him to.

Several years later, while in high school, my drunken teenage brother ran out of gas just as Ben happened to be passing. Happily recognizing Bobby, Ben stopped to help. Bobby screamed, "You made me hate myself!" and beat him bloody.

After Catholic school, Bobby ended up back at Benton, our old neighborhood school, where he became king of the bullies. He beat up every punk he could lay his hands on.

By eleven, he was running the streets at all hours, which, of course, we'd known. What we didn't know was that he was terrified every time his feet left our porch steps, just as I was. But he had to leave home if he ever wanted to be around other men. He doesn't explain his compulsion to run the streets this way. He just shrugs and says he wanted to see his friends, but I think it was more than that. Years too late to help my brother, I wondered what it would have been like to lose living with my mother, my hero, as he lost living with his father. What would it have been like having five brothers and no women to turn to?

In my junior year of high school, I had my only high school boyfriend, Robert, a classmate of Wina's from Beaumont in our old neighborhood. That year, she and I swirled at the center of a large group of guys who were his friends. There were so many of us, our girlfriends and his guy friends in tow, we made our own party everywhere we went. There might be eight guys over to bike-ride, play Ping-Pong, or eat the cakes Mama baked for them.

The guys abused him sadistically and Bobby dogged their footsteps like a pickpocket. They used him as a human dartboard, they locked him in their trunks and screeched around corners, they pounded on him with their fists. He loved it. When Wina and I tried to stop them, Bobby turned on us like a wild animal. During the year I had a boyfriend, Bobby had protectors. He locked himself in the bathroom and cried for joy when they hunted down and pummeled the teenager who'd mugged him. But Robert and I broke up and Bobby, again, lost the only positive male figures in his life. He hated me for "messing things up" with Robert.

Eventually, at about sixteen, he got so bad Mama found the money to send him to a psychiatrist. I hated him for the constant rewards he got for being a screwup. I brought home straight A's and Mama could barely be bothered to notice; Bobby managed to get one C among a rogues' gallery of D's and F's and Mama killed the fatted calf. I should have been the one sent to a shrink.

One day, Mama gave Bobby fifteen dollars and sent him out to Ladue, a ritzy, exclusive suburb of St. Louis. With her hard-earned money, he bought a tank of gas and a nickel bag and set off for the good part of town. Only Mama could have made such a request of him and lived to tell the tale. Only for Mama would he actually have shown up. Only for Mama could I so resent my own flesh and blood.

Bobby sat outside the splendid home of the white man who actually thought he could make sense of the madness inside his head, and smoked three joints. Through the haze of reefer smoke, he watched the gardener come and go, the black housekeeper converse with the black postman, the stay-at-home moms in their expensive peignoirs toddle out for the newspaper. Red-eyed and ravenous, Bobby rang the doorbell and watched the little white man's eyes grow round at the sight of the large, confused black man on his doorstep.

The nervous white man led him up the three flights to the converted office in his mansion and tried to do his job. He reassured Bobby that anything he told him was strictly confidential. Bobby could tell from looking at him that Mama had told him as much as she knew. OK, man, he said. Silence stretched out between them. The white man caved first.

"Do you drink?" the psychiatrist asked.

"Nah, man."

"Smoke dope?"

"Nah, man."

"Do you . . . fight?"

"Uh-uh."

The white man was at a loss. The two sat in silence while my mother's money ran out and my brother thought about how he didn't care whether he lived or died. He thought about all the times he and Packy had braced their chests against the shotgun barrels that were supposed to make them back down and screamed maniacally, "SHOOT ME, MOTHAFUCKA!" He thought about how obvious his death wish was, so obvious, in fact, that the worst hoods backed off. He thought about how worthless he felt and how he knew he wasn't good enough for his family. What he wasn't thinking about—and this was most important—was his father and how he was dead and how he loved, missed, and resented him. All those beatings, yes, but oh, all those times together working with tools and getting dirty. But does he drink, toke, or fight? Nah, man.

The timer dinged. My brother drove back to his life.

He was a maniac; who else has ever gotten thrown off his high school football team for beating up his own teammates in the middle of a game? He didn't think they were working hard enough. As he got older, he'd disappear so often and for so long, I'd been sure he was committing the worst crimes imaginable. A decade later, I found out the truth. Until our father died in 1977 when Bobby was thirteen, he was spending most of his time at 4933 Terry Avenue.

My mother had to force me to spend time with Daddy after their separation. I said perhaps fifty pained words to him before he died, all either "yes sir" or "no sir." He'd inquire politely about my schoolwork or general health, I'd offer up a dish of demure "sir"'s and count the moments until I was safely away from him again. We were like polite litigants trapped together in the courthouse elevator. I'd assumed Bobby's relationship with him was the same. I was very wrong.

Bobby spent five years waiting hours in the snow or humidity for the two buses it took to get back to our old home. A great deal of the time I thought he spent marauding St. Louis, he spent riding around with my father in his broken-down old truck.

I had hated him when he left our warm home swarming with

Gooches on Christmas Day, 1976. We had ham, turkey, dressing, greens and cornbread, sweet potato pie—the works. We'd been cooking for days and the house was filled with love and laughter, but still, he had to go.

Like an animal, he rooted with his bare hands among the pile of fried chicken, and I pictured him lying dead on the floor. "Merry Christmas, thug," I'd sneered. He gave me the finger.

Why was it that he could appreciate nothing that came from his own family? I'd pictured him toking up a Yuletide joint and trashing our gifts to him for his friends' amusement, even though he'd not bothered to buy any. I figured he'd be behind one of the tragic Christmas armed robberies we'd see reported on TV that night. Rather, he'd waited in the freezing cold for the bus and gone to have frozen turkey TV dinners with his father in an empty house.

Bobby spent Christmas night in my old room and listened through the open connecting door as Daddy coughed uncontrollably all night with the metastasized lung cancer that would kill him three days before my senior prom in 1977. Mama forced us to buy Daddy birthday, Christmas, and Father's Day presents; that year's was an industrial-size bottle of Old Spice. After he died, we found it still cellophane-wrapped and untouched in a box with every other unused gift we'd given him over the five-year separation. He died never knowing how to enjoy life.

That left my brother to finish his man-training on the streets. My father and those north St. Louis hoodlums laid the foundation. Puberty did the rest. He got bigger and madder and stopped cowering. He stopped blinking. He started fighting back. He started fighting for no reason at all. Sitting at our Maryland kitchen table, he remembered clearly the first time he fought back and the feeling of satisfaction it triggered, even though he was soundly beaten. "I beat that boy," he said, "till it wasn't nothing left of my Batman lunch box but the handle."

What made him decide to fight? Inspecting his beer, he said, "You know, Debbie, you just get tired. All I knew, I was tired of gettin pushed around."

So why did he stop fighting, stop marauding, give up street life? He shrugs the question off, as if reclaiming one's life is a mere hat trick.

My guess is he stopped fighting because he was again tired. Tired of being a teenage failure. Tired of being an able-bodied burden. Tired of self-elimination from his family. I think he wanted to come home to the mother who never lost faith in him, and to the sisters who did.

Once while we lived together, I planned to take my brother to an upscale D.C. bar, but it turned out that he didn't own a tie. I went door to door in my building and borrowed one. Then he annoyed me by dawdling with it around his neck. Finally he told me, brusquely ashamed, that he didn't know how to tie it.

My father taught him that hitting is the way to express disapproval, and that real men don't clean up their own messes. But he didn't teach him to tie a tie. Everything I learned about being a woman I learned from my mother and I consciously pattern my life after hers. My brother's legacy from his father is much more complicated.

MY BROTHER, THE RACE CONSULTANT

My brother's gifts to me, however, are unproblematic. I'd been so smugly sure of all the good I could do for him, it never occurred to me that he had anything to offer in return. I was his bridge back to the family and out to the mainstream, but he was mine across to my black peer group. Without him, making my way back to a sense of my black self would have been mostly mental. I lacked the courage to approach young black people I was unrelated to, especially in culturally specific settings. Older people have always approved of me since I am the quintessential dutiful daughter, but young people—I knew I'd be judged and found wanting, both racially and socially out of step. Also, I dreaded exposure to that special brand of negativity and defeatism which abounds in the black community.

With Bobby by my side, I could go to black gatherings on his coat-tails and be assumed cool. Often, his friends cocked an eyebrow at my speech patterns, but behind me, I would hear my brother bat cleanup for me with a simple "She cool, man." In any event, I was smart enough to know to keep my end of a conversation to a minimum. So I just paid attention, listened, and watched. Bobby was my race consultant. I'd shoot a quizzical look at him while one of his friends used ten "know what ahm sayin'"s in a row and he'd translate. One of his friends said I was "razor." I almost cried; I thought he meant I was cutting, a hard-ass, the very thing I was trying not to be. But no, my brother informed me. "Razor sharp" he meant. Well dressed. Oh.

I was dancing with one of his friends once to Teena Marie's song "Square Biz," except I didn't know who Teena Marie was, nor had I ever heard the song before. The guy said to me nonchalantly, "Square biz, baby." I said, "What?" "Square biz. You know . . ." and hunched one shoulder in the general direction of the DJ booth. I had no idea what he was talking about, but I was sure a liberty was being taken. Who was he calling baby? I was getting angry and the guy was looking at me like I was loud-talking him when Bobby walked over.

"'S jes the name of the song, Debbie," he said. To the guy he said, "She don't get out much. Know what ahm sayin?"

"Solid," the brother said, and they exchanged a complicated handshake.

I just shut up, smiled apologetically, and danced.

While Bobby dictated, I made slang flash cards—"sweet sixteen," as it turned out, was not a statutory rape victim but a measurement of some drug, cocaine I think. Or maybe it was a particular type of car. I could never remember. My vaunted memory struggled to handle these new inputs, but I persevered. Within days, Bobby made more black friends in my neighborhood than I had in the year before his arrival. Our doorbell started ringing. Within five minutes of hitting town, he'd found and programmed in the happening black radio stations; I alternated between them and the jazz station on my Walkman while working out. He never developed a taste for Billie Holliday and Count Basie, though. I found him shaking his head ruefully over my album collection. He asked me, "How come erbody you listen to is dead?" To my happy surprise, my brother's friends accepted me without comment. Most deferred to and overly respected me. I never mentioned my accomplishments, yet it was clear Bobby had been talking me up. I was like Dorothy at the end of the movie; I'd always had the power to go home. All that had stopped me was my own pigheadedness. I'd always wanted a brother and finally I had one. I'd always wanted to belong somewhere and now I did—the place I'd turned my back on.

I spent as much time as possible reconnecting with my brother—he had insights into the ground level of the community I had no other way of tapping into.

But Bobby wasn't just my path back to my community; he also gave me back my father. Always much too deferential toward me after our reconciliation, Bobby never argued or disapproved when I raved about how much I hated Daddy. He didn't try to excuse our father's iron control over us, or all the whippings over minor infractions, or all the needless deprivations. He'd just say, "Yeah, that's true," and begin another story about all the time I'd never known about that they spent together working, fishing, hunting, or just puttering in the basement.

He showed me a relaxed, everyday side of Daddy I never knew existed. Just the fact that he'd voluntarily spent time with our father floored and angered me. It also made me see just how wedded to my own opinion I was—how like my father. He also showed me that it was possible to hold Daddy accountable for his brutality while also acknowledging all the other things he was. If only I'd known about all those other things. Bobby told the stories of Daddy's beatings as readily as those of the good times. One story would be about being forced to eat rotted fruit because of the sin of wastefulness, the next about Daddy fighting off the rabid dog bearing down on Bobby. He took the good with the bad in a way that I still can't.

Accepting my brother back into my life was the easiest thing I've ever done. In no time at all, we grew close and have stayed that way, normal sibling wear and tear notwithstanding, in the decade since. My father, conversely, broke my heart all over again. I was so comfortable with the facile hatred for him I'd cultivated over the years that it hadn't occurred to me there was another version of the story. I carried around with me a depthless, one-dimensional TV movie of an inexplicably abusive father who reveled in the unhappiness he'd caused his blameless, abused family. Imagine my horror at finding myself laughing at funny things he'd done with Bobby or taking retroactive pride in some brave thing I'd never known about. I didn't know what to think; nothing he was telling me fit into the comfortable, inch-deep little tableau I'd concocted. For a smart girl, I was awfully confused.

I'd lie in bed remembering Bobby's stories of mundane hauling trips with Daddy and weep for no reason that I could explain. Nor did it help that Bobby had grown into the spitting image of our beefy father. More than once, I'd turn and find my heart in my throat at the sight of my father standing at the kitchen sink—chicken legs, barrel chest, square head, and all. I was furious that I was having a hard time holding on to my anger. I couldn't get him off my mind. I became fascinated by him and yearned to understand what made him behave the way he did.

Only then did I spend time thinking about the significance of his childhood, his historical context, his personality. I grilled everyone I could to find out more about him. I began to see that though I was legitimately angry at him, I was also sad. Sad for me and sad for him.

Then, while on a military business trip to Okinawa, I found I had Eddie Mack Dickerson dogging my heels.

From the time my taxi pulled into Kadena Air Force Base, I couldn't stop thinking about him. I found myself wondering where the battles were that he'd fought in. Where was the camp? Where were the caves they had to clean out of defenders one at a time? What did they do for fun? Were there hookers? Where was that quonset hut they destroyed when the Air Corps disrespected them? I sat drinking gin and tonics at the beachfront officers' club and wondered, Is this where he waded ashore, his rifle over his head, enemy bullets sinking into the chests of all the men around him?

Embarrassed and giggly like a little girl, I found myself tearing around the island going to bookstore after bookstore. Sheepishly, some silly part of me was hoping against hope to catch a glimpse of my long-ago marine father and his Tennessee homeboys smoking cigarettes or guarding POWs in a World War II photo. Okinawa abounded with photographic history books about the famous battle waged there, yet I could find none with even one picture of a black GI. The more I searched, the more enraged I became. Not even the several base bookstores had photos with black GIs in them. He might have died, I might never have been born, yet he was not fit to capture on film or be acknowledged by the forces of history.

He'd told us about how he and his homeboys had reacted when they were shown newsreel footage of the battle once the island was secure. All the blacks had been edited out. They rioted and flattened the quonset hut where the movie was shown. Forty years later, in his honor, I tore the head off every bookstore manager whose shop failed inspection.

I felt closest to him on the beach, so that's where I spent every free moment on that trip. I'd sit there and picture him wading ashore through that hellish barrage of enemy fire, the dead floating all around. How terrified he must have been, that young teenager fresh from the Tennessee cotton fields. He must have been sure he would die. And victory—total, utter victory—what must that have felt like? He must have felt like Superman.

And his family. For the first time, I wondered what he thought of us. I'd spent most of my life analyzing my feelings for him; I'd never wondered what he was thinking. For the first time since the day we left and I pitied him, I confronted the knowledge that we'd broken his heart.

But simultaneously, I was barraged with so many bad memories. It was physically painful, that game of mental tennis with my father as the ball, but I couldn't make it stop. First I'd have a happy remembrance of him, then a painful one.

I could see him sitting at the dinner table, laughing himself silly over a histrionic, cross-eyed choir director who visited our church. "I bet when he cry," he'd wheezed between guffaws, "the tears run down his back!" Mama tried to stop us from indulging in such un-Christian laughter at another's frailty, but there was no resisting my father's laugh. He'd laughed so hard, all he could do was rock back and forth helplessly in his chair. I hadn't laughed at the joke, I'd laughed for joy at my father's joy.

But when a first-grade playmate took a silly little squeak toy from me, more from playfulness than spite, he'd grimly repeated that story about how the Air Corps boys wouldn't give them meat. I knew what I had to do when he hissed that punch line at me: "Marines. Don't. Lose." I couldn't have cared less about the toy, yet I'd marched myself across the alley to oblivious little Garland Lee's house and started pummeling him the moment he opened the door. Marines and Dickersons. Don't. Lose. I cried harder than Garland did.

Daddy thought he was making me tough, and the irony is, he was. But my first use of my toughness was to squeeze him out of my life.

I cried and cried on a beach halfway around the world. I cried for my father and I cried for myself. Eddie Mack Dickerson was a hard man to love, but he was even harder to hate.

CHAPTER FIVE

IT ALL COMES TOGETHER

Officers' Training School, March 1985. In typical Air Force fashion, after waiting months for a slot, I had all of eight days to wrap up my Maryland life. Bobby and I'd had only a few brief months to repair our relationship; thankfully, we'd made the most of it. He returned to St. Louis and shortly thereafter moved to Las Vegas, where he's lived ever since, trouble-free and suburban.

I, on the other hand, got to reenter basic training. A more genteel, white-glove, twelve-week version, but basic nonetheless. Room and uniform inspections. Marauding flight commanders instead of TIs. Shoe polish and marching in the hot Texas sun. Memorizing convoluted regulations. Constant testing. Demerits for using a blue pen when the fine print said black. We were "Miss," "Mister," or "OT" and no one ever raised his or her voice, but then you don't need to in such a situation.

Just like in basic training, I threw myself into it body and soul. My feeling of anticlimax upon my selection for OTS notwithstanding, I wanted to be an officer with everything in me, sure I would be wearing Air Force blue till I was forced into retirement. After that, who knew, but till then—my Air Force, do or die.

I turned twenty-one in basic and twenty-six in OTS. Being older, prior-service, and a Dickerson, I did well. Where five years before I had excelled at basic fueled by a hysterical determination, this time it was a cold one, focused like a spotlight on the "butter bars" of a second lieutenant; nothing and no one could come between me and them. I would endure a twelve-*month* OTS to become the first Officer Dickerson. I was no more ambitious than that. For all my newfound sense of possibility and confidence, I was still thinking small.

I had no plans to end up with an exalted student rank—flight "fire safety OT" or "mail honcho" would have sufficed. I would have been happy, dutiful even, handing out care packages from home to my flight mates. All I wanted was a commission on my personal terms—doing the best job I could, causing no trouble but taking no guff.

It quickly became apparent that to survive OTS, the most difficult task would be simply remaining calm. The key to basic training was following orders thoroughly and with alacrity; those with leadership potential naturally ended up coordinating and directing others in accomplishing those tasks. The key to OTS, however, was time management and leadership. Prevailing as a group was as important as it had been in basic; but we potential officers also had to show ourselves to be capable of functioning without constant oversight.

The school tossed us into a high-stress, fast-paced, highly structured environment and told us how to survive it: prioritize. Again and again, we were lectured about time management. After the first two weeks, a great deal of our time was our own to organize. We had to create a path of order through the overwhelming number of tasks we were given to complete, none of which, standing alone, was very difficult. It's just that none of them stood alone. Our flight commanders tossed us piles of regulations and study guides that first day—wearing of the uniform, flight regs, squadron regs, group regs, wing regs, physical fitness requirements, the demerit system, academics, professional development, Air Force history, the honor code . . . it went on and on. We would regularly be tested on our knowledge of these documents as well as held responsible for the least violation of a reg, no matter how obscure.

Unlike the huge, open bays of my basic flight, at OTS we were two to a comfortable room on coed floors. The bathrooms were single-sex but otherwise there were men all around. No attempt was made to put all the women together on a floor, and they only told us once that no "fraternizing" would be allowed. OTS was the most gender-neutral place I've ever been. Our unisex barracks uniform was squadron shorts, white T-shirt, flip-flops. Underwear not optional. We saw each other at our worst every day during the first two degrading "chicken stripes" weeks; it was hard to see each other as sexual beings after that. When we ran the confidence course (again), I had trouble getting over a high wall we had to rope-climb. The people behind me couldn't get over until I did, so I was heaving and straining and getting nowhere. Suddenly, a big, strong, and undoubtedly male hand landed on my butt and pushed. I scrambled over the wall, utterly unconcerned with whose hand it was or what its owner might have been thinking at the time. I didn't even look back.

Lights-out was at eleven. Unlike in basic, you could go to bed before that, but given the near impossibility of completing all our tasks, more than a few minutes early was a forlorn hope. Focused on the big tasks like reg memorization and mastering the push-ups which would bedevil me the entire twelve weeks, I usually managed fifteen minutes or so early on the theory that nothing could be accomplished in so little time. But I watched my roommate one night methodically folding socks, organizing her briefcase, and making lists right until the clock struck eleven. Fifteen minutes seemed a lot longer to me after that, and I accepted that OTS was really, truly a full-time job. About halfway through, after we'd proved ourselves, things lightened up and I sometimes got as much as an extra hour's sleep. But until then, I never wasted another moment.

THE MOANERS' BENCH

Our flight commander, Captain Lowery, called me in to give me my evaluation. Beaming, he told me he wanted me to compete for a squadron position.

It was basic training all over again. I begged to be passed over.

I wanted a commission, not a command. When I told myself I could do anything in the Air Force, I didn't mean all at once. I wanted to become an officer, then cast around for ways to the top. I had no intention of shooting for the moon at OTS, failing, and being shown the door. In basic, they'd been desperate to rebuild after the Viet Nam drawdown: you had to impregnate the base commander's daughter or smoke a joint in his office to get shipped back home. At OTS, if you wanted to leave, you could SIE (self-initiated elimination) as quickly as they could complete the paperwork. Not only that, if you appeared not to have the right stuff, they'd ask for your SIE, then force you out themselves if you demurred. I was frantic to remain unnoticed.

Just like Technical Sergeant Harris's had, Captain Lowery's proud smile turned to disgust. Maybe it was disappointment.

"So, you want to be a 'low-key OT,' huh?" he sneered.

Hell, yes! I thought.

Among ourselves, we lavished praise on the OTs who managed to keep their heads low and graduate with the same butter bars the most "strack" OT did. I had to mount a convincing argument that I wasn't trying to evade responsibility but rather was trying to focus as seriously as possible on the basics, unworthy as I was, to be sure I'd make a fitting officer. I tried to convince him that I was barely keeping up and had to stay focused on just that, graduating.

Lowery pulled a pad to him and began to write, narrating aloud ominously: "OT Dickerson, despite her demonstrated excellence and natural leadership, refuses to assist her flight in accomplishing its mission. Preferring her own leisure time and . . ."

I drew myself to my full height, stood at my tallest "attention."

"Sir, I'd be honored to compete for a squadron position."

We exchanged salutes and I marched away. At least this time, I didn't cry in the hallway.

I had to be an officer. I had to. I was mad as hell about being forced into this competition—which, as Eddie's daughter, I saw as the world trying to keep me from becoming an officer—but there was nothing I could do but try my absolute best. Captain Lowery backed me up every step of the way. The Air Force didn't just tell me I could achieve if I wanted to, it showed me how.

Captain Lowery gave me the applicable regs so I could prepare for the boards; in the meantime, I redoubled my efforts in everything else—academics, athletics, room inspections, personal hygiene and posture, bone density. Whatever.

Flight commanders assign flight jobs based on their assessment of their OTs' aptitudes, then nominate some, like me, to compete at the squadron level. That board sends the cream of the crop on to compete at the group level. The group selects for its level, then sends the three remaining OTs on to compete for the top three wing jobs; these are announced in front of the entire wing at the graduating class's last commander's call. Each level had its own process, which I had to master to win. In the end, it all came down to meeting the board of current leaders; each picked its own successors based on flight commander recommendations, our OT records, but most of all on their personal assessment after "eyeballing" us. There were probably eight board members and perhaps fifteen of us being evaluated. The board would pose essay-type questions and we each had to answer one of our choice. The questions would range in subject from current events to the significance of different aspects of OTS's training philosophy.

The afternoon we met the board, I met my competition for the first time. All white, all male, all oozing confidence and bonhomie. Perversely, it relaxed me. There was no way little old black Debbie from north St. Louis was going to be chosen over these white boys, not by a board full of white boys just like them. Never gonna happen. All I wanted was to acquit myself honorably and show Captain Lowery that I'd given it my all.

In the anteroom where we waited, some protocol OT came out and briefed us on the procedures for reporting in to the board and for answering the questions. It was meant to fluster us (otherwise it would have been spelled out in the regs for us to study): something like, march in, about-face, salute the flag, about-face and say "Sir, OT Dickerson reports as ordered, sir," assume parade rest between questions, salute before speaking . . . on and on. They wanted to see how we responded to pressure.

Several of my competitors panicked, begging the OT to repeat the sequence and frantically pacing about, working out their choreography. Watching them, I realized it would be best to just do whatever I did confidently, without hesitation. It would matter less that I forgot to about-face than that I was sweat-drenched and tentative. My father taught me that. "If you gon be wrong," he'd say, "be wrong the right way." Once when I was small, without a hint to us that anything was amiss, my mother calmly called a cousin to come baby-sit, waited for her to arrive, then drove herself to the hospital in crippling pain from internal hemorrhaging after major surgery. This bunch of college boys was not going to see me sweat.

We marched in and took our seats. While the current OT wing commander explained procedure, I had another of those moments.

I could see everything and everyone in the room all at once, like through a fish-eye lens. I never moved, yet as I "sat at attention," I could see up and down that row of scrubbed, white, male faces. I could look across the room and see *that* row of scrubbed, white, male faces. And I could see my own glaringly brown hands on my womanly brown thighs, as ordered. My brown heels locked at a forty-five-degree angle, brown spine ramrod, brown breasts jutting as proudly as 34B's can. Dignified surroundings. Comfortable conditions. Respectful treatment. The flag symbolizing America's acknowledgment that she needed me and what I had to offer. Open-ended possibilities.

I belong here. I earned this.

I had clarity. I had confidence. Not based on besting others, just a confidence based on knowing that I could do this. I could do anything I needed to. I could handle myself with dignity and these white men could do whatever they were going to do about it—judge me fairly or not. I wasn't scared. I wasn't intimidated. I wasn't invested in their external validation. I could do this, but I didn't need this. They could select me or not. Either way, I was going to feel just fine about myself. I was going to work hard regardless of the outcome and the world could reward me or not.

Tension crackled from everyone on my side of the room but me. Uncertainty about what questions we'd be asked was beginning to take a toll on me, though. What if I waited too long and let a question I had covered go by?

Hyperaware, I remembered something from my childhood. I had to be baptized before I could become an actual member of the church I'd been attending from birth. When I was ten or so, at Emmanuel's yearly revival, my parents decided it was time we all got baptized and "join church."

Starting one Sunday night and continuing every night that week until the following Sunday, revivals were frightening, nightmarish events. The adults screamed and moaned with even greater vehemence than usual; the ministers ratcheted up their fire and brimstone to horror-movie proportions. It was weird being at church on a Tuesday night at midnight. Worse, the unbaptized had to sit up front all alone without our parents on "the moaners' bench." Everybody stared and pointed at us and we were viewed as if demons rode on our shoulders. Adults exhorted us to repent our evil ways and preached at us nonstop. What if we died unbaptized? Straight to hell, young lady!

Die? Me? What fiends I thought them.

Each night, after terrorizing us for hours, they'd set up chairs at the altar while the donation plates went around and "open up de arms a de choich." You had to get an adult to pray with you at the altar before you could sit in the chair and ask to be baptized, pretty please. That was the only way to get off the moaners' bench. It was such a nightmare, I just sat there night after night while all the other kids dragged one of their parents up to the altar and ended the torture. But I was frozen. I couldn't move. Every night at home, Mama begged me to ask for her like everybody else already had on the first night, but I couldn't open my mouth, I couldn't move my legs. I just hoped it would eventually end without me having to exercise any volition.

The last three nights, I was all alone on the moaners' bench. I had nightmares for years about it. The longer I put it off, "the deeper the sin sunk down" in me, old-timers cautioned. If we'd been eastern European peasants, they'd have made the sign of the evil eye and thrown garlic at me. Only Mama showed me compassion; the other adults thought it was the "debil" in me. The other kids thought me a moron. Finally, on the last possible night, after all the sermons had been aimed directly at me by name, I finally forced myself, sobbing with terror and humiliation, to go get Mama to pray for me.

Before the board chair got three words of the first question out of his mouth, I was on my feet.

"Sir! OT Dickerson would like to answer the question, sir." I didn't know and didn't care if those were the right words.

To my surprise, my competitors were demoralized. Their faces turned red, their eyes grew wide, their lips pursed. Conversely, every member of the board was looking at me like I'd just thrown myself on a grenade.

"Perhaps I should actually give you the question, Miss Dickerson," the OT squadron commander joked, and the board chuckled approvingly.

My competitors were squirming. Adding insult to injury, I got a softball question—something like the significance of athletics and how

I thought that helped build good officers. It was a total freebie. Finally, all those Dead White Men and my fancy vocabulary paid off. I was eloquent and, I realized, unafraid of public speaking.

Two minutes before, I might have been on a higher plane of enlightenment and above such petty competition, but watching their faces fall—I was loving it! It was true, still, that I didn't need a fancy title to know who I was. But damn, it was good to win! It was another victory, like beating Sister Flight's dorm chief downstairs every morning, and victory is intoxicating. Habit-forming.

In the anteroom, waiting to be called back in for the results, I was roundly congratulated. My competitors were gracious and generous. They assured me that I would go on to the highest levels and none of them chalked it up to affirmative action. Several asked me to coach them on public speaking and deportment. I was ashamed of my racist assumptions.

Along with several others, I was sent forward for the group competition. Lowery and my flight mates were ecstatic. My fame preceded me at the group competition. Even in the anteroom before we went in, my competitors were both deferential and proud of me. Talent and leadership are acknowledged in the military and these men gave me my due.

I answered the first question there and at the wing level; no one made a move to claim a question until after I'd spoken. Then, in what I took to be the highest compliment, they lunged to be the next speaker. That's leadership, I realized: a good example. I resolved to set a good example on purpose, though, instead of inadvertently.

Three of us were finally selected to compete for the highest positions: OT wing commander, deputy wing commander, and group commander. It was like the Miss America Pageant; it was just a question of who was queen and who the runner-ups.

I was far from done with my fraud syndrome and self-limitations, but it was clear I had to rethink some things. I was not at all convinced I could handle one of the top three positions, they were so "highly visible." Among our duties would be mingling with top officer brass at ceremonial functions, running the nine hundred OTs, and, last but hardly least, staying on top of our own personal OTS requirements—OT colonel or not, I wouldn't be exempted from anything any other

OT had to do, but I would have extra duties they did not have. What if my grades fell? What if I forgot something little like a zipper and got my 341 pulled (the ultimate training horror) because more was expected of me? How would I get it all done? Though I was what OTS called a "PFT animal," I still had yet to accomplish the twelve push-ups required for female OTs. It was embarrassing—I'd have no legitimacy with the OTs. In the midst of my angst, once again, the Air Force showed its brilliance.

Before the wing board, we three were required to attend a mixer with the outgoing wing and group staff. I was irritated at the extra duty: I still had shoes to shine and regs to memorize. Had it not been obligatory, I'd not have gone.

I showed up for the mixer sure that the outgoing OT wing commander and staff would be luminous like stars or, I don't know, spout Sun Tzu, or have the Stars and Stripes tattooed on their chests or something. But they were just guys. Worse, they were just OTs.

They had great grades, great athletics, and oozed drive, but they still spent the mixer griping about unfair room inspections, sleep deprivation, and the flight commander who just wouldn't lighten up. Several were openly studying from the flash cards OTs cart everywhere.

Those guys had to study and shine shoes and march around in the hot sun just like me. They had no magic: all the smarts in the world won't let you pass an Air Force history test you haven't studied for. They won't iron your uniforms just right and they won't do your push-ups—only I could do those things. If I studied and ironed and exercised, I could do all the same things they did. They were just people—talented people—but talent alone can never be enough.

Listening to all the griping, I could see that it really was in my own hands. Even the highest-ranking OTs bitched and complained and whined on the phone with mom, then they got off their butts and did the work. That's the only magic there is.

I was selected OT wing commander.

BOTTOM RAIL ON TOP

That same weekend, I was "bedposted."

My upper-flight OTs "nuked" my room. When I came back from learning that I was OT wing commander, the number one OT among the nine-hundred-plus there, I found my room had undergone a surprise inspection. The report was replete with demerits, more than I'd gotten in any previous three-week period, more than the worst sad-sack OT got.

Funnily enough, my roommate's side of the room remained perfect while my side had been sabotaged—drawers hung open, nothing was flush with the edge of anything else, and there was actual trash under my bed.

I got the message: you can't make it alone.

Harsh though it may have been, it gave me time to think while my buddies, my whole class, fled to our first authorized off-base weekend and I, the new "wing queen," was on lockdown in my room.

Being OT wing commander gave me a sense of responsibility that filled my every waking moment. It was such an honor, such a position of trust, such an expression of the Air Force's commitment to fostering and endorsing talent wherever it might be found, that I knew I could do nothing to bring dishonor on myself, my flight, my flight commander, my squadron, my group, my wing, my fellow OTs. It was never off my mind.

Not that I found the responsibility oppressive. On the contrary, once it was settled and the Air Force's decision was made, my fears were calmed. I was the daughter of Johnnie Florence and Eddie Mack: I had no choice but to see this through with dignity or SIE. To that end, I determined two things—one negative, one affirmative.

First, I decided that I would not respond to any agenda other than the Air Force's. Initially, I had spent a lot of time paranoically mind reading: who was out to see me fail because I was black? because I was female? Should I avoid the other blacks or seek them out? avoid the other women or seek them out? Would they expect favoritism, score-settling against the whites and the men? Speaking of that, didn't whites and men deserve a little "in your face" attitude anyway? (I couldn't help thinking of the slave who escaped to fight for the Union and saw his former owner being led away in chains by Yankee soldiers. "Bottom rail on top now, Massa!" he'd crowed.) Shouldn't I try to prove to everyone that a black female could do as well as a white male? But how to do that? Maybe I should focus on assuaging the fears of the white males, let them know that I was Air Force through and through.

There was no way out of thoughts like that. Whatever else could be said about such a focus, it was surely true that it gave my volition, the volition which had propelled me to high office without any assistance from those to whom I mentally kowtowed, to others. This self-limiting conundrum led to my second, affirmative guiding principle as OT wing commander.

I decided to focus on living up to my position rather than on all the ways I might fail. If I failed, too many important things failed with me and I would not let that happen. (There had been a few black or female OT wing commanders before me, but not very many. I didn't ask for the particulars and no one offered the information. Race never came up in the selection process or afterward, as far as I know.)

My position gave me a sort of low-intensity bravery that is hard now to describe. When you're acting only in your own behalf, it's reasonable to play the odds and not exert yourself beyond your comfort zone if there's little to be gained. But I felt that I had to go for broke in every situation; the other OTs didn't need me showing them how to be a low-key OT—that came naturally. At the same time, I was also determined not to be a little tin-soldier GI Joe having napalm for breakfast and sleeping with my combat boots on. As with that confusing procedure for meeting the board, I believed that the point was for me to try my damnedest but in the most openhearted way possible. I didn't want to be merely right, my actions merely sufficient. I wanted to push my limits as sincerely as possible. That was as much as a leader could ask of any subordinate, so that's what I determined to give. My uncomplicated best, no more, no less, no excuses.

Over the course of that weekend, I inventoried both my head and my room. The wing staff was housed in "Club Med," a special suite of rooms in the headquarters building. I'd have to move there, away from my flight but to a single room on Monday, so I used my bedposting as an opportunity.

I emptied my room of everything I could do without. The regs say what you can and can't have. In typical OT fashion, I'd hoarded everything allowed by regulation—blow-dryer, curling iron, limited amount of makeup, etc.—and focused on stowing it in accordance with the room inspection regs. Now, I decided to turn the reg on its head and live with as little as possible. If it wasn't going to help me be a better officer, it was out of there. My drawers went from jam-packed to nearly bare.

To my surprise, I didn't miss any of the things I threw out. Rather, it was freeing; out of sight truly is out of mind. I'd see female OTs wearing makeup or fancy hairdos and think, Why? With the limited amount of time, with the tiny margin of error we have . . . why? Holding on to those things was holding on to civilian life and that was the last thing I wanted. There would be time for the extras later. After I was an officer.

Physical fitness was the only area I had any doubts in. Unlike basic or the active-duty Air Force, OTS was a very athletic place. Everybody had to meet the minimum requirements, like everywhere in the Air Force, but at OTS, going above and beyond the PFT requirements got you "merits" (which you could subtract from your demerits) and set you apart. Being considered a "PFT animal" was just one more way to push yourself; also, to be DG, you had to excel in every category. The OT wing commander ought to be a PFT animal; it was as simple as that.

At OTS, there were constant PT requirements, which led up to seven PFTs, a mini Olympics. You had to pass every event in at least one of the PFTs to graduate. I came to OTS in incredible shape from three years of serious running, aerobics, and weight training. I aced each component of the PT program except, to my chagrin, the twelve push-ups required for women.

Strong as I was, I just couldn't do men's push-ups. So, like everyone else who couldn't pass the PFT, I was placed on remedial PT. (There's no stigma associated with remedial programs in the Air Force, only with not trying.) I had to report for upper-body weight lifting. It was a joke at the gym. I could lift as much as that program called for one-handed and whistling a happy tune. It was a question of mind over matter. In my mind, men's push-ups were too hard, therefore I couldn't do them.

In every spare moment, I did push-ups. In my room upon waking, between classes, before bed. Against walls, between chairs, off the side of my bunk, in our classroom during breaks. Some days I could do thirty push-ups. Some days, two. And I finally passed the sixth PFT. My flight danced for joy right there in the dirt.

The very next day, I was unable to do even five push-ups.

Mind over matter.

IN THE TRENCHES

Far and away, the best thing about OTS was my flight mates and the camaraderie born of our joint travails.

We had no choice but to live, work, and play together, no choice but to work out our differences, no choice but to support each other; if you didn't, you'd be left hanging when you needed backup. But it was more than just the survival instinct. It was becoming a vital part of something much bigger than yourself. You'd do things for your flight that you'd never do for yourself because there was no way to opt out without dragging the entire flight down with you. The Air Force made me part of something larger than myself, that had a glorious history, and that ensnared me in bonds of familiarity and joint effort.

Like athletics. Our entire program was ingeniously geared to building up the confidence of those of us, male and female, who had avoided or underachieved at athletics. Also, it was another means the Air Force used to inculcate leadership and team-building. Knowing that traditional sports would just have the usual jocks come out on top, the Air Force made up games. Flickerball was a combination of basketball and football. One pitch was a mutant form of baseball. The rules were bizarre and intricate (and tested), the outcome of the games tabulated and ranked, but ultimately beside the point. Playing was obligatory. Not only that, each position rotated so everyone had to play every role from coach to umpire, to timekeeper to quarterback. No riding the bench, no waterboys or equipment managers, no letting the jocks always carry the ball.

I'd always chosen solitary sports and dreaded the team sports that were unavoidable at OTS. Left to my own devices, I'd have coasted (I had few enough demerits to absorb a few here), but then I would have let my flight down—it was always obvious when someone was coasting. I had to at least try to help score points because that was our mission.

In the end, I enjoyed the sports and got as gung-ho as the next OT about winning. If I fell down, or missed a ball, or caused the team demerits for forgetting one of those crazy flickerball rules, I gave not a thought to my dignity, just to what it would do to our standing in the game. When it's about the group and not about you, you rarely stop to think about you. And in so doing, you find that you can do more than you ever thought possible.

When I had to tackle the confidence course for the second time at OTS, I went all out knowing that the black female prior-service OT wing commander's progress would be of great interest. I attacked the obstacles like a maniac. As I bore down on the water obstacle, I could see the rope we were supposed to swing across on hanging still in the middle of the brackish pond. I couldn't possibly reach it.

I can't swim. I am terrified of water.

So terrified that, in basic, I had seen that rope swinging toward me for exactly what it was—the blessed lifesaver that would keep me from drowning. I'd timed it perfectly and swung to safety in one hysterically balletic movement. But now, I was the designated role model—and that cursed rope wasn't swinging toward me. It was miles from my grasping fingers.

The flight commander manning the obstacle wasn't looking my way and there was no time to await instructions. The rest of OTS was running behind me—everybody had to swing on that rope and I couldn't hold things up. There was no help for it. I gritted my teeth, pumped my legs as hard as I could, and dove for the rope that was so very, very far away.

Thank God I didn't end up going headfirst into that disgusting water—I went feet first. The photo I was presented with shows me going for my dip with outstretched arms and an odd smile on my face. My head is held high and my tippy-toes are just touching the water.

When I surfaced, the throng lining the pond was hooting with laughter.

"OT," the flight commander gasped between guffaws, "I'da swung the rope to you. Everybody else waited—but not you!" He waved the grappling hook he used to retrieve the rope; he'd dropped it as I approached and was looking for it when I made my great leap forward.

I laughed, too. My worst physical fear—water—and I'd faced it. My worst emotional fear—public humiliation—and the phrase had lost its force. My mother had kept having babies even though the doctors said it would kill her. My father had jumped off that troop ship. Sodden and shaking but still moving forward, I felt their proud presence as I made my giddy way to the next obstacle amid the back slaps and shoulder squeezes of my fellow OTs. I lived every day at OTS buoyed, challenged, and comforted by the knowledge that I was doing my family proud, that I was making their sacrifices count for something.

But I had more fears to face. Project X is an open-air facility of eight or ten different exercises, each blocked off from the other's view by high walls. We were placed in teams of three to ten, depending on the exercise, and had to figure a way out of some scripted scenario against a stopwatch. We were handed a card which explained that we were the crew of a bomber downed behind enemy lines, for instance, and had to make our way back to friendly territory. Or the mission might be an escape from a POW camp across a raging "river" marked on the ground. One of us might be designated wounded and have to be gently carried, even if it was an all-girl team but for the "injured" six-foot-two, 220-pound former linebacker on a stretcher. There were walls, ledges, minefields, ropes to swing on, "burning building" façades to jump from—MacGyver-like ingenuity was required to figure out what the pair of gloves or the iron bar or those six short lengths of rope we were given were for. But it wasn't our ingenuity that was being tested, it was our ability to work as a team under pressure. As with the sports, everyone was required to play every role, from squad leader to comatose deadweight. There was a "school solution" to every scenario and it was our job to find that solution. The flight got a merit for each scenario we mastered.

I ended up atop a goalpost-like structure, all my team members on the other side waiting for me to swing across the divide on a rope before the "enemy patrol" was due by.

I am afraid of heights. I get dizzy on a ladder. I'm more afraid of water, but not much more.

But if I didn't swing on that rope, thrown across an even higher third goalpost and anchored only by two flight mates' body weight, we wouldn't get the merits or a leg up in the Honor Flight competition. We'd fail. Because of me. I would have eaten the demerits in a minute, but my flight . . .

I made every person on that other goalpost, the one that was at least one hundred feet away and twenty feet in the air, say: "Debra, I will catch you." Not "Miss Dickerson" or "OT." Debra. As the stopwatch ticked off the last of the few seconds we'd been alloted, I closed my eyes and let go.

My feet never touched that goalpost. Every member of my team had some part of my body and I couldn't have cared less whose hands were where.

Daddy wouldn't have asked for their assurance—he'd rather have gone splat on the pavement—but I had no such qualms. I'm not a sharecropper, just the daughter of sharecroppers. I know how to meld the old and the new. Still, I know he'd have been proud, because I got the job done, however I had to do it.

Once I became OT wing commander, I had been afraid that my flight mates might freeze me out, but to my amazement, quite the contrary happened.

Twice during OTS, the second time at about the nine-week point, we had to write letters evaluating every other member of the flight on their strengths and weaknesses. OTS called them "peer evaluations"; "peer smears," of course, to us. They were supposed to be constructive and anonymous. But I don't believe in anonymous statements so I signed all of mine, which made the exercise excruciatingly difficult and time-consuming. Criticism, after which you will have to live and work with the person you've criticized, is hard work.

I was very worried about my peer smears. I'd gone out of my way not to overshadow my mostly young, mostly non-prior-service flight mates. The last thing I wanted to do was be some know-it-all GI Joe jerk bossing everybody around and boring one and all with my war stories. I gave advice and help when unavoidable but kept even that to a minimum. Yet they were so young and untrained, there'd been many occasions when flight progress was at stake and I saw no choice but to be somewhat dictatorial. In fact, Captain Lowery had counseled me about it early on, telling me it was the "retreads"' duty to lead. But how were the "initials" to learn, as I had in basic?

Once I became OT wing commander, I was even more hesitant to throw my weight around. I stepped in when it seemed needed but otherwise stayed mum. I bit my tongue often. But with peer smears winging their way toward me, I girded myself to be told off for my bossiness. I was sure that, from the safety of anonymity, I'd finally get the comeuppance I certainly deserved from their point of view, even though I'd tried to walk a restrained line.

I was right. They told me off. I got twenty letters chiding me for having withheld so much of my knowledge, leadership, and experience. It was frustrating, they wrote, to have me stay so much on the sidelines when I could have cleared up so much and told them more about what to expect in the Air Force. I'd thought I'd been overbearing; they thought I'd been maddeningly unassertive.

I didn't ask my other prior-service flight mates if they got the same critique, but given that we were a low-key bunch that didn't throw our weight around, they probably did. We despised the other prior-service types who swaggered around inflating their records and trying to both impress and micromanage the initials. We gauged our own behavior in opposition to those "beggar, lifer, puke" losers, warriors at OTS but chairborne clock watchers, no doubt, back in their units.

My peer smears weren't in the least mean but they *were* disappointed. In them, I was praised and congratulated and great things were prophesied for my future, but they made it clear that I had failed—no, *cheated*—my flight mates by refusing to be more of a leader.

I crammed as many war stories as I could into our final three weeks and taught them every trick I knew about Air Force survival. Especially the one I learned at OTS: Always go first.

On graduation day, July 3, 1985, Captain Lowery escorted my family to watch from the stands as I led the wing in the graduation parade. I had informed them of my position, but the words held little meaning and I didn't try to explain. When they saw me lead the parade, though, with all eyes on me and nine hundred people awaiting my commands, they got it.

"Long way from Miss'ippi," Mama murmured, that thousand-miles-away look on her face.

I suppose she was fantasizing about what it would be like to have my opportunities. To travel the world, and preside at meetings where she could overrule men and white people. To speak with loud confidence and make demands of important people. But I couldn't give her any of those things. All I could do was make a comfortable home for her. I browbeat her into quitting the vending machine factory and moved her to the burbs with me as soon as I got settled.

That day, though, she tried to melt into the crowd, but I held on to her and kept her by my side while I shook hands and greeted dignitaries. The general called her ma'am and complimented her on my accomplishments. My blend-in-with-the-wallpaper mama didn't blush or stammer. She looked him in the eye and said, "What else would she do but what needed doing?"

CHAPTER SIX

FULL CIRCLE

I wasn't worth a damn until I was thirty.

It wasn't until then that I got some perspective on how all the contradictory parts of my makeup could combine in a way that would allow me to capitalize on the opportunities for which my forebears sacrificed. Making peace with my family, my community, and myself gave me both a sense of personal freedom and a heightened sense of community responsibility. I didn't lose my baggage. I couldn't. All I could do was make room for it.

No one's as zealous as a convert, and as I became increasingly consumed with the plight of the working class and my narrow escape from it, my magazine and newspaper subscription list expanded. I was in a constant state of political agitation. Even though I was moving farther and farther away from the poor with every accomplishment, my heart wouldn't stay where my head was. At last, I was suburban and professional, but everyone I loved was a slave to the business cycle and to events on the front page of the morning newspaper. My late-blooming political awakening had forged a surreal connection between the politico-historical frameworks in my head and the news of the day. Philosophy and political theories were not buried in my junior-high unconscious background since I hadn't been exposed to them then; they were foreground. I couldn't experience anything in a vacuum. Nothing "just happened" for me.

My head spun as I unraveled current events to trace them back to their origins in federal housing policy, migration patterns, or Jim Crow restriction, once de jure, now de facto. I'd talk with a family member as

I packed for a six-week intelligence-gathering trip around the Pacific (at a generous per diem) or gathered materials for the congressional budgeting exhibit I was preparing in the name of the United States Air Force and feel lost in a political limbo. I had the feeling we were all characters acting out roles in history books that hadn't been written yet—the peon laborer, the first-generation professional, the pink-collar typist—hostage to whatever deals got struck in Washington. Health benefits, no health benefits. Workmen's comp, no workmen's comp. Union? No, Right to Work. The very programs through which the taxpayers subsidized my undergraduate and graduate degrees were facing extinction as Congress looked for ways to cut the budget. Simply talking with my relatives became profoundly political and fraught with revelation.

Bobby, humiliated and drained on the phone after a waitering day spent in a cheap polyester uniform taking abuse from both managers and customers. Certainly, he should have worked harder in high school, stayed out of trouble, equipped himself for a better job. Now he has the rest of his life to pay for decisions he made at fourteen while living in a black boy's hell. He wasn't a child of the middle or upper class; he had no margin of error.

My youngest sister crying on the pay phone outside her cashier job at a you-buy-it-you-bag-it, generic-brand-only discount supermarket where you shopped directly from open packing crates. Her *former* cashier job. She'd been forced to watch while the manager she'd stood up to publicly searched her locker and purse. He even unwrapped her tampons. That he found no stolen goods made no difference. She was fired on the spot and threatened with arrest. All this for minimum wage.

The bittersweetness of watching my mother blossom when, for the first time since she was fifteen in 1942, she could stop working. Months to talk her into moving in with me. More months to pressure her into believing that she could trust me—trust the fates, trust that she had value other than as a workhorse—and quit the factory job she immediately found in San Antonio. I didn't remind her of my frequent promises, twenty years before, that we'd be bougie someday. She remembers. At 4 A.M., the sound of her whirring sewing machine and her tuneless, happy hum would lull me back to sleep. Free from an overseer and endless debt for the first time in forty years, she couldn't produce enough with her own hands and on her own timeline. She became a master seamstress and ceramist of exquisite skill. There isn't a home in our far-flung family without examples of her work. All that talent buried for all those years and she's so far from alone. Black clerks snarling and sullen from the safety of their pointless but secure DMV jobs. Surly black security guards fuming as they sign you in and out of buildings. Grown men making a teenager's wages washing dishes. How stifled the working masses are. How, pardon my Marx, alienated from the product of their own labor.

Home on leave, I went with a friend to sign the papers on her new apartment. The white owner made us stand on his porch in the rain while he conducted our meeting from the doorway of his hip, high-rent-district home. He lectured her on paying her rent on time like she was a kindergartner threatening not to nap. I asked about the faulty door locks. "Safety is a state of mind," he said airily. I indicated the sturdy locks on his door and asked what state *he* lived in. He looked bored. I asked about the cockroaches so numerous they fell from the ceiling, the peeling plaster, the water damage. He looked annoyed. I asked to use the bathroom. No. I asked for a drink of water. He held the lease an inch from my friend's face. Asked her if she had a problem, if she wanted the apartment or not, made no difference to him. She squeezed my arm. I shut up.

My homies couldn't afford to get mad. They couldn't even afford to dream. I could. I did.

It wasn't enough that *I'd* escaped. In 1983, I hated to come home because their "choices" so infuriated me. By 1986 I hated to come because I was so infuriated *for* them. Was a life of simple dignity, whatever your aspirations or status, too much to ask?

The complacent heartlessness of my new peers, both in the workplace and in public opinion polls, chilled me. The honest ones took a myopic, "not my problem, it's every man for himself" attitude. The rest seemed to think they were well off because of their innate superiority and their clear-eyed acceptance of personal responsibility. Yet the reality is that the ghetto would explode if the majority of its denizens didn't exercise ramrod control every day of their lives. I felt more humble, more fortunate with each passing day; too many of my fellow members of the middle and professional class seemed to feel more entitled. Politically overstimulated though I surely was (all read up and nowhere to go), I didn't want to give up any of my perks, I wanted *more* people to have access to them. A willingness to work hard, as my mother's life proved, was no guarantee of a decent living, and it maddened me that this was how discussions about economic justice were framed, not in terms of fundamental fairness but around the reality-defying notion that poor people are poor by choice and not mostly by circumstance, that historic oppression and political gamesmanship don't largely determine who gets what.

Without having consciously chosen to, I felt ever more connected to those I'd left behind. I'd made it over the Berlin Wall, I'd ridden an inner tube to Miami; I felt more like an exile than a native, grateful and guilty for having escaped, cosmically deputized to be a living reminder of those still captive. Listening to the poor being insulted and dismissed was listening to my mama, my siblings, my childhood friends, being insulted and dismissed—how could I just go to the mall, just wash my new car? But then exactly what was I doing for them besides haranguing hapless office mates and making things worse by meddling in their affairs?

I was devouring journals and nonfiction to understand the pass America had come to and toying with a vague, titillating notion of entering law and politics. The corporations had their congressional mouthpieces, the black bourgeoisie had theirs. Why didn't poor blacks?

I added the whole raft of political talk shows (*Meet the Press, Face the Nation, The McLaughlin Group,* etc.) to my source list. So as to avoid commercials and superfluous TV, I taped all the shows and smoked watching them in the wee insomniac hours. God how they galled me with their glib dismissals and crocodile tears over the little people's travails. No wonder I couldn't sleep.

As always, negative examples opened up whole new vistas of possibility for me. Through the papers, I'd follow the black political class openly selling out the black masses for greater access to power, or, worse, to assuage their own self-hatred. I'd gnash my teeth while white suburban representatives acted as marionettes for defense contractors and separatist, exclusionary white residents. Dairy farmers and international conglomerates on the public dole. Ethanol subsidies, money *not* to farm. Yet a poor kid can work hard, think she's excelling, and graduate valedictorian of a ghetto high school without ever having performed a science experiment or written a footnoted paper. At the college she dreamed of while others sold crack, she finds out she's laughably unprepared. It physically hurt to watch our elected representatives subvert the common good for the benefit of a few, already privileged reactionaries.

How hard could it be, how much brains could it really take to do that? I'd fume and think. How hard could it be, how much brains could it really take to beat them, at the polls and in the halls of Congress? Just as with college and becoming an officer, or going for a graduate degree, the better I did in life, the closer my contact with elites, the more doable their accomplishments seemed.

Who was fighting for the black poor? The black political class claimed to, then, once elected or appointed to high office, embraced affirmative action at Ivy League graduate schools as the best way to help blacks stuck in the neighborhoods. Fighting for busing instead of fixing neighborhood schools, or even starting schools of our own instead of constantly begging whites to associate with us. Fighting the eviction of troublemakers and criminals from public housing, defending murderers, stifling internal critiques. Policies that make a lot of sense when you're drafting them in your office at Yale or the Longworth Building, but not when you're listening to footsteps behind you as you scurry from your tenement apartment to the bus stop. Not when you hear from another elderly relative newly burglarized by a knucklehead much more likely to be represented for free by a black lawyer than she was. They couldn't even keep patio furniture, landscaping, or a kiddie pool in their yards without some thug boldly making off with it, but black leaders couldn't figure out how to fight *that* everyday battle simultaneously with the more nebulous one against white racism.

Just as I'd needed the Air Force to fill my selfish need for a noble, meaningful mission in life and not just a job, I began thinking that working for the betterment of the working class would make me happy. The conspiracy against it was obvious, both because of my state of hyperpoliticization and because I was such a recent escapee. I hate bullies and the middle and upper classes steal the working class's lunch money every goddamn day. It made me frantic. I scratched my TV screen flinging shoes at Reagan during his State of the Union address. Reading George Will and Joe Klein in *Newsweek* made me fume and, ultimately, cancel my subscription. The history books I devoured made me cry.

Though I knew I was obsessed with race and economics, I had only the vaguest idea that it might, or should, lead me somewhere. How does one even "enter law and politics" anyway? Thinking I could do something about the plight of the black poor was like thinking I could cure cancer—noble but pretty egotistical. The notion embarrassed me in its grandiosity and messianism.

Also, community-minded though I was becoming, I was still quite concerned with the direction of my own life. My future was bright, but far from solidified. The "Who am I? Why am I here?" questions still plagued me, though now in a positive, measuring way. I actually had hope, born of confidence and achievement, for my future. I'd always had desperation. Now I had calm cunning. All I needed was direction.

I still believed then that the Air Force was the best place for me—constant challenges, upward mobility, travel, good benefits, lots of responsibility, little institutional racism. Nothing in civilian society could rival it. I felt strong and capable, and, most important, humble. But I was still frustrated by my distance from the everyday world of black folk. Socializing has never come naturally to me, and without my race consultant, I was at a loss as to how to proceed. San Antonio was a terrible place to decide to exercise my Négritude.

A tiny percentage of the population, and a very quiescent one at that, blacks were actually difficult to find there. I refused to give up my hard-won spot in the middle class; that meant refusing to frequent ghetto bars. I already had a ghetto home back in St. Louis, I didn't need another. I wasn't going to seek out the hood just to prove something. I wanted what I'd earned—full access to all of American life and the cushy environs I could afford on my military salary and generous benefits.

Also, it was a very interesting dynamic to be black in a city where Hispanics were a numerical majority, whites the power majority, and blacks so insignificant as to escape notice. The Hispanics were the niggers in San Antonio; white racism was directed at them. They'd be blamed for crime or depravity anywhere in the city. Occasionally, some white Air Force person expected me to help him insult them.

An office mate's wife complained about the theft of two wrought-iron porch chairs saying, "There were a couple of green-carders working down the block."

A white master sergeant gave me an inquisitive sideways glance before adding, "The problem is jail don't mean nothing to those people. They have family reunions in there." They waited for my reaction.

This was a victory of sorts. My uniform, comportment, and officer's rank had promoted me to a "daylight white": almost, but not quite, one of them and therefore eligible to participate in the oppression of the lesser orders.

"I've heard tell that white folks, on rare occasion, have been known to break the law. Some of those 'green-carders' might well have been in America for hundreds of years. When did your ancestors get here?"

I refused to assimilate by joining in racist initiation rites. It's a short trip from "beaner" to "nigger."

I joined the Tuskegee Airmen, a black officers' community service and social group. It was named after the black flying outfit formed against much white opposition during World War II. They never lost a bomber they escorted.

Quickly, it became apparent that it was more about a pecking order and the in crowd than anything else—my high school SOBI all over again (and also a preview of HLS's Black Law Students' Association). I went to a Tuskegee Airmen picnic early on. The men clumped importantly together while the women eyed me. No one spoke to me but the president. At the (admittedly only two) meetings I attended, I was horrified to hear agenda items tabled yet again that had been in limbo for months. Sign-up sheets for the various projects sailed round and round endlessly with few signing up to do the work. They never failed to list their membership on their résumés, though.

The problem is careerism. Officers are always looking for "OER fodder." To be competitive, your Officer Effectiveness Report needed to show lots of additional duties, like military-related community service organizations. No one's heart was in these things.

Next, I tried simply networking at my base, Kelly, an HQ command with a few blacks. I tracked down every one I heard about and stopped every one I saw in the hall under the rank of lieutenant colonel (I couldn't socialize with senior officers or enlisted). I'd expected we'd all be overjoyed to connect and create a haven away from our overwhelmingly white, albeit benevolent, world. I envisioned a lively circuit of weekend barbecues, card games, and to-the-beat dancing. I pictured involvement in the black community with substantive community service projects we really cared about and events we actually enjoyed. I was realizing how important it was just to be with other blacks and to not lose touch with, or become contemptuous of, the grass roots. I also looked forward to the careerist multiplier effect of all the inside info we could share with each other from our disparate perches in the intelligence community. Instead, I was surprised by how unfriendly they were. In fact, there was hostility.

The military is an incredibly competitive place; the officer corps even more so. Impressions count for a lot in the service; the mere suggestion of seeing ourselves as black first, Air Force second, terrified them. Blacks who were succeeding at the system, I was learning, often did so by distancing themselves from other blacks. I actually saw fidgeting black majors look over their shoulder to see who was seeing them talk to me; they were terrified that they would be seen as somehow distancing themselves from the Air Force. Turnabout really is fair play—that's exactly how I'd seen it when the Head Negro tried to involve me with other blacks at DLI. That was exactly how I'd felt to be one of only two or three at Skivvy Nine—white people would know I was different, better than those other blacks. I was a good black. I was like them—worthy of respect. I'm not suggesting that they were self-hating, just that their concern with their careers made them willing to separate themselves from other blacks so they could stand out. It was hard to get visibility in such a competitive environment; this was one cynical way to do so.

Invariably, if a clump of three or more of us formed in a public place at Kelly, nervous jokes like "We better break this up cause we're scaring the white folks," or "No more than four in one spot, now. You know the rules," were never slow to surface and provide cover for drifting off. Another part of the problem was the competition for black male officers, in critically short supply and therefore by definition desirable regardless of looks, temperament, or career. The men knew they were a hot commodity and often interpreted my overtures as amorous, the women as nefarious plots to get close to their men. Most of the black officers there were on "joint spouse" assignments which allow husbands and wives to be assigned to the same unit or at least the same base or city. Most of the couples at Kelly were joint spouse; otherwise, you're assigned as an individual. There is a great deal of infidelity in the military—nobody trusted me and I can't say I blame them. I wouldn't have trusted my military spouse far from my sight either—temptation is built-in and unavoidable in uniform.

By far, though, beyond romantic concerns, nobody wanted to abet the competition; there was value in being the only one in a unit. Blacks bemoan the "one nigger" syndrome in American life wherein one black per institution or career is allowed to achieve greatness and that's supposed to be enough for the rest of us. In the military, perversely, blacks often tried to enforce the "one nigger" rule. Too often, a black who was doing well wanted to be the only one in his office, command, or even career field. (I saw this with women, to a lesser degree, as well.) If they couldn't be, they could at least freeze you out and try not to be in the same place at the same time with you. I was competition. Blacks continually lament the coldness and cronyism that typifies whites' way of doing things, but we're no different when we get the reins in our own hands.

I was appalled by how careerist they were; I never believed that a checkmark in someone else's column was a minus in mine. There's room for everyone to succeed and talent will out. Besides, all-white groups weren't seen as suspicious—why should all-black ones be? They wouldn't, I believed, if we'd just stand our ground, but we never did. Frequently, I heard insignificant events analyzed through the prism of cutthroat competition. For instance, I'd be chatting with some black officer about a party or a community event and they'd dismiss it saying, "I don't see how that's going to help me get promoted." I was all about getting promoted too, but not to that degree. Nobody can argue that blacks don't make the most of the military, and I was proud of us—but there *were* other things in life.

I gave up on plugging into a community of black officers—if there is such a thing, I probably fenced myself off from it with my head-on attempts to gain entry. Even so, ever the daughter of Eddie and Johnnie, I tried one more brave but naive thing before giving up on prying my way into a black community.

I went alone to bars. The very few women I knew were all Air Force, all married, not interested in nightlife. I had no choice but to go alone or stay home with Mama.

I girded myself with feminist reasoning to stifle Daddy's voice telling me I was a harlot, and spent a few nights trying to find some black middle-class nightlife. Looking back on it, I can't figure out how I summoned the fortitude to go out alone more than once; perhaps the difficulties made me stubborn. But I wouldn't do it again, not in the prim heartland. If a woman insists on acting like a man (i.e., moving about at night without a male escort) she is a presumptive whore and deserving of the male violence she is all too likely to receive.

I'd park under lights and very close to the entrance, even if I had to drive around till someone left. Even so, men, who for some reason like to congregate around their cars in parking lots, yelled terrible names, threw things, or taunted me with rape threats ("You know you want it") as I made my way unescorted. Their comments made it clear that my being out alone at night where the fertile congregate meant I wanted sex. I may have been out of GI Korea and that prostitute-rich environment, yet as long as I was without a man or a group of women, I was undeserving of respect.

I refused to scurry. I refused to look away. I refused to respond in kind. I did, however, put a baseball bat in my trunk and a switchblade in my purse. I was tired of taking abuse, tired of being afraid, and tired of waiting passively for my next victimization.

In Korea once, a white GI followed me as I left the Stereo alone at 2 A.M. With no help in sight, I angled my path gradually, and when he'd followed me to the middle of the deserted street, I whirled to face him. Taken aback, he stammered something about wanting to tell me I had a great ass. I just stared at him, waiting to see what he'd decide to do. He scurried off.

In Maryland, there was a spate of rapes at the nearby mall area I frequented for its movies. I cowered at home for a few weekends, as the local authorities and Bobby recommended. Then, furious at my purdah, I resumed my outings while openly brandishing a tire iron and making evil eye contact with every passing male. I knew I looked insane. I was *hoping* I looked insane because I was ready to hurt the next person who tried to stop me from going about my business simply because I have a vagina.

San Antonio was no different. During his first visit, Bobby, of course, found the happening black dance club immediately. While I waited at the bar for him to finish a seduction attempt, a man sidled up and asked to buy me a drink. I declined, knowing that Bobby would return and start trouble. To atone for not having protected us as teenagers, he now tries to kill any man who talks to his sisters. In a club environment, where men are particularly stupid, I knew a confrontation would likely get ugly. For the entire time Bobby was gone, that man stood six inches away calling me vile names and threatening me since "I thought I was too good." Knowing that Bobby would kill any man he saw me struggling or arguing with, I never said a word. I never broke eye contact, but I never said a word. Bobby came back and the man vanished into the crowd like a wisp of smoke.

I was tired of taking abuse, tired of being afraid, and tired of waiting passively for my next victimization.

I didn't know how to use the switchblade I carried, but I did know that cowards would crumble if I stood tall. (Also, I knew that many whites think all blacks are street savvy and familiar with weapons—they'd assume I could handle such a ghetto tool and back down.) If they didn't, what could I do but go down fighting. Paw Paw used to tell us how to fight our way out of a crowd: "Just grab one of em. Any one. Beat that one plumb to death no matter how many licks the others give you. The one you're whipping will make the others back off." That was my plan—to leave scars and go down with my eyes open. The very thought of cowering at home like I had no right to move about my own country made me sizzle. I was afraid, I'm *still* afraid, of men and their violence, but I'm just not going to let it keep me home.

Determined to avail myself of the mainstream I had battled so hard to enter, I made the rounds of San Antonio's nightclubs and discos. What pitiful excursions those were. On my solo nighttime excursions, rarely did I encounter other blacks; when I did I was barely tolerated. I sometimes found a table of three or four black women trying to do what I was doing—find young black men to connect with. The problem was that I was equally interested in connecting with young black women. I'd ask to join them and they never refused, but they were never friendly. I couldn't understand why they didn't welcome me—at least we could make our own fun even if we couldn't connect with black men. But instead, I'd come back to the table from the ladies' room to find them huddled, arguing about how best to ditch me. If a black man asked me to dance, I could hear their indrawn breaths and tooth-sucking as I moved toward the dance floor. Ditto, but for different reasons, if it was a white man.

I gave up on befriending women—they were simply on a manhunt when I was on a comprehensive Negro hunt. I'd have been happier to find girlfriends than a boyfriend.

On the rare occasions when I saw black men, they seemed physically incapable of meeting my eyes. I'd shoot them a big smile and welcoming toss of the head. They'd frown. Often they'd leave.

Buoyed with feminist brio and naive thickheadedness, I'd cross the dance floor, sure they just hadn't seen me, or sure I could convince them that I'd settle for solidarity; there was no reason we couldn't unite racially, if not personally. I tried to give them the long-lost-sibling treatment, but they angrily shrugged me off. Then, I figured it out. They were looking for white girls and I was cramping their style.

The night I finally got it, one of the brothers on a two-man white-girl-reconnaisance mission turned his back pointedly. The other seared me with the evil eye and snorted: "I cudda went to the West Side for this."

Payback really is hell.

Intellectual loneliness was the worst of it. I had too much ambition to stay home, too much drive and too little patience with human foibles to be well liked, opinions too divergent from my peers' to be comfortable. I knew my "daylight whiteness" was limited, and every day there was another way for that to be made clear to me. The white boyfriend who removed all the photos with me in them from his photo album before going home on leave. The volleyball game where my coworkers said nothing when someone complained about a shot that went too high: "I aint no nigger." Going out for beers with my male coworkers and listening to them vent their frustration at the lack of "decent" women.

I knew for sure that something had to give the day my office mate Lindsay and I attended a special meeting for female Air Force officers.

Rarely were meetings of this kind held during the duty day. Sans discussion, it was considered dangerous, divisive, and non–Air Force for women or minority groups to hold segregated meetings, let alone on Air Force property. Insofar as GIs congregated in these ways, they did so sotto voce, off duty, and off government property (usually we didn't do it at all). Billed as an "informal lunch talk," it was a daring thing for these two colonels to do and we appreciated it. In the end, though, it scared me into entrenched insomnia and pushed me irrevocably toward separating from the Air Force.

At the lunch, we managed to seat ourselves in rank order as GIs always will. We lieutenants positioned ourselves at the foot of the table. Then captains, then majors, then light colonels. The two "full-bird" colonels sat at the head of the table, chain-smoking and gravelly-voiced. It was like my first board at OTS; I had a fish-eye view of everything and everyone, everywhere in the room.

I couldn't help seeing that we lieutenants, being fresh to adulthood for the most part, had few weddings rings between us. Most of the captains and majors were flashing rings, but only one of the light colonels and neither of the full colonels. None of the colonels had kids.

Trying to relax us enough so that we would speak freely with them about women's future in Air Force intelligence, they joshed around, engaging in male-like one-upmanship and exchanging show-offy jokes about each other's Mercedeses, big houses, and elaborate vacations. What they failed to kid each other about, though, was vacationing alone. Driving alone. The lack of a husband or family to greet them at their luxurious houses after a hard day in the trenches. These realities were clear from the content of the jibes and their lack of rings. So utterly had they accommodated themselves to the male structure we all coveted entrée to, they seemed barely women. I kept expecting one to cough up a hock of phlegm and spit it on the floor, the other to itch at her crotch. No doubt it was my penchant for overdramatization that made me see them as so masculinized, but still, I did a mental head count and realized that of the few female Air Force generals, only one I could think of was married. Much the same went for the few female full colonels.

I sat at the end of that table with the lowly lieutenants and saw my future pass in front of my eyes. No husband. No kids. Especially given that I was the only black in the room and overage at that. Not to mention overopinionated and highly politicized. If I did marry, almost certainly I'd have to give up my Air Force career—many more civilian men were marrying GI women and following them around, but the odds were against it. Many of those captains and majors might soon be mustering out when the Air Force tried to send them to Germany for four years just as their civilian husbands were getting entrenched in a company. Or, if they stayed in, their careers would take a backseat to their GI husbands'; no way could they both be maximized. Worse, many marriages, whether between two GIs or a GI and a civilian, became pseudomarriages as the family endured years-long separations rather than lose the time put in toward retirement. To my mind, a family that wasn't together wasn't a family—that's not a mind-set compatible with military life. It was fine for a single person, but I didn't want to be single forever.

I had to at least consider striking out on my own, security and public approval be damned. I wanted both a family and fulfilling work. There was something I was supposed to be doing, I knew that as clearly as I knew I was alive, and the Air Force, much as I valued it, as ungrateful as I felt for thinking of leaving, was not it. Not anymore. It was an invaluable part of my maturation process—second only to my parents—but it was just about time to move on. But to what?

Thinking about leaving the military—my home, my redeemer, the only place that ever believed in me—was terrifying. I scrambled for ways to bind myself more firmly to it, like distracting myself with a graduate degree. Every officer is required to get one to progress (that's why there is no shame in acquiring a master's from a diploma mill). Because of Atticus Finch and the pioneers of the civil rights movement (and probably because of my father telling me I couldn't do it), I wanted a J.D., but San Antonio had no night law school.

I settled for an M.A. in international relations at St. Mary's University. My assignment "dream sheet" said "anyplace overseas is better than anyplace stateside" and I was still trying to get overseas. I knew I would always be an autodidact; what I learned formally would only supplement the learning I'd always do on my own. A graduate degree in domestically focused political science would be somewhat redundant, while one in a rigorous IR program would both expose me to a new strand of political science and put me ahead of my peers, who tended not to take their graduate studies seriously. A grounding in international politics would best prepare me for that happy day when I would join an overseas flight crew and ensconce myself in a down-

and-dirty, front-line flying unit. Then I'd be too busy to ponder the fate of the black masses beyond sending a check to the United Negro College Fund, or mentoring some diamond-in-the-rough kid like me on the weekends. After retirement (2000 at the earliest), I'd think again about a more personal involvement, perhaps teaching. Perhaps in local office. But that day, I hoped, was far off.

I chose St. Mary's because it was private, had small classes, and had the most stringent admission requirements (a week of audited classes at the more expensive Trinity failed to impress). I wanted to see if private schools had more to offer than the public school I'd attended and I wanted serious classmates.

I immersed myself in the political and economic classics at St. Mary's. I had misread the course catalog and thought basic graduate economics (a subject which had baffled me as an undergraduate) a graduation requirement. After one class, I was mesmerized. In the end, eighteen of the thirty-six hours in my master's program were in economics.

Though my elementary school education laid an excellent intellectual foundation for me, I'd received almost no instruction in philosophy. Discovering it and economics in grad school was the final layer in my growth as a thinker. I read everything from Plato to Rousseau to Aquinas to Mill to Marcuse to Ricardo, Marx, and Veblen. I didn't just read the assigned chapters, I read the entire volume and went back for the authors' lesser-known writings. I had no social life. I never had, so I didn't miss it. I just read, thought, wrote papers, and argued politics with anyone who came near me.

Politics kept me so agitated, my cigarette input doubled; my brain whirred so I couldn't keep my hands still. Smoking gave them something to do while I argued with the thin air at home, lectured my long-suffering mother on the intricacies of the omnibus spending bill pending on the Hill, or in the car while analyzing the radio news.

I was politicized to the teeth, unable to evaluate any social phenomenon apart from its place in the sweep of history, probably the only bona fide radical in uniform. When a pimply-faced movie theater operative demanded to search my backpack for reasonably priced contraband food (it contained only Marx's *Das Kapital* and Veblen's *The Theory of the Leisure Class*), I bombarded him with such a furious lecture on constitutional law and the rights of man, he ran off and I proceeded victorious to see *Weekend at Bernie's.*

Besides working out, movies—sometimes three, sometimes four a weekend—were my only outlet. I'd buy two tickets, come out of one movie and go right into the next at the multiplex. Then I'd go home and read some more. When not studying, I sewed, knitted, and crocheted at a prodigious rate. Being stuck stateside and forced to be a bureaucrat, I was desperate for some creativity, something real, something not fraught with ambivalence, something I could feel and produce in my life.

I had so many projects going at home and was so frustrated at work, I reported for duty at 6:30 or 7 A.M. and I ran out of the office each day at 3:30 or 4. By the end of my three years there, I was driving home at lunch to put in a sleeve or block a new sweater or speed-read a few chapters. I knew that Daddy had trained me to be a prisoner in my own home, but by the time I unlocked the door, it was too late. I'd learned to roam free in my own head and to look to family for human contact. I had never picked up a phone, dialed someone local, and said, "What are you doing? Want to go shopping?" It never occurred to me. I called a sister or cousin long-distance instead. Trained to keep busy, I have never once been bored or at loose ends. Lonely perhaps, but never bored or aimless—there's always something that needs doing.

Being raped didn't help. I could hit the gym and two movies before dark on the weekend if I got an early enough start and I always did. I was militant about doing what I wanted to do but I avoided moving about at night if I didn't have to. There might have been a club in my hands but there was also still a target on my pelvis. I didn't go out at night alone to prove some feminist point. I was just trying to live my life unmolested (which is my definition of feminism).

Books and the knowledge they contained continued to keep me at a fever pitch of intellectual excitement. Once I discovered *The Economist,* I never again had an unagitated moment. It enabled me to carry the whole world around in my pocket every week to obsess over at my leisure. There was just so much to be concerned about.

After my Damascus Road undergrad political awakening, I considered myself a hard-core leftist and was looking desperately for fellow travelers. Outside of the middle-aged professoriat, I never found them at St. Mary's. I started night grad school at twenty-seven, graduated at thirty (my grandfather remarked that I was "the graduating-est somebody [he'd] ever heard tell of"). Once again, I girded myself to face being the "grandma" of the group. Instead, I was continually amazed at the anti-intellectual small-mindedness of the young people in my classes. Though it *was* the Reagan eighties, when it was cool to be dumb and selfish; I suppose I shouldn't have been surprised.

In answer once to a professor's call for unrestrained brainstorming, I made the obvious suggestions of increased, incentivized mass transport and carpooling as remedies for San Antonio's intolerable and growing traffic congestion. A twenty-one-year-old honor student allowed to take the class gasped and breathed at me in horrified wonder: "That's *communism*." She said "communism" as if it were "necrophilia."

Another young twenties type gave an impassioned speech about how much he liked being able to deviate from a planned route to hit McDonald's or a mall if the mood struck him. That would be much more difficult on a bus or train. How he liked being able to drive alone singing at the top of his lungs if he wanted to without other carpoolers interfering with his unfettered freedom. His personal convenience was the only variable in his analysis. I pointed out that these were not arguments addressing the problem of traffic congestion, which had been our assigned task. I asked him how we could fix something we all agreed was a problem without being willing to make some sacrifices. He, with the other young conservatives, rolled their eyes. How funny. The lone military person was a liberal. All the college kids were conservatives, if you can dignify their self-concern with a political label (they did).

Nor did they work hard. Few did the reading, even fewer participated in class discussions. A few of our professors responded by asking precious little of us. I was shocked when my economics professor laid out the requirements for the end-of-course paper (at the first class, when he'd mentioned the required paper, four of the twenty of us present got up, left, and dropped the course). He distributed handouts printed in insultingly large type, spelling out the style manual we were to use, the minimum number of footnotes (a paltry five), the minimum number of pages (five. In graduate school, for goodness' sake) as if we were fifth graders. He barely mentioned the topic, all he cared about was the format. Months later, when papers were due, half the class was a no-show. He collected the papers of the hardy few, then, disgusted, sorted through them one by one.

"Mr. Jones. How many footnotes did I require?"

"Five."

"How many do you have?"

"Three."

"Miss Smith. What style manual did I require?"

"Turabian."

"What did you use?"

"APA."

"Miss Baker, how many pages were required?"

"Five."

"How many do you have?"

"Two."

Another class required us to present our papers. The professor told us that we couldn't just thumb through them, that we had to structure a separate presentation from them. Those who even turned the paper in, let alone on time, just strolled up and thumbed through their paper randomly reading paragraphs. Whenever a paper was due, from my seat up front I'd watch my peers saunter up for extensions (some professors didn't even dock the late submissions a letter grade—had they, there would probably have been a riot).

Since Southwest, I had never missed a class. I even structured my many business trips around my class schedule. I've never turned a paper in late or asked for an extension. I would watch their sorry (young!) asses and wonder: Maybe they're right and I'm wrong—why bother? Am I really a freak? How could they take their educations so lightly? Mind and body—that's all we've got to work with, so don't take them for granted. Why not give a damn?

I watched the parade of students offering excuses, nearly all of whom sauntered off with the same A's I earned, and envied my brother his forthrightness in beating up his football teammates mid-game for slacking. If I'm to teach, I thought, I won't be aiming to teach lazy, ungrateful, overprivileged wretches like these. Better community college and a hardy student population that gives a damn.

At work—well, I loved my military family, but open-minded they were not. Clear-minded, but definitely not open-minded. If it wasn't traditional two-party, winner-take-all, every-man-for-himself mytho-Americanism and fundamentalist Protestantism, they weren't having it. They never gave an inch, not on anything. They drove me crazy but I admired their tenacity. For their part, they thought I was a bleeding-heart liberal living in a dream world. One said, as if a thunderbolt of clarity had struck him, "I know what's wrong with you, Debra. You want things now that can't happen until after the Rapture. You want a paradise on earth and that can't happen until Jesus comes back and separates the lions from the lambs."

They could accept that Jesus walked on water, they could accept that He had risen from the dead, and they could accept that He was coming back to lead them all to glory. But they couldn't accept that we could clean up the corner of Fifth and Elm, that we could show a little initiative and provide quality education and health care to every kid in America—*that* was pie in the sky.

They believed what they believed with all their hearts, though. I thought they were so brainwashed by the status quo as to be unreachable, though neither of us stopped trying. Many was the time that half the office would crowd into my cubicle to debate me on some leftist firebomb I had lobbed while waving some obscure text around. The height of my affection for them came the day I looked up to find them smirking and crowded into my cubicle doorway, each jockeying for a position from which they could observe my reaction to their own little firebomb.

My immediate supervisor, whom I respected and loved, was the leader. Triumphantly, he slapped a book opened to a highlighted passage on my desk.

Obligingly, I read aloud (something like): "The triumph of communism is the starvation of millions. The tragedy of capitalism is the starvation of a few. Winston Churchill."

The "gotcha!" expressions on their faces broke my heart. I felt such a surge of affection for them and of gratitude for getting to be a part of something so firmly grounded, so believed in. My simply having read their capitalist apologia aloud was deemed a victory. To them, the words themselves were incontrovertible proof of the inalienable rightness of "the system." Even a child should be able to see it.

I couldn't steal their moment.

Unimpressed, I thought, Very pithy, very Churchillian, very empty. I'm not arguing for communism, just Christian fairness and kindness.

"Well said," I said aloud.

Crowing forgivingly, they scattered, satisfied with their staunch defense of the status quo. (When Uncle Sam started forcing GIs out to balance the budget a few years later, well . . . that was a different story. They sang a different tune then.) I loved those guys and would have done anything for them because they would have done anything for me, politics be damned. I would have trusted them with my life, but I rarely cut them the kind of rhetorical slack I did in that special Kodak moment. They'd have been disappointed if I had. They didn't hold my tirades against me. Rather, they enjoyed our jousts because they reinforced their bedrock belief in 1950s press-release America.

We argued like cats and dogs most days. When the dust settled, nobody changed his mind and nobody questioned anybody else's patriotism or sanity. We'd fight off and on all day after I threw out some incendiary quote from the Bible or the Constitution (which I carried everywhere with me after I read that Thurgood Marshall had) that I knew they weren't aware of. I'd try to force them to concede the plain, subversive meaning of a passage in Luke or a founding document. They'd patiently explain why the words didn't mean what they obviously meant. Then we'd go off to chow en masse or to give each other rides somewhere. We all knew and socialized with each other's families. We all covered for each other when one of us needed to be out of the office and unreachable for some undisclosable reason. Nobody called in the thought police, nobody ever started a whispering campaign against me (liberals later would, though, when I questioned the party line). Nobody ever mentioned my politics in a performance appraisal (it didn't occur to them to). Nothing slopped over into our duty performance. Because I was Air Force through and through, my politics weren't held against me. They knew I was thinking of leaving, but until then I made no bones about my commitment to the Air Force, so they made no bones about their commitment to me.

Though it may seem counterintuitive, there's a greater tolerance for eccentrics in the military than elsewhere. I knew an Army guy at the NSA who built a sandbag enclosure around his bunk in the barracks, shaved his head bald, growled, ate MREs morning, noon, and night, and generally acted like a deranged commando. We chuckled at his antics because he was, in the performance of his duties, the consummate office-based soldier. If you wanted something done, you asked him to do it, freak or not. In the same way, my extreme politics and my open disappointment with my assignment (I wanted to be overseas working with flight crews—being office-bound gave me too much time to think dangerous thoughts) were affectionately tolerated because I made it clear that they would in no way affect my attitude toward my duty. My thoughts were my own as long as my attitude and behavior conformed.

The true test of the military's tolerance for individuality came when the Supreme Court heard the case of the Texas protester who'd burned the U.S. flag. We had a nearly daylong office debate about that, including a visiting colonel. Everybody counseled me not to repeat my opinion (of course the First Amendment covered his actions, however reprehensible) outside our group. But the subject came up when the visiting colonel was there and I spoke up, respectfully. He was momentarily taken aback, then just nodded—at my right to respectful dissent on an abstract issue, not at my opinion—and engaged me. I began every volley with, "With all due respect, sir. . . ." My politics never affected my career because I never let it affect my professionalism. I'd have cut out my own tongue before I disparaged a military operation, a military policy, or a military leader. Aloud, that is.

I had nothing but time to think. My chairborne, far-from-the-action job took up half my time at best. Even that half-time was filled with mind-numbing paperwork and meetings with contractors focused on bleeding us dry.

Also, as my existential anger and confusion waned, I lost another outlet for blowing off my excess energy as my workouts began taking up less and less of my time and concentration. Now, I was just working out like a woman who wanted to look good in her clothes, not feel good in her skin. Finally, once I graduated from my master's program in August 1988, my conscious thoughts were no longer occupied with grand, universal themes. That intellectual, footnote-happy edge was off, though my political focus, built now on the proper educational foundation, was keener than ever. I needed new challenges.

Desperate for adventure and to prove myself on the front lines, I stalked the captain in charge of assignments. Again and again, she told me that we were in another cyclic drawdown and everyone was being forced to do three to four years on station. PCSs (permanent change of stations) are very expensive because of the generous allowances; it was one of the biggest sinkholes in the military budget and therefore a prime cutback target. No way could I leave with less than three years on station. When I pointed out that my office buddy Lindsay, a second lieutenant, had been at Kelly a year less than me, a first lieutenant, but had an assignment to Berlin, the captain's face hardened. Only she could have worked that assignment; only a stiff-necked Girl Scout like me would have rubbed her face in what was either favoritism or incompetence. There was no chance of my getting out of Kelly now. Stonily, she intoned, "Air Force needs come first," and sent me away. I knew she had all sorts of leeway and was just refusing to use it on my behalf since I'd put no effort into courting her.

I detested her with all the Old Testament force I could muster. She was everything I hated about the good-ol'-boy aspect of the service. Whenever I saw her, I gave her my stone face; it heartened me to see her turn away flustered. There was no way around her without strong protectors and I had put no effort into developing those, so sure was I that hard work and devotion to duty were sufficient. I spurned those officers who had built their careers on a superior's coattails and I refused to call in any chits. It was like my not wearing my decorations at OTS; my record should speak for itself. Only suckers file a dream sheet without having a higher-ranking mentor bat cleanup for them. Suckers, and high achievers, I thought. I was wrong.

But even as I fought to get overseas I was having more and more trouble visualizing an Air Force future for myself. My political maturation had led me to revisit my Cold War "West good, East bad" simplistic mind-set. Our Central America policy made me queasy—the Nicaraguan contras the "moral equivalent of our Founding Fathers"? I already had problems with the Founding Fathers, what on earth was I to think of a bunch of hereditary, oppressive elites whose only claim on our support was their penchant for killing in the name of capitalism?

After I was commissioned, the Humint (human intelligence) branch had tried to recruit me for my language aptitude. When they (rightfully) refused to guarantee that I wouldn't be trained in Spanish and sent to Central America, I chose not to volunteer. Was any capitalist government really better than any left-leaning one? What about our sponsorship of the repressive El Salvadoran government and their sponsorship of death squads; did they learn any of their techniques from U.S. military trainers, people I served with? How does that comport with our vaunted love of individual liberty, supposedly America's most valuable export? I was a committed Cold Warrior in the same way that I was a committed meat-eater: I eat sausage but I didn't want to see it made, and I certainly didn't want to make it myself. I'd grown up hating and pitying the Soviets and had inherited the USSR. Central America was happening right before my eyes and I was blinking rapidly.

It was difficult to find a side to support in those quagmire situations, and I couldn't stop fretting over my own role in history: was it better to have blind faith in our elected leaders and follow any lawful order or to decide on a case-by-case basis? I could quote Thomas Paine, Malcolm X, Descartes, or Clausewitz to prove either proposition. Soon, we'd be fighting strongmen oppressors we'd only recently helped to create, like Noriega and Saddam Hussein. Apoliticism is a requirement for a professional military if it is to remain under civilian control and I was questioning the party line in a very personal way. I was making mental lists of places I had to refuse to go, missions I couldn't in good conscience support. That's not acceptable for an officer in an all-volunteer military. The Air Force stayed the same but I was changing.

More selfishly, as the Iron Curtain began to crumble and the military had to cast about for new missions to justify its budget, I recoiled at our growing loss of dignity and lack of high purpose. Defeating communism was a reason to get up in the morning. Was tracking dolphins with Navy sonar equipment? Boot camps for juvenile offenders?

To my horror, I was critiquing the Air Force I'd once unquestioningly revered. I needed more than a nonflying, non-medical-corps female could possibly accomplish there. I needed an institution dedicated to pursuits of the highest order and with which I wholeheartedly agreed. There was no use admitting I could blindly follow any and all orders. I couldn't anymore. They should never have invested in making me feel so powerful.

I spent three years trying to escape Kelly Air Force Base, each day resenting more and more my inability to make my own decisions about my professional life. I was at the mercy of a captain who hated me. While I might not always be hated, I would always be at the mercy of arbitrary forces when it came to the most important details of my life, like where I could live and what job I could do. Ironically, the Air Force had made me so ambitious and so well educated I couldn't be content with what it had left to offer me, though God knows I tried.

Feverishly, I redoubled my efforts to find a job that would keep me interested, invested, and unconflicted in the service. I volunteered for every outlandish posting I could find—instructor at the Air Force Academy, diplomatic postings, recruiting, OTS flight commander, a second master's full-time at the Sorbonne (I still declined to become a Humint officer, though). I lobbied the assignments captain relentlessly for the two assignments I most wanted and had the least chance of getting—Iceland and Turkey. Both were "trip-wire" outfits strategically located to buttress our commitment to NATO. Both were reserved for experienced captains and hotly contested. Both were less than two years; separating was becoming more and more certain in my mind and it needed to be sooner rather than later.

But I had been handpicked and deemed officially "essential" at Kelly, working as I did on an intelligence project ranked in the Air Force's top ten list. Every week I was getting yelled at by the places I'd applied to for wasting their time once their requests for me were summarily bounced back. My superiors were apologetic but firm. Air Force needs come first.

Like a child singing full-voice to keep herself from hearing the monster in the closet, I threw myself into a whirl of additional duties and extra training to keep from questioning my secure place in the service. But it was all to no avail. I couldn't keep my fingers in my ears. I wanted a future with no limits. I wanted to create a field of endeavor for myself that incorporated creativity and intellectualism and community concern, though I had no idea what that might mean. So I fought those thoughts. It had taken me all my life to find the Air Force, and the thought of being on my own again, without that strong, societally valued identity, left me weak in the knees. It was the Reagan eighties and America loved me and my uniform and that used to mean everything to me. Yet I was tortured by half-formed thoughts of doing great, unlimited things, things I could only do as a civilian. But a civilian what? I had no idea.

It was like being schizophrenic, in the grip of those two mutually incompatible urges: stay! go! stay! go! But every day it became increasingly difficult to drag myself into my office at Kelly to shuffle papers after another sleepless night spent trying to read the future. One day, some portentous event would tell me to stay. The next, another portentous event would aim me toward the door.

At the beginning of one month, I attended my language school friend Dave's graduation from the Air Force Academy. He honored me by asking me to pin his butter bars on, administer the oath of office, and commission him. After the graduation ceremony, he introduced me to the young black honor grad who had been the class's cadet corps commandant, the equivalent of my OT wing commander (plus a brutal three years and nine months). The training staff was complimenting him in front of his gaggle of exultant relatives—just as Lowery had me in front of mine—while he modestly fidgeted a silent "aw shucks." He remained politely mute, kept his head discreetly lowered, his body language self-effacing. I looked at him and a GI aphorism sprang to mind: "Save the watch because the boots are already gone" (i.e., buried in bullshit).

That kid was bursting to do a victory dance, bursting to scream I BEAT ALL YOU WHITE MOFOS. ALL YOU THIRD-GENERATION GENERALS' KIDS. ALL YOU LEGACIES WHO DIDN'T NEED THE FREE EDUCATION LIKE I DID. ALL YOU MIDDLE-CLASS PUKES WHO NEVER DOUBTED YOU BELONG HERE. I BEAT YOU!!!!!! I could feel it in my overachieving, gratification-deferring bones. But the good manners his mama and the Air Force had taught him forced him to keep his peace. Four years. How hard that kid must have worked just to graduate, let alone excel.

As we were introduced, he held his hand out politely to shake mine, but I left him hanging. I let a long, awkward moment spin out between us and held his perplexed eyes.

"It's good to win, isn't it?" I said wolfishly.

I was thinking of my father surveying the enemy dead on Okinawa. Hell, the *friendly* dead of which he was not one. He must have felt like Genghis Khan because that's how I felt every time I snatched something from someone else who had as much right to it as I did. Where but in the Air Force could I ever acquire such opportunities to best a valorous competitor?

He struggled but was unable to keep the triumphant grin off his face. He made a fist with the hand I refused to reduce to a bourgeois shake and pumped it in the air for just a second. YES! Then, that housebroken smile returned and we parted, knowing exactly what had passed between us. Maybe I was wrong. Maybe he was a general's kid. Either way, he had a victory dance coming.

The Air Force was a wonderful place for black people.

At the end of that month, I attended that special meeting for female officers.

The Air Force wasn't such a wonderful place for women.

I was buried alive in my own life, anesthetized by a fat paycheck and bourgeois trappings. I had to stop muffling what my heart was trying to tell me. It was time to move on.

But that was so much easier said than done. If I left the Air Force, I knew it had to be for something free-form. I imagined myself tied to a desk at some bank like the one I had worked at before Mizzou and shuddered. Yet I still had no idea what I should do. Nearly thirty and there I was trying to figure out what I should be when I grew up: Doctor? No. Nurse? No. Teacher? No. I took personality tests. I researched careers from astrophysics to zoology. Finally, I believed I had the persistence and talent to be whatever I wanted and nothing struck a chord.

I signed on with a few head-hunting firms that specialized in former officers and was inundated with calls and letters, but it all sounded so pointless, so dry. Secure, but meaningless: management consultant. Secure, but repugnant: CIA. More mid-level management positions in industry than I would ever have imagined, but who wants to peddle soap with the Palmolive people or push papers around as a GS-12 government bureaucrat? The Air Force beat any of the things I was offered hands down—at least that was about more than just a paycheck.

I decided to approach the conundrum from the other way around. Since I didn't know what I wanted to do, I could focus on what I didn't want. I could focus on how, generally speaking, I wanted to live since I didn't like the way I had been living. But what was it exactly that I didn't like? If I could build my life from a kit, what would be in it? What did I want?

I carried index cards with me and scribbled down every thought or occurrence that annoyed or pleased me, every observation or insight into my own nature. To my surprise, the answers came quite easily: I didn't want anyone telling me what to do again, ever. As long as my military superiors had been benevolent, I hadn't resented their intrusion into my life. But when I didn't get what I wanted (we called this the "Burger King, have-it-your-way mentality"), I could no longer shrug it off. "Air Force needs come first" wasn't working as my mantra anymore.

I looked in my closets. Full of the exotic South Asian clothing I collected but never wore. I wanted a life where I got to wear them.

I looked in my jewelry box. Funky trinkets that never left my bedroom. I wanted to wear them too. Ankle bracelets whose tinkles announce my presence and toe rings that serve no purpose at all.

What I didn't want was to wear a uniform ever, ever again.

Or panty hose.

Or anything with a constricting neckline.

No more polyester.

No more alarm clocks.

No more meetings of more than three people.

No more meetings that didn't result in a firm plan of action, the failure to accomplish which would result in punitive measures against the malfeasor.

The power to reject joint projects and/or the power to mete out punishment (i.e., expulsion from the endeavor, group disapproval).

No more meetings of longer than twenty minutes.

No more commutes of longer than twenty minutes.

No more commuting by automobile.

No more shared office space.

No more hair-straightening.

No more living in the suburbs or any car-dependent city.

No more taking arbitrary orders from random superiors.

I want to be the idiot in charge.

I want to produce something tangible for a living, something with my hands.

I need a mission.

I hate clock watching.

I hate clock watchers.

I am stiff-necked, judgmental, and unforgiving—need work that allows for that.

I care about the character, talent, and drive of the people in my life.

Something that involves other diamond-in-the-rough black people like me.

I want to set my own hours.

A job that doesn't feel like a job. A job that feels like my life.

A job that I am.

Sentences like these made perfect sense to me.

I read self-help manuals like *Do What You Love, the Money Will Follow, Swim with the Sharks Without Being Eaten Alive,* and *How to Retire at Forty-one.* I subscribed to business magazines and looked into mall pretzel franchises. I wanted to be in charge, whatever it was I ended up doing, again for negative reasons—I was tired of taking orders from people whose judgment didn't impress me. I could do as well (but at what?) and not be annoyed in the process. I thought and thought and thought and finally noticed what was missing from my many scribblings: Money. Position. Fame. Power.

My subconscious had given me the foundation on which to structure my life while I searched for my one true calling (the existence of which I never doubted).

Autonomy.

That's what I was really looking for in my life.

Autonomy.

I would trade money, title, fame, everything—as long as I could be in the driver's seat.

Taking responsibility for myself—apart from the military, a corporation, a husband, a well-off family which could rescue me—was at once terrifying and a complete relief.

I wasn't going to starve. I wasn't going to become homeless. I would do whatever I needed to and I didn't care that people would think little of me once they knew I waited tables or sold T-shirts from the trunk of my car for a living. I knew their eyes would slide right over me once they heard me answer the "What do you do?" question with "I make dresses with my mama and sell them in church basements," and the thought no longer shamed me. It was like the OTS board. I knew I'd do what needed doing no matter what others thought or however they treated me.

I was ready to flip burgers, make lattes, or sell T-shirts on the highway off-ramp rather than tie myself to a desk, operating room, or space capsule doing something I hated. Or even doing something that merely bored me. I wanted work that felt inseparable from my life, something I'd do even if I won the lottery. Something, the more I thought about it, that I could do from home because I had come to abhor office life, especially commuting and meetings. But until I figured out what that something was, I was ready to wash cars, herd sheep—anything I could do largely on my own, anything I didn't dread waking up to face. I'd come to hate Sundays by then, because I had to go back to work the next day. I refused to live the rest of my life that way. Most everyone I could think of—from senior officers to my cousins at the post office—hated his job. I was resigning from that club.

Recounting it here makes it all seem very simple and straightforward, but I truly believe this is the point at which I developed hypertension. I had black circles under my eyes and talked to myself. Aside from myself to worry about, I still had family responsibilities—I wasn't some Kennedy who could just disappear and find herself with the aid of an expensive shrink. My relatives thought I was crazy for thinking of leaving the Air Force after a decade, especially when I'd made officer, but I was after that examined life.

After about two years of sleeplessness and neurosis, I had to take the plunge and get out. I had no idea what I was going to do with myself but I knew I would do whatever necessary to survive and live up to all my responsibilities, however I had to do that. I knew I was doing something ridiculous, but even so, I felt wonderful. Calm. Hopeful and excited.

After much list-making of potential home-based careers and potential ways to fund said careers, I had decided to do what professional students always do when in doubt: go back to school. This time for a doctorate or a J.D. What I wasn't saying out loud was that I was sheepishly entertaining the notion of running for local office back home or teaching at a community college, notions I deduced working backwards from the idea that I was supposed to be doing something about the working class. Why else couldn't I get it off my mind? The ghetto needs living, breathing role models they can see and talk to. Bill Cosby on TV was as foreign and otherworldly to them as any white elite, his accomplishments correspondingly exotic and unimaginable. What they needed was successful, well-educated people in the neighborhoods to demystify the process. As well, both were occupations you controlled yourself, for the most part, and which allowed for great flexibility. Best of all, they were inherently meaningful and outward-directed. Even though I'd come a long way emotionally, both seemed grandiose statements I might not be able to live up to, so I kept them to myself as I typed up my separation paperwork. I wasn't ready to submit it yet, but I had to make my commitment to leave real. That night, I fell immediately to sleep for the first time in years. My insomnia disappeared.

Watching my mother work longer hours than any factory had ever required of her at her own projects made me appreciate the extent to which working people are deprived of any creative outlets or of even the most basic control over their own actions. Black grandmothers have to cringe before twenty-something restaurant managers to get permission to see a doctor or go to a PTA meeting. (That's why they so often take their frustrations out on the customer. I often let my turn go by in a low-level government office or retail environment rather than face an angry, dis-expecting black woman behind a cash register or computer screen. Black comedians do entire routines about the bad attitudes of low-level black service workers.)

As well, most have neither the time, the money, nor the breadth of vision to avail themselves of cooking classes, singing lessons, community theater, and the like, so their self-expression is stifled in its infancy. At the same time, the inner city is awash in working folk selling their hand-sewn pillows and kente-cloth-wrapped everything, weekend fish fries, kitchen-table beauty salons, backyard mechanics. Willette, the black hairdresser I patronized in a white shop, never smiled, never laughed, and was so softspoken I routinely had to ask her to repeat herself. Once she opened up her own (illegal) salon in her house, she blared gospel music from eight speakers as I bent over her kitchen sink. Her kids did their homework across the table from where she set my hair in rollers. She was so full-throated, I couldn't believe it was the same woman. I asked her if she thought she could make as much from home as from the high-traffic district of the old shop. "I DON'T CARE!" she yelled. "Long as I can feed myself and the kids."

The business ventures I looked into, coupled with my community-mindedness and the entrepreneurship struggling for sunlight in the ghetto, reminded me that what poor people need most of all is money. The second thing they need, though most don't even dare to dream of it, is some measure of autonomy.

My mother filled every flat surface in our house with her handiwork and tools. She could not at first bring herself to part with any of the trophies of her new freedom, but eventually I was able to persuade her to peddle the overflow at flea markets and craft fairs. There were often more vendors at these events than customers and bargaining was fierce. Most had day jobs. My mother invested so much time and money in her craft, she always lost money. But the people who profited no matter the turnout or sale price were the people running the event and leasing the spaces.

What if I created a space for black women to earn extra money, exercise some blessed decision-making, and express themselves all at the same time? I remembered how my mother scuffled to create memorable Christmases and back-to-school collections for us. Usually, she either went into debt or took a second night job. What if she'd been able to spend her nights dressmaking or throwing pots at home with her family, then bring them to someone like me to sell for her? Usually, poor people just take another dead-end, low-wage McJob that keeps them from their families. What if I created stall space, some rented long-term, some just as needed during an expensive family crisis or to buy new furniture? Women like Willette could move her basement hair salon here and rent-to-own space from me. I could encourage, or even require, them to take an apprentice, some woman trying to get off welfare or newly released from jail. Entrepreneurially minded strivers could run a snack bar, offer accounting services, do deliveries. The local jobless could provide security. I could network with downtown big business to support vendors in spinning off their own ventures. Most ghetto businesses are off-the-books, but I'd insist on all the legal formalities (like taxes); that means I'd need to help them with basic bookkeeping. Might as well do GED classes on the side. Voter registration. Military personnel from the many local bases to do mentoring, tutoring. There must be lots of embezzlers and inside traders who could do their community service with me, teaching about the stock market or the legal system. Bugger self-esteem training—self-esteem comes from accomplishment: offer math and citizenship classes, encourage them to take the ghetto back from the knuckleheads. Citizen crime patrols. Identifying promising local kids and grooming them for leadership. Not just telling people they should aim high, but steadying the ladder for them while they did so.

How hard could it be?

I was asking for a separation date six months off, mid to late 1989. By then I'd be safely ensconced in a Ph.D. program somewhere studying political economy, or in law school, or running for local government, or substitute teaching at a ghetto high school while selling homemade pies door to door at night to fund my school board campaign. I was open to anything, as long as doing it made me happy, left me largely in charge of myself, and kept me engaged with other forward-thinking people. My big plan was substitute teaching. I could decide day by day, school by school, whether or not to work, and earn just as much as I needed to get by.

My separation paperwork burning a hole in my briefcase, I set the following Monday as the day of submission. Tingling with nervous excitement, still, I felt at peace for the first time in years. It was such a relief to not be going round and round in open-ended circles. I didn't know exactly what I was going to do. I just knew I would do something—my commitment to my mother alone would ensure that.

I wandered down to the cafeteria and who should I encounter but the captain who'd kept me a prisoner at Kelly by refusing to work an assignment for me. I was so serene and resigned to stepping off the cliff of my own future, I spoke warmly to her and inquired about her family. It was hard for me to even remember the hostility I'd harbored for her. She was so surprised her eyes widened like saucers. We chatted amiably. When I got back to my desk, my phone was ringing.

"You'll never beat out all the fighter jocks for the intel chief job in Iceland. Still want to go to Turkey?" she asked.

I took the discharge paperwork out of my drawer and tore it up. I knew I was still going to get out, but just not until I'd had my last overseas hurrah. I was ready to take my destiny in my own hands. But first, an adventure!

JUST FOR THE HELL OF IT

My fifteen months from June 1989 to October 1990 assigned as chief of intelligence, Ankara Air Station, Turkey, were the best of my career. I'd done no research about the country apart from its military significance, yet I was still hearing voices. My instinct told me it was the right move.

With a small band of other young officers, I traveled all over the region and saw sights thousands of years old. I drank from St. Paul's local well in Tarsus and visited the protoconvent where Mary lived after Jesus' crucifixion. I saw places like Spain, Egypt, Bulgaria, Cyprus, Greece, Syria, and the medieval walled city of Dubrovnik. With my friends, I saw the whirling dervishes (they're slow and mesmerizing, not high-speed and manic). I watched the sun come up over Nem Ru mountain with its ancient stone heads lying about like a giant child's discarded toys and wondered about the peasants who must have died by the thousands dragging them up the mountainside. On a train platform in Budapest, a young Gypsy man threw me a devilish kiss and led his troupe in serenading me (much to my boyfriend's disapproval)—they looked right out of *National Geographic* and yet they thought me exotic! Wherever my (white) boyfriend Erik and I went, there was so much gawking, he used to joke that he was going to get a T-shirt that read "Yes! She's That Color All Over." There are supposed to be lots of Africans in eastern Europe, but we encountered very few (and virtually no women). When we did, it was clear how mongrelized African-Americans have become after three hundred and fifty years in America. The Africans stared at me, too.

We drank Turkish beer and bought lots of gold and handwoven carpets (even though I knew that women and children slaved making them, often involuntarily). We lived like kings on our military pay and thanks to Turkey's ever-worsening inflation—for twelve dollars a month, I had a cleaning lady. For a few bucks more, she'd have cooked too, but I was rarely home.

But all this was a sidelight to my military job, by far the most satisfying of my twelve years in uniform. Our air station was there to support and defend our commitment to the southern region of NATO. I was assigned to DO, the Directorate of Operations, as chief of intelligence. I wrote the intel annex to the war plan for our region and developed plans for supporting and directing troops that would have to deploy to the region in a contingency. We expected our enemy to come from the Soviet Union, but it was deteriorating at such a rapid pace, we began to wonder if there'd be much for us to do at all.

The highlight of my job was the weekly intelligence briefings I delivered to General Grove and his almost entirely male and middle-aged staff. It took me a couple of weeks to get my legs under me, but in very short order my briefings were standing room only. I enjoyed them tremendously. It was exactly the type of challenge I relished. There was a piss-and-vinegar full-bird colonel who loved to play "stump the dummy" with me, asking questions he thought I wouldn't, but should, be able to answer. He cut me no slack, and trying to anticipate his demands—it was a point of honor with me to have no questions asked at the end of my presentation—kept my briefings razor sharp.

Rather than stage fright, my problem was a lack of nervousness. Once I'd done my homework on the region's military situation (which I continually monitored anyway with help from my headquarters at Ramstein AB, Germany), what was there to be nervous about? Had I had to lecture on physics, I'd have died a thousand deaths, but knowing I knew more than my audience did in my area of responsibility—where's the edge going to come from? I found myself leaning on the podium, not standing up straight, my mind wandering from a presentation I'd memorized and practiced to the point where I couldn't listen to it anymore. I wasn't strack because it just came too easily. I ran across an article about Al Pacino. In it, he said that he didn't eat before a performance, that hunger gave him an edge.

To sharpen my own performance, rather than work efficiently on my presentations all week, I'd just file away items I thought I might brief in a special file. As always, I made sure to keep abreast of all developments, keep my map file stocked, my weapons slides up to date and complete. Then, the afternoon and night before a briefing, I whirled into action, knowing I had exactly enough time, but no more, to pull it together. I was a tornado, running around, gathering final up-to-date info, making my presentation slides, orchestrating with the airman who handled the briefing room infrastructure. I'd work till late in the evening, go straight to bed, back up again at five. Lots of black coffee but no breakfast.

Hungry, overcaffeinated, and heading for a line after which I would be dead (0800 sharp), only then would I run through the briefing a few times, keying from the slides I'd made the day before. I allowed myself no margin for error. Since I didn't have time to choose my words carefully and memorize, I'd have to rely on my wits and thorough background knowledge to pull each briefing off. It was a high-wire act and I loved the high. I made the odd mistake here and there (I recall being unable to find Riyadh, the capital of Saudi Arabia, on my slide even though I'd placed a huge gold star on the spot). What fun.

Keeping up with the dissolving USSR, Lebanon, the standoff between the Turks and the Kurds, the Turks and the Greeks, the Greek Cypriots and the Turkish Cypriots—not to mention the likes of Muammar El-Gaddafi, the western Sahara, and the Israeli-Arab conflict—I had more than enough to monitor. It was the perfect job. I got to indulge my love of history, research, international politics, and public speaking every Wednesday morning at 0800 hours. I relied on *The Economist* as much as I did the intel infrastructure at Ramstein.

But reality was never far off and the reminders to remain in control of my own life were everywhere. Since my mother hadn't wanted to move to Turkey, I was maintaining two households. I arranged to share an apartment with a male Air Force nurse in Ankara only to have his boss, the hospital commander, order him not to move in with me because it might look bad to the Turks. There were no single female officers to share with, so I was stuck footing the bills alone. How I longed to be in control of the intimate details of my own life, how I longed to be the idiot in charge. The biggest reminder was yet to come, though.

To keep me operationally ready, my boss sent me to join a stateside unit deployed for a long exercise in the countryside of a NATO ally. That brief experience made me reflect on the murky status of women in the military and on my own personal and feminist evolution. It also steadied my resolve to separate.

During my first few military years, I had consciously eschewed female frippery. I'd completely identified with the down-and-dirty ethic of my new world and felt that acting like a man was the route to the top. I wore fatigues and combat boots, cursed, smoked, drank my beer from the bottle, didn't carry a purse. I was one of the boys.

Then, without consciously having decided to, I made myself over and started wearing makeup, pumps, and all the jewelry allowed by regulation. Skirts, never pants. I tailored my uniforms, painted my nails, wore perfume. I enjoyed seeing eyes widen when I entered those all-male, all-white, all-pilot meetings. In the secret world of electronic combat, those guys seemed to forget that women existed. Somehow, people were always surprised that the Captain Dickerson (I learned not to use "Debra") who'd written the intelligence annex to the war plan had legs. It was sweet to watch them fight the urge to rise, then give in to the one to pull out my chair and open my doors. At the coffee break, some middle-aged major would always pick up my lipsticked cup and josh in mock flirtation, as if with his daughter's friend, "Now whose could this be?"

With equal measures of spite and affection, I'd enjoyed their befuddlement and played it for all it was worth. I knew they could only stare for just so long and then they'd have to start listening. By the time they did, they'd be eating my dust. I'll always believe that standing out in this way while also being good at my job helped me.

Knowing I was close to the end of my Air Force history, and knowing that my gender was a large part of the reason I'd be leaving, I thought about all these things while on deployment. Life in the field, for even just a few days, was a raw and unusual experience. So relevant were these issues of femininity, sexuality, professionalism, and power in that highly charged environment, I couldn't get them off my mind as I tried to sleep on my cot in our tent at night. Living in a coed environment in the field was an eye-opening, bullshit-free experience. Had my mind not already been made up to leave, those few days would have removed all doubt.

By the time I arrived, the unit had been in the field for a month. There were 383 men, 3 enlisted women, and 2 female officers including me. We lived in a Tent City—it looked just like the *M★A★S★H* set but was actually very comfortable.

The other female officer had a husband stateside whom everyone knew. She was having an affair with one of the pilots, and the whole camp, except for us women, treated her like dirt. Her lover was, of course, exempt from disapproval. I could have told her that there are no secrets in Tent City and that it was a rookie's mistake to get involved with any of those guys. I knew that any problems (like rape) would be deemed her fault, no matter the circumstances. I knew that indulging her sexual urges would brand her a whore and undermine her authority no matter how much whoring they were doing. And they would know about it. People all but spat after saying her name.

I, on the other hand, was treated like a vestal virgin. When we weren't flying, we were partying and each group had a party tent. Many drank to the point of incoherence and physical collapse, which was all perfectly acceptable as long as their work didn't suffer the next shift. I knew better than to drink or dance and spent those evenings fending off advances, chaperoned by my male deputy. He obligingly stayed too close to me to allow for any serious breaches of decorum and, for his pains, was routinely referred to as "bitch," "pussy whip," and "the captain's puppy." He shrugged his tormentors off with all the boredom of Mata Hari being interrogated by the Gestapo. To the others' credit, they never name-called him with any vehemence or disgust. His acquiescence was the price of their grudging acceptance. (His colleagues no doubt knew what I had suspected from the moment we met: I'm sure he was gay, though we never discussed it. Once, while hiding in his tent, he made big moon eyes and bleated, "But, Debra, they neeeeeeeeeed you." I laughed so hard they found me.)

Every tent we entered would go quiet for a moment, then men would move forward like the palace eunuchs to deposit me in a seat of honor. They'd ply me with beer and then exchange reverent looks when I'd ask delicately for a diet Coke. Men—married, single, engaged, or openly whoring—would ask me pretty directly for sex and then nod approvingly when I'd remind them of my boyfriend in Ankara. (I wouldn't let Erik visit. If I left camp with him for a hotel, if I were sexualized in any way in that bare-bones emotional environment, I'd be just another whore and my authority would be compromised. Worse, my safety might be compromised.) Clearly, I was being tested and rewarded with the gift of approval for being a nice girl.

Once they accepted that none of them was going to get any, I became everyone's big/little sister, mom, daughter, surrogate wife. The blacks especially claimed me. (I was also the only black officer.) I tried on innumerable gift sweaters and jewelry. I edited letters home. I read letters from home for hints of infidelity and gave advice to the lovelorn. I felt foreheads for fevers. I was Woman. I was a natural resource.

From the time I arrived, I spent not one moment alone. You can't knock on a tent flap, so men started yoo-hooing me at first light. By my second lap jogging, I'd have a detachment in tow. An attentive cohort waited for me as I emerged from the shower tent in my robe. If they couldn't find me anywhere else, they'd move down the line of wooden latrines calling my name.

By the second morning, the commander was refereeing the seating arrangements at chow: "You Red Horse guys had her yesterday. Give Supply some time." Solomonically, he inclined his head, and I reported to the Supply table to bestow the balm of virtuous female presence. (The enlisted women were smart enough to know to ensconce themselves as "one of the guys" in their work units. No one from outside that unit could come near them.)

I borrowed a pilot's coffee cup one day at work and he stopped me when I tried to wash it before returning it. "No," he said. "Leave it." He placed it on his desk next to his wife's picture. After that, men asked me to drink from their cups and I saw my lip prints on filthy cups all over camp.

I was frightened the entire time I was there. I was furious the entire time I was there. No one ever suspected either because I knew I would ruin myself, personally and professionally, by showing it.

I was afraid because I knew that one pair of form-fitting jeans, one hour of spontaneous pleasure, would rob me of both my good name and my effectiveness in the job I'd earned. I was afraid I'd risk one beer and wake up again with a drunken GI pounding away at me—you can't lock a tent flap either. I was afraid I'd start screaming the fury bubbling up inside me into every sweet, milk-fed American man's face that passed me on the muddy paths between our tents. I hated them. They could simply be GIs while I could only be a female GI. I would never be truly free in the military.

I was newly determined to get out but I couldn't do so from Turkey; war with Iraq was looming and I was, again, declared essential. I was on indefinite hold as to when I'd be able to separate. It was just as well because I had been having so much fun, and then was so side-tracked by the war that we in the Middle East could see coming from some distance off, I'd made virtually no decisions about my future. I still didn't know what I was going to do and knew I needed the time stateside to make the transition. In any event, with the war against Iraq percolating, I had no intention of leaving when I might be needed, especially if things went badly.

I applied for an operational assignment back home and once again was punished for my excellent record. Just like in my damnable assignment to Kelly, I was once again being forced to push pencils, this time in the worst place I could think of—the Pentagon. It was a coup to win an assignment to the Pentagon as a junior officer and everyone was overjoyed for me. Everyone but me. I'd rather have been debriefing pilots at Bugtussle Air Force Base in a swamp or living in an igloo at the Arctic Circle Air Station than fighting turf battles over who got to shine some general's boots at the Pentagon.

As the world knows, Saddam Hussein invaded Kuwait in August 1990 and we went to war against him. Even before that, though, the situation in Turkey was fraught with danger. Over the Martin Luther King Day holiday that year, when Erik and I returned home from my first-ever ski trip, we found his apartment blown to smithereens by a terrorist car bomb. A Saudi Arabian diplomat who lived in his building was the target, but so what? The military community was required to travel to and from work in civvies and to vary our route each day. A secular Muslim nation situated at the crossroads between East and West, Turkey was a frequent battleground between interregional secular and fundamentalist Muslim factions. In the 1970s, kidnappings and assassinations involving Americans had been far from infrequent. But by late 1989, life was good for Westerners in Turkey. Once the war broke out, though, our "good-time Charlie" lifestyle went right out the window. Eventually, we'd even lose a few people to terrorism.

Given that Turkey borders Iraq, my one-man intel shop was immediately overwhelmed with more work than any one "man" could handle. I requested reinforcements from Ramstein Air Base, Germany, U.S. Air Forces in Europe Headquarters, and two men were on the next thing smoking to Turkey. They ended up staying "in country" longer than I did.

Far too soon, the war was over for me. With my rotation back to the world imminent (October 1990) just as things were heating up, I moved to block the arrival of my successor. Even though every GI understood that this was a war about cheap oil, paid for with the suffering of long-oppressed Iraqis, politics went out the window for me once we were at war. I may have serious bones to pick with my country, but it's still mine. Also, I was not unaware that there was likely to be an adventure or two in the Persian Gulf War unfolding before my eyes. I convinced my superiors that it was better to leave an experienced intel chief in place with the war raging than live through what might be a deadly learning curve with a newcomer.

If only I'd thought of it sooner, because my replacement (also a wily prior-service captain) pulled the oldest GI trick in the book. He went underground and incognito. Obviously, he feared exactly what I was pulling—not only stealing whatever glory might be in store during a wartime, front-line posting but also robbing him of a personal role in aiding the war effort—and put me in checkmate. He outprocessed from his base early, went on a protracted leave, and left no forwarding information. I tried desperately to track him down so I could have his orders cancelled, but alas. I went to work one morning and there he sat in my office waiting to relieve me of duty. He successfully, albeit nicely, blocked my attempts to get an emergency increase in Ankara's intel billets to two so I could stay. He parried my attempts to keep even a minor role in the day-to-day intel affairs while I waited for my rotation date. I would have done exactly the same. Damn.

All too soon, I found myself beginning my last year in the United States Air Force at the Pentagon. I took over management of the conglomeration of intelligence programs that included the one I'd worked on at Kelly AFB. That meant that I inherited a team of ten people who'd been in the war zone since ten days after the Iraqi invasion. These were people I'd worked with in San Antonio, in one case a young mother with a civilian husband, an infant, and small children at home. She was team leader. The responsibility kept me up at night. The only way I could think of to sleep again was to volunteer for the war zone. I was terrified they'd approve it but I couldn't send anyone, let alone former friends, anyplacc I wasn't prepared to go myself. But unlike in *M★A★S★H,* where Major Houlihan was always getting overnight reassignments, the real military doesn't work that way. I wasn't even allowed to fill out an official request. But at least I could sleep again. (All my team members made it home safely.)

Or I could have if I had not hated every moment of every hour of every day I spent there at the Pentagon. I never had a clue how to be effective in a place like that, where everything is subtext and behind-the-scenes machination. Secretaries, let alone lieutenant colonels, bested me in turf battles.

Which is not to say that I never had indecisive moments about staying in. After all, were I to play my cards right, my military future was limitless. I spent as much time as any other ambitious young officer fingering colonel's eagles, even general's stars, at Clothing Sales. But reality always came knocking at the door. Like being told that, because I'm black, it was unlikely I'd be chosen as a White House escort officer.

With my separation paperwork once again gathering dust in my desk drawer, I was looking for signs that leaving was a mistake. Turkey had kept me happy for a little while longer; might not something else? I found myself in a briefing room at the Pentagon with more than fifty of my fellow officers, yet not one of them objected when the major recruiting for this extra duty decided to tell this truth. When I'd asked why there were so few blacks in the prized annual photos he displayed of the escorts with the presidents, he'd first pointed out, rightly, that blacks were relatively few. "You have to understand," he added, "these escorts are seen as representing the United States to all sorts of foreign dignitaries and, well . . . you know."

Aghast, I'd waited for the room to explode, but the next officer just raised his hand and asked about the time commitment, the opportunity to hobnob with the guests . . .

Most surprising was the attitude of the few other black officers present. Though I was near tears I was also furious, and made myself sit through the entire presentation so I could confront the briefer. While we waited, I tried to mobilize the black officers to make a stand. I expected them to be furious at the major, at the Air Force, at cosmic injustice. They were furious all right. Furious with me.

"You know better than that," one seethed, and turned his back. "What did you expect him to say?" another hissed evilly, too low to be overheard. Others checked to see if the white folks were watching and rolled their eyes like I was a naive child. They moved away to shun me, to distance themselves from my career-busting militancy. I had broken the "one nigger" code of conduct: my job was not to buck the system head-on but to compete with them to see who'd be the one nigger in the photo (there was always at least one).

I left without confronting the major. Why bother? He was right. The spots for blacks would be held to a minimum, and the competition for those spots would be so fierce it was unlikely I'd be selected, because, well . . . you know.

Twelve years in uniform, yet I was not fit to represent my country. Just like my father forty years before, I was airbrushed, albeit before the fact, from our national consciousness. What was the real difference between that and the whites-only Laundromat of my youth? Erik listened helplessly when I called him at his Pentagon office in tears. I submitted my separation paperwork red-eyed and haughty.

As if all the portents weren't fully in place, then the William Kennedy Smith rape trial happened.

Until that moment it had never occurred to me that the outcome of my rape prosecution might have been different. Not once had I looked back in relief that he hadn't gotten away with it. How could he—he raped me and he knew it. To me, all that was required was for me to stand up and name my accuser; of course he was found guilty.

But all the Spineless Worm would have had to do was deny it. Had he not confessed, I realized as I watched that lying cad on television, he wouldn't even have gotten the slap on the wrist he did get. It would have been my word against his and he would have gotten off scot-free. I would have been even more humiliated than I was. It wouldn't have taken Dershowitz to make me look like the delusional nymphomaniac and vengeful harpy who can't face up to her own raging hormones that every rape victim is made out to be.

Didn't you spend the whole evening with him?

Didn't you defend and protect him? Come on now, you were flirting with him, weren't you?

Hadn't you been drinking for hours? Didn't you tell him you'd leave the door unlocked?

Weren't you already cheating on your boyfriend?

Why didn't you scream? Wouldn't the neighbors have heard you?

Why didn't you notify the authorities right away instead of going to sleep?

Didn't you stop to curl your hair the next morning? Weren't too upset, were you?

Didn't you lie in your statement—an official legal document—when you called the boyfriend who didn't care whether you lived or died your fiancé? What else are you lying about?

What a trusting fool I'd been. Thank God I'd had no idea what I was doing when I pressed charges.

I was aware that I had not dealt well with the trauma of my rape. When the Kennedy Smith farce unfolded on television, I feared it would force me into an emotional crisis. I couldn't get it off my mind but I didn't want to alarm my mother. I'd never told her and I didn't want to alarm her with a breakdown now. So I packed her off to visit relatives. I took leave and watched the trial on TV, waiting to fall apart. But that's not what happened.

I wasn't sad. I didn't cry. I didn't have flashbacks but I did have trouble sleeping. I was too pissed off to doze off.

The Smith trial affected me more than the Clarence Thomas–Anita Hill debacle, though both were galvanizing. Having always eschewed identity politics as counterproductive, I now felt forced to revisit that decision. As well as I'd done, I would always be seen as black and female, regardless of all the other things I was. Sometimes they'd work for me, sometimes against. But they would always be relevant. A lifetime of incidents convinced me that, though my instinct is to see myself simply as an American, I feel forced to see myself as African-American, as female.

I see it this way: in military intelligence, we weren't necessarily concerned with where our own forces actually were at any given moment. What we wanted to know was where the enemy *thought* our forces were. That's what's going to start a shooting war. In terms of my personal and political well-being, it only partially matters what I think I am. It's what my overlords think I am that really counts. That's what's going to get me shot at.

I'd played the game the mainstream, middle-class way, but it made little difference when push came to shove. I tried to buy my way in by abandoning other blacks, abandoning other women, by learning their language, adopting their ways. It worked, and it didn't work. We are a nation of factions. We should frame our decisions in terms of what's best for America, but we don't. It's what's best for farmers, what's best for my district, what's best for homeowners, what's best for noncustodial divorced fathers—what's best for me. To make matters worse, those who claim to speak for the inner cities, where my heart truly lies, too often have hidden agendas, debilitating baggage, or are simply untalented but well-connected apparatchiks.

I knew I could do better.

My goal, my selfish desire in choosing my next step, was to find a way into the public realm, to find a way to help unempowered women and blacks be heard. Not to get on TV, not to cavort with the rich and famous, not to declare myself the leader of a group of people I would avoid personal contact with at all costs. I knew I could do better.

My idea to create a venue wherein neighborhood blacks could substantively improve their lives never left me. It wasn't clear, however, what sort of education I needed to get there. Since I knew nothing about business (and wasn't interested in business per se, just the autonomy that entrepreneurship afforded), I knew I'd need the cachet of a fancy degree to give me credibility both with the neighborhood blacks and with the local leaders I intended to shake down. Also, I simply love school and wanted the full-time, daylight, hang-out-in-the-student-union experience I'd never had. All I could think of was a doctorate with internships spent learning about grants, local government, and running a foundation.

It all came together the day I happened upon a profile of Thurgood Marshall in *Washingtonian Magazine.* I bolted upright in my chair.

That man changed America and he did it with a J.D., the degree that highly verbal but amorphously talented people get when they don't know what else do with themselves. I had to have one, too.

I had no intention of practicing law. To me, the law will always be State Farm forcing me to pay for an accident that destroyed my property and injured me even though they admitted it wasn't my fault. It will always be Chrysler laughing at me secure in the knowledge that the law would do their dirty work for them. The law was the official blessing on my relatives' summary dismissals and evictions. The law made my rapist play volleyball for two months instead of punishing him. But that's precisely why the powerless need to learn how to wield the law, to protect themselves from the powerful who create and control it to protect their own interests. The very idea of practicing law left me cold. But a J.D.? That idea warmed me. The law persecutes the poor but education saves them; a J.D. I didn't intend to directly use was the perfect antidote to the persecution. I'd been around enough to know that those initials behind my name were all I'd need to be deemed officially capable of any endeavor I undertook.

Pragmatically, I also realized that if I got a doctorate, I could teach but I couldn't write a contract or sue an oppressor. But if I got a J.D., I could teach, I could write a contract, I could sue anybody who harassed me. For better or worse, attorneys can do anything in America. I could run a corporation, a nonprofit, a hospital. I could run for office or I could run a university. I could defend the falsely accused or prosecute the predators. I didn't understand how the legal profession worked then, so I also thought I could eliminate the need for a staff lawyer at my foundation if I could write and administer my own contracts, negotiate leases, incorporate nonprofits, and the like. Thankfully, I didn't understand enough then to know that it would take many years of practice before I could function as my own attorney.

With blissful ignorance, I looked at that photo of Marshall and heard the same voice I'd heard in basic training. This is it, it said. Attorney.

I never had another moment of doubt. I knew I didn't want to be a lawyer but that I had to go to law school. I was confident that, until I was ready to open my own organization, some opportunity to work for the betterment of the grassroots African-American community while thoroughly enjoying myself would present itself. I stopped reading *The Economist* and started reading *Ms., Essence, Black Enterprise,* and any other periodical, article, or book having to do with the forward movement of striving women and blacks. My international focus dissipated entirely.

Ironically, though it was my idea to attend law school, I had to be prodded to apply to the Ivy League. Erik, the Princeton-educated son of privilege, demanded to know why I was applying to Tulane and Emory but not the Ivy League. I had no reply. In the silence, I remembered that when he and I had first met in Ankara, I asked him if the language of the Princeton diploma on his office wall was Spanish. It was Latin. We were worlds apart.

For all my raised consciousness and hard-earned sense of wide possibility, the Ivy League had never crossed my mind. I'd thought myself bold and freethinking for applying to private law schools, but Yale, Harvard? Even when I was contemplating a doctorate, the University of Missouri at St. Louis was the only school I considered. I could only hold one personal paradigm shift in my head at a time—Ph.D.'s and J.D.'s were holy grails. Ivy League Ph.D.'s and J.D.'s? It made my head hurt to think about it. Self-doubting and neurotic to the end, I applied to eleven schools.

Accepting admission to Harvard Law School was my first consciously political act. It was the first and only time I ever benefited from affirmative action. Harvard routinely turns away students with perfect LSATs; after two weeks of evenings studying at my kitchen table (I was still on active duty), I ranked in the 81st percentile (i.e., only 19 percent scored higher). I had tested early to give myself enough time to readjust my strategy if necessary. Having scored so "low," I was planning to take a prep course when Erik stepped in again.

He cranked up that privileged-white-boy network they always deny the existence of and we made the crass calculation that, with the rest of my record, I would be admitted just about everywhere as is without troubling myself with a prep course, as do so many of Ivy League admittees. I thought long and hard about taking the course and raising my score simply on principle, but in the end decided to coast on affirmative action. As a younger woman, I would have relished besting the LSAT, if only so I could make whites eat crow whenever affirmative action came up. In my thirties, I'd learned to conserve my energy. It was there for me to take advantage of, so I did. I took the easy way. In my case, it's definitely true that affirmative action allowed me to avoid working my hardest.

I remain ambivalent about affirmative action, though. I had never benefited from it before because my record was outstanding, yet I was always thought to have done so. That used to infuriate me until I realized a few things. First, that it only infuriated me so because I craved white approval. Second, that whites seem to have no trouble living with the knowledge that minorities believe them to be the historic and continuing beneficiaries of built-in affirmative action; if they can shrug it off, so can I. Third, whites will believe you needed affirmative action to best them even when they can see you outperforming them. Affirmative action supporters are often among the most patronizing and dismissive. Too many whites need to believe all blacks are innately inferior and will do so despite the evidence of their own eyes. Now, having accepted that you can rarely change people's hearts and minds, only how you allow them to treat you, I don't care what white people, qua white people, think.

I'm still ambivalent about affirmative action, though, because I believe in the merit system. Or I would if it actually existed. Merit is not what determines who gets what, elite protestations to the contrary. As well, we have no way of gauging the merit of the marginalized. Nor do I accept that a white kid with perfect LSATs and no other accomplishment is more qualified. While I'll admit I got into Harvard through a loophole, I would never have gone had I thought myself unqualified; test scores can't possibly tell a person's whole story. I had no fear of Harvard or of those with higher LSATs. Qualified respect, but no fear. I had no qualms about facing them in a courtroom, a boardroom, or the op-ed page. Non–Ivy League lawyers beat the pants off those prepsters every day in court, every day within their own law firms. Your LSAT score won't help you during final argument.

As much as anything else, though, it maddened me that the debate focused on the interests of the black bourgeoisie; by the time they are applying for college and graduate school, the die has long been cast for the vast majority of blacks. They're destined for mailrooms, french-fry vats, and the backseats of squad cars, not Ivy-covered walls and spring-break ski trips. The genius of the black bourgeoisie is its ability to pass its interests off as the interests of all blacks. The focus should be at the other end, on primary education for those minorities who don't live in the suburbs, attend private schools, or have mentors guiding them to the mainstream. I saw little real difference between the well-off blacks demanding help getting into Harvard and the whites trying to keep it all to themselves by keeping everybody else poorly educated and self-hating. If it's got to be "us" against "them," I'm going to make sure my team wins.

Through my studies and ruminations, it had become clear to me that the way out and up for blacks was education and entrepreneurship. Conservative and pessimistic at my core, I had no faith in government-based solutions, if only because governments change. Hard work, to my peasant mind, is the only thing that can be counted upon to work. Better for us to take the reins of our destiny in our own hands and alter our relationship to the status quo fundamentally rather than at the margins with welfare, sporadic job-training initiatives, affirmative action, and the like.

I knew that it was partially the loss of hands-on neighborhood access to blacks who had made it that was responsible for conditions there. It appears to be impossible for most of those outside the inner city to understand how alienated many of its denizens feel from the mainstream, but it's all too true. Having a well-educated, well-traveled Ivy League grad living and running a neighborhood-based remedial education and entrepreneurial development center two doors down would make it that much easier for them to believe that they too could do big things. When I was reassigned as an officer, I made it a point to leave my office door open so all the enlisted blacks who "happened" by as word spread could get a good look. Black officers were still few, so I knew what they were thinking as they checked me over from head to toe like a new breed of black person—*Maybe, just maybe, I could do that too.* Black pilot friends told me that invariably when enlisted blacks on the flight line spied their dark faces at the controls of a fighter jet, the troops would stand straighter, salute more smartly, make a point of going the extra mile. Real role models with concrete accomplishments—and not just pampered black elites working their connections to get ahead—give black people real hope.

Also, Harvard would allow me to confront head-on the negativity and defeatism too many of us rely on to excuse our mistakes and our apathy. Only someone like me could look them in the eye and call "Bullshit" to their protestations that "the man" won't let you get ahead. What they needed to realize was that the man can't stop you from getting ahead, not if you're determined. Mae Jemison, the black astronaut, would always seem larger than life when seen from a TV screen. If they saw her down the block mowing her lawn and schlepping groceries in between interviews, people would find it easier to believe that they could do what she had done.

Also, I knew that having a Harvard J.D. would give me a penis. A white one. Harvard Law School would make me an honorary white man for the first ten minutes of a business meeting, long enough for me to demonstrate my mettle. Without that, a black working-class female with night school degrees would have a much more difficult time building bridges between the government, educational and financial communities, and the black community. No one knew better than me that getting ahead was as much about having the right connections and the proper items on your résumé as anything else. I knew that Harvard turns heads and raises appreciative eyebrows.

Finally, I just plain wanted it. I needed to best Harvard. Though it would have chewed me up as an eighteen-year-old—because it would have—I had to experience that which had so terrified me as a young person.

In the end, I was hounded by law schools. I was flooded with calls, letters, scholarship offers, and personal attention. This time, I had lively conversations with all comers and was amused when they sicced their Black Law Students' Association presidents on me. I was admitted everywhere but Stanford and terminally wait-listed at Yale.

Somewhere, my father was laughing at the thought of me in law school, let alone Harvard. Not at me but with me, because I thought it was pretty damned funny, too.

Next, I went looking for scholarships. I buried myself in the stacks at the public library and applied for about a hundred and fifty different awards. Months later, I got a phone call from the Earl Warren Scholarship office administered through the NAACP Legal Defense and Educational Fund. Valhalla, for me, having been established and directed for so long by Thurgood Marshall himself. I'd applied for their biggest award, $1,500 (a year at HLS costs about $30,000). They were calling to find out if I'd compete for a new $30,000 award they'd just established (this was only its second offering) through a joint venture with Shearman & Sterling, a major New York law firm. It had set aside its winnings from a pro bono lawsuit. Soon, I took my first trip to Manhattan for the competition. I came home a winner.

Just like at OTS, I pared my possessions down to the indispensable.

Part of my dilemma had been figuring out how to hold on to all my identity-buttressing possessions while making such a profound lifestyle change. I had to accept, though, that I couldn't. It all had to go because I couldn't take anything with me. I couldn't afford to maintain anything, not if I was to be free. Autonomy meant responsibility. It meant minimalism.

I paid off my mother's car, sold mine, and gave her everything we didn't sell, donate, or pitch from our cushy trilevel Lorton, Virginia, town house. I paid off my few bills and emptied my bank accounts, my IRA, even the savings bonds I'd bought as a green airman. My life looked like the Oregon Trail, former treasures jettisoned at every turn. I never missed any of it. Walking away from all my possessions was a heady experience—I felt so free I sang as I made my last trip from the homeless shelter I gave my library to. I was astounded remembering how hard I'd schemed to hold on to all those . . . those things when it was so clear that everything I really needed was in my head and in my heart.

Mama had decided to move to warm Charlotte, North Carolina, where my oldest sister and her family live. Born to be best friends, Erik and I broke up, then moved in together as roommates in Arlington, Virginia. For the first time since I was sixteen, I didn't have even one job, wasn't taking even one class.

PARTY PEOPLE

I was discharged in early 1992. While I waited for the next adventure to begin, I cast about for a way to get my feet wet in activism. I couldn't afford not to work but I was determined not to get just some job. When a DNC fund-raiser called to hit us up for a donation, Erik talked me up to the caller, stressing my admission to Harvard Law School. Just as I'd gambled, Harvard opened doors before I ever arrived on campus. Soon, I was meeting with the volunteer coordinator. You have to have connections to get a job there, so I jumped at the chance to stuff envelopes and field constituent calls without pay.

It immediately became apparent that I have no future in party politics. Having never yet encountered a problematic professional situation that talent and hard work couldn't cure, or a poisonous office environment I couldn't remain on the fringe of, I just focused on my work. The money would come eventually. I understood about paying your dues and had no qualms about not starting at the top. Soon, they were promising me the next opening. When Mark Gearan, the executive director of the Democratic Governors Association and a senior Clinton adviser, needed an assistant for the duration of the campaign, I was the only choice. Now I encountered the first problematic professional situation that talent and hard work couldn't cure, the poisonous office environment I couldn't remain on the fringe of.

Yes, I should have realized that a political organization would be intensely political. That everyone, especially in an election year with West Wing offices dangling like luscious fruit, would be mud-wrestling for position. But I was leaving in September, why wrestle with me? Yet the DGA staff barely tolerated me, barely acknowledged my existence. I wasn't attacked or sabotaged, just regarded with great suspicion and frozen out. One, now a big shot at the White House, wouldn't even reply when I spoke to him. It didn't matter that I was DNC staff, not DGA, because access is the gold standard in politics and I had access to Mark and to anyone he had access to if I wanted to play the game. I answered Gearan's phone and had access to his Rolodex (which *did* contain the names and numbers of everyone who was anyone in Democratic politics. I used to flip through it in awe). They must have imagined I was buttonholing George Stephanopoulos and James Carville for private chats and circulating my résumé to their private fax numbers so as to coattail Mark to the White House. I wasn't. I was simply taking messages and totaling taxi-cab receipts while waiting for law school to start. I was just trying to learn whatever I could for my own activist future back in north St. Louis.

The blacks at the DNC dismissed the DGA staff as racist, telling me to watch my back, that the DGA had never had a black staffer. The blacks at the DNC were among the most disgruntled I have ever encountered—most seemed to think everything and everyone was racist, especially the DNC and the Democratic party. In their defense, it is true that while lots of blacks pushed mops and delivered mail at the DNC, few were professionals. On the other hand, one of the few black male staffers, and one of the loudest grumblers about white racism, so thoroughly sexually harassed me (calling me "Tootsie Roll" and "lollipop" while licking his lips), I hated to come to work. There for only a few months and forced to file a sexual harassment complaint against one of the only professional blacks at the DNC? I was too much of a tribalist to do it. (Instead, I went ghetto on him and handled it privately.) But who else has he done that to? What young girl new to the ugly ways of brutes like him? I shudder to think that he may well have pressured some unsteady young woman into being alone with him (he was relentless in the face of weeks of direct requests for him to stop).

My biggest disappointment was that I never had a conversation with anyone there about America, helping people, or ways to fund more Head Start slots, just about ways to advance our own careers. I was as ambitious as anyone on the planet; it just seemed to me that by focusing on the work, both the accolades and the personal satisfaction would come. They saw it the other way around—first get the gig, then think of the work. Everyone talked *politics*—what the Republicans were up to, how Clinton should run his campaign—but few talked about ideas, philosophy, real people's lives. I'd expected idealism but found mostly bureaucracy. Of course, I wasn't trying to make a career there. I could afford idealism.

Still, it was a very cynical place. There wasn't even an 800 number; constituents had to pay to have their voice heard. I let them talk and lied to them that Ron Brown, DNC chair at the time, would personally hear of their concerns. He wouldn't. I sent out canned letters in response to the many we got from constituents, canned letters that were an insult in their nonresponsive bureaucratese.

I helped administer the summer intern program, unpaid jobs at the DNC for college students. It turned out that some are less unpaid than others. One daughter of a famous Southern politician kept calling asking me about her slot and her paycheck. I tried to tell her that those jobs didn't pay and that since I hadn't seen her application, I was pretty sure she wasn't going to be an intern. Frustrated but ever polite, she fretted, "I don't *do* applications. You don't understand!" She was right. I didn't. I was given a few names and instructed to pass them directly on to a senior staffer. That woman and several other children of the rich, famous, and well-connected not only "won" those coveted, hotly contested slots, they were paid. All their fathers were millionaires.

It should have soothed Mark's DGA staff to see that he treated me like office furniture. No one abuses a desk lamp or fax machine, and Mark, a true gentleman and genuinely nice man, never abused me. He just treated me like a desk lamp or fax machine—useful for performing low-level administrative functions and possessing no feelings. I had no qualms about totaling his receipts or fetching him lunch. He was a busy, hardworking man with a lot on his mind; often, I brought him lunch or sodas without his having to ask. He was so busy, in fact, he barely used me. I was bored out of my mind, but all I could do was wait for work. Assistants are always promised that they'll get to do substantive work, and it's almost always a lie; either you do nothing or nothing but scut work. So be it. Frustrated or not, I was in it for the adventure, I still had a place in the HLS class of 1995. Assisting him at the party convention in New York, I told myself, would be reward enough. Surely there would be real work to do there, and what exciting circumstances! In the meantime, I just read the paper, answered his phones, and hung with staffers who were also nice people.

There's a cafeteria in the basement of the DNC operated by an Asian family. I used to go down there just to watch the young black girl they had out front work so hard sweat poured down her face. Toiling away at her dead-end job, she just tried so diligently and cared so much. Mangling her verbs and dangling her participles, she sang out all the regulars' orders before we could speak. She scrubbed tables and counters like they were her own, she unpacked potato chips as if they were for starving refugees. The owners rarely gave her direction, they didn't need to.

All that talent, all that drive, all that willingness to work. No, all that *need* to work. If she were to commit a crime, or smoke crack, or have babies she couldn't support, we'd design programs around her. Instead, she was a ghetto kid who did everything we asked of her—high school diploma, no black marks on her record, backbone of her family and her neighborhood. Her reward? Invisibility. Complete disregard. All her talents left undeveloped. Consigned to the steam table for the rest of her life. How long will it be before the light goes out in her heart? How long before she's snarling at customers from across a DMV counter and scheming to get away with as little work as possible? How long before she "upgrades" to a mailroom or a security guard's uniform and the midnight shift reading trashy black novels? She'd do better to rob this place, I'd think. Then she'd get some attention.

I used to look at her and think: Come away with me.

But where?

Watching the mid-level DNC operatives around me, I realized that I was out of my league and gratefully so. Most had senators, their Choate roommate's CEO dad, or their trophy wife's aristocratic sorority sisters pulling strings for them. As we got closer to the convention and looming victory, the jockeying for postvictory positions was nauseating. Mark traveled constantly and took few of the hundreds of calls that came for him when in. He returned virtually none. People gave up and had no choice but to give me the message to pass on. I took many a long-winded, whiny, or nakedly bloodthirsty call, some from people soon to be occupying slots in the Clinton White House. I hope to never again witness people behaving so badly. People called who'd gone to third grade or Boy Scouts with Mark and who now wanted a job in politics. Mostly, though, it was party insiders wanting me to pass messages to Mark about "something very, very bad you should know" about a competitor. They'd bray that so-and-so muckety-muck had promised some perch to them and they damn well better get it. Muckety-mucks called to have me tell Mark that so-and-so is his son's best friend and, well . . . you know. Many kissed up to me shamelessly, trying to buy my help with fake camaraderie or promises of their future patronage. O beautiful for spacious skies.

As summer and the Democratic National Convention in New York neared, Mark was promoted to being Al Gore's campaign manager and the air around him thickened with excitement—the press of bootlickers was unbearable and his phone rang nonstop. One young woman joined the queue of Mark's never-returned calls. Soon, she was calling twenty times a day and desperate enough to try to enlist my aid, something about a job that her mother, the best friend of a DNC pooh-bah, had arranged. Mark never told me anything so I couldn't help her. Eventually she started showing up. I gradually came to understand that she was assisting Mark too. Except she, who was neither yet twenty-one nor a college graduate, wasn't answering phones. She was doing research, going to meetings with Mark. Once we got to the convention, which I expected to be my payoff for having been a faithful lackey, this young woman was accompanying Mark to high-level strategy meetings, riding in motorcades with him, showing up in the background on the evening news. I, on the other hand, got to sit doing nothing in the staff room while everyone kept asking me who that was that had my job.

I was completely demoralized. Pure and simple—my feelings were hurt. What hurt most was knowing that Mark wasn't a bastard. It never registered with him that his giving a bigwig's daughter a cool job that (let's face it) any bright person could do meant more than that now said bigwig owed him a favor. I didn't even exist on his list of people or things to consider.

I was through the looking glass in a world where basic civil behavior and decent manners had no meaning whatsoever. And why was that? Because I lacked importance. I had no protectors, no name. I was nobody. But this wasn't personal. It wasn't about hurting me. It barely concerned me. I was an ant. No one sets out to step on ants. That just naturally happens when they roam among giants.

I had to face the fact that I lacked the stomach for politics.

The man who'd parceled out jobs like mine at the DNC had taken a liking to me and listened helplessly while I cried on his shoulder about having been so unceremoniously, so publicly dissed.

"Debra, this is how this world works," he said. "Mark likes you. He told me so. Imagine what might happen if someone was actually gunning for you. Get out now because this is nothing to the things I've seen. Go on to law school and don't look back."

Mark never called for me, so I stopped even going to the staff office. I went shopping. I saw Broadway shows. I watched the convention on TV. My only joy was terrifying my replacement whenever she happened to cross my path. All I had to do was give her the look of death and she ran. Too bad mom couldn't steal someone else's backbone for her.

Outside Madison Square Garden one day, I struck up a conversation with a black female attorney on Hazel Dukes's staff. Dukes, since disgraced, was a NAACP grande dame and a well-known New York State politician of long standing.

She asked me about the paucity of blacks in leadership positions at the DNC, Ron Brown and Alexis Herman notwithstanding, and on Clinton's senior election staff in general. I had to admit that there weren't many. I was elaborating that the *real* problem was less the lack of blacks per se than the lack of committed activists who thought beyond their own thirst for power and proximity to the powerful. As it happened, Dukes walked by and proved the point for me.

The woman called her over and asked me to tell her what I'd just told her. Just a few sentences in, Dukes interrupted.

"You're wrong," she scolded. "I'm *very* close to Governor Clinton. Just yesterday, I was on the private plane. I talk to him all the time, he considers me a confidante. I've been to the governor's mansion."

I, I, I, me, me, me.

There was a self-satisfied simper on her face. She preened and looked around as she spoke to see who was looking at her, clearly hoping to be recognized, preferably by a news camera crew.

"Ms. Dukes," I said, "don't you think you might be being bought off with a few perks? So you rode on the private plane, how does that fix inner-city schools? What did you all talk about, real issues or how good the meal was? I know who's in those strategy meetings with Clinton and it aint you, it's hardly any of us."

She sighed dramatically, then rolled off a list of the usual-suspect black politicians who'd been with her on the candidate's private plane, how Clinton called to wish her a happy birthday, etc. She never offered an analysis of the role of blacks in national Democratic politics that wasn't about her own individual importance or one of her equally hooked-up professionally Negro politician friends. We both thought the other a complete fool and parted with mutual disdain. With leaders who can be bought off with a plane ride, no wonder the Dems take the black vote completely for granted.

The night of Jesse Jackson's speech to the convention, I was the only black in the DGA's jam-packed skybox at Madison Square Garden. There were three Hispanics, all uniformed waiters. The air was giddy with incipient victory; everyone knew we were going to beat the Republicans. I was among the few listening to Jackson orate about the poor and the downtrodden; most were partying way up in the air, above it all. A young woman who was shepherding one of the elderly party grandes dames (a famous old-guard politician's sister) tapped me on the shoulder.

"Another mineral water, please," she asked sweetly, and indicated the wheelchair-bound old lady.

I was in evening clothes. The waiters were in uniforms. I had a drink in my hand. The waiters had trays in theirs. I was doing nothing. They were working hard. I pointed to them as the polite young woman waited politely.

"*That's* a waiter," I said. I pointed to myself. "*This* is a Harvard Law School student."

I never heard the end of Jackson's speech. I went off to law school and never looked back.

CHAPTER SEVEN

BREAKING RANKS

This was the frame of mind in which I arrived at Harvard Law School: militant and distrusting. Of my putative allies. The official enemy I understood quite well.

Washing up on the shore of the Ivy League was a surreal experience. Wonderful. But surreal. Something amazing happened every day of my first semester there, like finding out that one needn't work very hard at Harvard Law School.

Many students never work another day over the next three years once admitted to HLS. As the saying there goes, "Times passes and so will you," or "The hardest thing about HLS is getting in." Gentlemen's B's and C's were de rigueur.

To my surprise, it was a fairly unintellectual environment. People cut class for weeks on end but they didn't do anything interesting instead; they watched *Melrose Place,* slept a lot, and bitched about how much they hated HLS. They read schlock books, when they read, and the men were the least manly I'd yet encountered. The typical uniform for my average male classmate was rumpled Harvard sweats straining over a beer belly. The women put a hell of a lot more effort into their appearance and constantly bemoaned the lack of male interest. The male classmate who fit this description was also very likely to be catching the "fuck bus" from Harvard to Wellesley so he could date teenage undergrads who listened in rapt silence when he spoke. Watching a group of barely shaving, barely tall-enough-to-ride-the-teacups-at-Disneyland Lords of the Universe swagger around the Hark (our student union), one friend of mine remarked, "Screw perfect LSATs. What this place needs is a height requirement."

Having worked hard throughout prep school, high school, and college, many of my classmates considered graduate school their chance to relax and reap the benefits of their neurotic-compulsive, overachieving youth. Most of my classmates were just there to get drone jobs in mega–law firms, which is what gave HLS a "vo-tech" air not unlike that at O'Fallon Tech, where I'd prepared for a secretarial career. It was confounding to me to hear twenty-year-olds planning to be unhappy, scheduling it in on their day runners like a doctor's appointment. They'd say the most amazing things, like "You're going to be miserable anyway, so you gotta make sure you get the most money." Even more didn't know why they were there at all, just that it was the only item remaining unchecked on their external-validation to-do list. To be sure, HLS had its hard-charging social reformers, rabid conservative activists, and serious scholars, but it was the sad sacks I was unprepared for. The twelve years since kindergarten spent unimaginatively grades-focused robbed too many of them of the ability to *feel* their educations anymore. But how could anyone take Harvard for granted?

My classmates threw the school newspaper and the weekly admin newsletter we got on the Hark floor, never mind that the cleaning staff—most our parents' age—always placed huge bins strategically. The floor was white with discarded paper on Thursdays and Fridays. They openly read newspapers in class, carried on pointless conversations at full volume, and drowned out the last five minutes of every class snapping their binders open and shut putting their things away. Professor Meltzer, our criminal law professor, kept us late one day to finish a point. One of my young classmates stormed dramatically out, furious. He was waiting right outside the door to fume with his friends. A professor would be teaching his heart out, trying desperately to get people to participate—they'd just let him twist in the wind. I'd be thinking, Hey, the guy's working up there, and raise my hand. I only got called on Socratically twice in three years because I readily participated. One of the most dedicated teachers at HLS, Professor Rakof, was walking backwards while making a point once and tripped. The class tittered. These, my betters?

Most professors called on students randomly in their assigned seats, so the cowards "backbenched," i.e., sat in the unassigned back row of our huge classrooms. This though most professors were perfectly pleasant and helped you arrive at a passable answer. God forbid they should have just looked the professor in the eye and said, "I don't know." Some profs picked a row at the beginning of class and cut a swath down it. Twice, I saw women in the chosen row scurry red-faced out of class rather than be called on. How many of them had perfect LSATs? Twelve years of real-world contingencies and briefing senior officers who'd rather bite your head off than let you take a breath took the starch out of Arthur Miller and Alan Dershowitz for me. I respected them but I had no fear of them (Miller is the tyrant; Dershowitz is beloved by students).

I was very serious about my studies at HLS (as were many of my classmates), especially the first semester of the first year, which pretty much decides your entrée into fast-track law. Many at HLS affect to hate the place; that's immaturity and upper-class "cool pose," I think. They would have kidnapped the dean's mother to get in, yet they acted as if they'd been shanghaied by a press gang once they got there. I had the time of my life. I knew exactly how fortunate I was. As well, I was blown away by the luxury of time and resources that faced me. Never before had I had only one thing to do—I had more free time in law school than I've ever had before in my life. I'd been helping out at home, working, and going to night school for so long that, faced now with a few hours of classes and studying each day, I was dancing in the streets. Also, being older, I knew how to organize my time and I knew how to stay cool under the pressure of HLS's dreaded Socratic method. Every day, I was whispering grateful prayers of thanks to my parents and to the United States Air Force—I'll never face tougher standards.

The first thing I did was join BLSA (the Black Law Students' Association). It did not go well. I hate working in groups (they're never serious enough) and I hate meetings (ditto); the Air Force is the only organization I had ever joined voluntarily. Second, I was eleven years, on average, older than everyone else. Most of them were at least middle class, and, of course, there was an in crowd that put all other in crowds to shame because so many had (or claimed to have) important connections. From one moment to the next, BLSA was a fashion show, a politburo meeting, a hotbed of revolution, a social club, and a refuge from the white world we'd chosen. In short, it was a typical association of pampered twenty-somethings who couldn't decide whether or how to take themselves seriously.

From my crochety point of view, it was all very undergraduate. I'm critical of them, but I actually felt maternal toward them. I could see them trying on different personae (which, after all, is what college is for) and trying to gauge others' perceptions of them. One minute they were upper class and blasé about Gstaad, the next they were ghettofied and "down with the peeps, know what ahm sayin?" I understood that. I certainly wasn't the same person at thirty-three as I'd been at twenty-two and I'd certainly tried on and discarded several mutually exclusive personae; it didn't seem fair for me to assert myself (something told me they didn't crave my leadership the way my OTS flight mates had). Also, I was pretty sure I'd be blown off if I tried since I rarely saw things the way they did.

BLSA, by charter, exists for the benefit of its members and God knows they didn't need my help looking out for their own best interests. Anyway, I was always putting my foot in my mouth with them. Once, I was talking to a black classmate who is the son of a judge. I liked John; he never pretended to be a ghetto boy and never troubled himself much with what other blacks thought of him. We were so far apart in life experience, though. He'd come from California and was bemoaning the expense of relocating his things. I suggested he do what I'd done—get rid of all his possessions except for the bare necessities—and replace dishes, furniture, and such at thrift stores. He stopped mid-step and looked at me like I was recommending we eat from garbage cans. I withdrew the suggestion.

As always, I was clueless as to how to navigate the social shoals of large groups. By the end of the first few weeks, the social doors were shut. There'd been a black admittees' weekend in April which I'd thought extravagant. Most everyone else had come, though; the cliques had clicked before I knew what was happening. Since cliques have personalities, the window of opportunity quickly shut on establishing an atmosphere of open dialogue at BLSA. In the end, my high tolerance for solitude was my biggest impediment to social mobility; I voluntarily spent 90 percent of my time alone happily reading, renting foreign films, and working out. But when Bobby visited, I barely saw him. I was terrified the campus cops had him on lockdown for being big, black, and obviously non-Harvard. Instead, he'd melded right in with my classmates. For days after his visit, my phone rang with people looking for him. He simply expects to fit in, and so does.

Also, Bobby was exotically "authentic" and I wasn't, even though we're siblings, raised in the same household. Knowing he was a huge rap fan, I took him to a panel on the significance of hip-hop held at the beginning of his visit, before anyone knew he was my brother. Wide-eyed with stunned disbelief at the pomposity and postmodern gobbledygook he was hearing, I couldn't help laughing at him.

"Welcome to my new world," I said.

"You need to think about moving," he joked back, shaking his head.

I finally persuaded him to offer his own comments. Even the rappers on the panel hung on his every word. People tripped over themselves trying to draw him out, "down" as he was with street lingo, the bona fides of a waiter, and a rough-hewn "street" exterior. I, indeed anyone who criticized them (especially women), was routinely cut off, ignored, and generally dismissed. I got the back of the hand several times as "not understanding the typical black's reality" from millionaire rap stars and Exeter grads, presumably because I both spoke mainstream English *and* disagreed with them. To our great amusement, Bobby and I were specifically contrasted (him: relevant; me: irrelevant) several times, with comments such as those recommending I spend more time with "real brothers" like him.

I forced myself to go to BLSA meetings for my first year, though I dreaded them more and more as time passed. They were typical students—no meeting ever started or ended on time. No one had ever accomplished the task he'd agreed to perform. No one could disagree with the party line without having his Négritude questioned. Why is it always that the biggest oaf has the loudest mouth, the most forceful personality, and is so persuasive to people who are perfectly reasonable away from the group?

At one meeting, we were debating our response to both Colin Powell's speaking at graduation and the gay students' group's plan to protest. He was still chairman of the JCS then, and his opposition to gays in the military was a hot topic. The gay students' group had sent us what is one of the most diplomatic, neighborly, and reasonable letters I've ever seen explaining why they'd be protesting his visit and assuring us that it had nothing to do with race, only that one slice of his politics. Whoever penned that letter has my admiration, writer to writer.

A consensus seemed to be forming that we could take the protesters at their word and stay out of it while we formulated our own response to his visit. One of the Beautiful People changed before our very eyes from suave party boy to Malcolm X lite. Spittle flew as he lapsed into field-hand-speak and fulminated about how "the white man come up in here and we house niggers s'pozed to run do what he tell us." It went on and on. Any minute, I expected him to break character and lead us in laughter at his joke. He finished his spiel and turned back to the Beautiful Woman he'd been romancing before he took the floor.

It was unhelpful, it was an act, and it was silly. Part of me wanted to laugh and part of me wanted to cry, because it's forceful personalities like his that dominate the discourse in the black community and signal the rest of us to conduct ourselves in this defensive, self-conscious, dishonest, and ultimately masturbatory manner. To our credit, even though he wasn't the only person who saw it this way, we published a letter supporting Powell in glowing terms but also supporting homosexuals' right to serve their country. Many more of us disagreed with the Head Negroes than made a point of it, obviously.

At BLSA meetings, I'd sit with two older friends (one ex-Army) who were also doing their best to go along with the program. Afterward, we'd go for drinks and try to make sense of the ridiculous things we'd just heard. Except for sporadic appearances, none of us stuck it out much into spring semester. As another friend put it, "For them, there's only one way to be black and it aint *my* way."

Blacks at HLS were in a difficult spot and I felt the strain as much as anyone else. We knew we were in a high-visibility situation and we all fluctuated between being representatives of the race and being selfish individuals. This led to some silly and some harrowing situations. More than anything else, though, Harvard is a silly place and the politics often reflect that.

Here's a typical scenario: in our first year crim class, one of the least impressive black women who ever lived objected on racist grounds to Professor Meltzer's hypothetical involving unopened crates of stereo equipment in a tenement apartment and the likelihood of their being stolen. Being both dumb and a bad loser, she wouldn't let it go, so the class ended up having to vote as to whether we thought it more likely that said boxes in a mansion or in a tenement were stolen. I could have strangled her.

In a housing law and policy class, Professors Jean Charn and Duncan Kennedy were detailing the history of ethnic housing patterns in the Boston area in the pre–Civil War period and how government policies affected them. This same woman accused them of racial insensitivity because they failed to account for the housing patterns of the large numbers of blacks she claimed lived there then. The next class, the professors (two of the most activist leftists at HLS) distributed information detailing how less than 2 percent of the area's population was black during the relevant period, and therefore insignificant in our discussions. This woman and her all too numerous ilk were excellent arguments against affirmative action.

This woman was actually dumb (a rarity at HLS. Lazy, we had lots of, but even the laziest usually was also frighteningly smart); disingenuousness was a much bigger problem. In another crim class, the usual argument erupted about police harassment of blacks. Professor Meltzer, to his credit, handled one of HLS's most controversial classes with firm grace; we never knew what his opinion was, yet he orchestrated the class discussion with precision, bringing out all sides of the debate while (pretty much) keeping the lid on. In this instance, however, I can't help feeling he dropped the ball.

Again Professor Meltzer asked for a show of hands: how many people had been stopped by the police? Nearly every hand in the class went up (not mine, though; I've never been stopped for other than traffic infractions and never been badly treated). Whites looked around with smug jubilance at the forest of arms in the air. But the inquiry ended there. Professor Meltzer didn't ask why they'd been stopped, how they'd been treated, or whether they'd been charged with anything. Suspicious, I took an informal poll and found out that most of my white classmates whose hands were raised had in mind perfectly benign episodes at their Ivy League campuses or chichi neighborhoods where the police had actually helped them. The context of the debate was adversarial police stops, yet that crucial element was ignored.

While I think the professor's lapse was just that, a lapse, disingenuousness and hypocrisy were rampant at HLS, not least among black students. Professor Randy Kennedy, black and a well-known criminal law and social theorist, was often dismissed by black students as an Uncle Tom and a sellout. I wasn't familiar with him so I listened carefully early my first year to a group discussion about how his failure to publicly join the faculty diversity movement proved his self-hatred and cowardice.

"Why does he have to weigh in? Why does he even have to have an opinion on faculty diversity—just because he's black? Maybe he's focused on other issues," I said.

But they had an "amen corner" going, most agreeing with each other that Kennedy's silence condemned him as an Oreo. Few even addressed my argument that the First Amendment applied among blacks, that you can't presume to know what his silence means, and, most of all, that he had the right to not believe in (or not even care about) faculty diversity as long as his reasons were intellectually defensible. They were so cruelly dismissive of him, I found myself in the library researching him; who was this man who was so viciously dissected and found wanting?

I liked what I read; Kennedy is a free-range intellectual, loving, but not beholden to his tribe. I dropped off a package of my own writing to him and he asked me to become one of his research assistants. He was the first person to publish me, in his (now defunct) journal *Reconstruction*.

From my perch as his research assistant, I got to see many of the same students who spit on his very name queue up to suck up. They came for those all-important letters of recommendation and for the grant money he controlled. Basically, they came to turn him into a connection they could trade on since he was a nationally prominent intellectual, a Rhodes Scholar, and Thurgood Marshall's former Supreme Court law clerk. Butter wouldn't melt in their vituperative mouths as they puckered up to win his favor. One woman, who had just the night before derided him as "incog-Negro" and said she had no respect for him, was quite shocked when I stepped out from behind his door and asked her to share with him the interesting conversation she'd led last night at the BLSA meeting. I curried favor with professors, too, but only those I respected and always with a stack of my own work in my hands. Why come empty-handed for help?

Professor Kennedy was clueless as to the vipers in his nest; how could he not be, given the calculated dishonesty he faced? He'd mention some student he was helping with a clerk- or fellowship, and I'd have to bite my tongue. Once, after one of these Oscar-worthy performances ended, I teased him, saying, "When I was in the service, I always wondered if senior officers could tell when their asses were being kissed. Now I know: you can't. I'll have to remember that when I'm rich and powerful."

He had to chuckle, if ruefully. Most of them were probably only saying what they needed to say to be cool, in any event. Parroting the party line is rampant behind Ivy-covered walls.

The other nonparticipatory blacks I knew tended to also be either loners or involved in pursuits BLSA blacks had little use for (like heavy metal music); even so, we'd all bemoan our inability to fit in racially. Eventually, though, we gave up. The politics and social arrangements just played themselves out in a way we couldn't stomach and we drifted off to the activities that came naturally. Our absence, however, often made us racially suspect (just like Professor Kennedy's not toeing the party line on faculty diversity). That no longer silences me or affects my behavior—it just hurts. It hurts because the disapproval is of the playground variety—the Head Negroes make it known who is outside the pale and quickly punish those who fail to cut the offender off. You know it's juvenile and inexcusable, and yet you can't quite shrug it off. Even when I have little respect for them, as was true with those untested youngsters at Harvard, there is something about seeing other blacks' eyes go slanted in negative judgment when I break racial ranks on a matter of principle that wakes in me a pubescent need to pretend to be something I'm not. I resist it, I leave like minds to think alike, but it saddens me. From the start, I was suspect.

I joined a study group with four men, all white but one (he left the group later), all second-careerists except for one (but Patrick is an old man at heart). I chose them for their maturity, seriousness, and open-mindedness; I couldn't be in a study group where I wasn't free to speak my mind without being frozen out as either a political or a racial heretic. We met every day first year to study and argue for two to four hours, then I'd go back to my one-room, shared-bath in Wyeth Hall and study for four to six hours every day. I was in heaven. Such a luxury—all I had to do was think, read, and debate. I studied so much, I had to intensify my eyeglass prescription three times. The eye doctor at University Health Services actually laughed when I "read" the eye chart for her. Then she said, "First-year law student?" I hold it as a matter of pride that I did permanent damage to my eyes. And then grades came out.

First-semester first-year grades at HLS determine your future in the law to a significant extent. Certainly, for those whose goals in the law lie on the well-trodden path, they determine the next five years. Law review is largely decided by those grades coupled with a grueling writing competition. Grades and law review determine, for the most part, clerkships, the fast track to academia, and access to the best firms, government jobs, and prestigious public interest organizations. While one need only remain upright and conscious to get a B at HLS, earning a first-year A means you are indeed something special. I made B's.

For a couple of days, I was reeling, as were the other 95 percent of us who were now officially no longer the smartest kid in class. I got over it by writing about it in the school newspaper, the *Record*. First semester, the ridiculousness of daily life at Harvard had seemed so surreal to me, I'd written two humorous pieces about it for the paper. They'd asked me to do a regular column, but I'd declined because I thought it would interfere with my studies. Now, realizing that I could make those same B's with a lot less effort, I began a weekly *Record* column that I continued until graduation.

To this day, I have no idea why or how I started writing. I'd always done it effortlessly but never saw any future in it, if only because writers were gods to me. I never studied journalism and, at Mizzou, I dropped the only creative writing class I ever took after two weeks because it was so inane (the girls were writing bodice rippers about voluptuous redheads with one green and one blue eye and star-shaped birthmarks on their buttocks; the boys haiku about their bowel movements). Virtually overnight, though, page after page poured out of me;

I suppose it was finally having the luxury of entertaining thoughts not directly aimed at survival. In any event, I knew somehow not to try to figure it out and I still haven't tried; it's the only thing in my life I'm unself-conscious about.

The process of becoming a writer was a sublimely seductive experience. Little by little, writing crept into my thoughts like a cat burglar through a skylight or like the voices goading the insane. Lucky for me, my voices forced me to put words down on paper, not set empty warehouses on fire. I'd find myself walking through Harvard Square talking and laughing aloud to myself, forced to run home and boot up my computer. I worked most of the summers to help defray tuition, so I got up at dawn to write before work. The last third of the first and the full second half of my second summer I took off to write full-time, giving up $1,500 a week to do so. I left dates early to write. I woke up from REM sleep to type one sentence which had come to me, then went back to bed. I'd find sentences scribbled on notepads all over my room that I didn't remember writing. Writing made me a very unreliable friend and just a little bit crazier than I already was, because it made me not care what else I had to do to make the writing possible. Writing is like sex with someone whose sensuality overpowers you. I resist it even though I want it because the only way to experience it fully is to let go fully. So, I resist even though I know I'll enjoy it once I yield, but not *until* I yield. I was a pushover; I always gave in. By third year, I was skipping classes for the first time in my life and showing up unprepared (but never backbenching). I was writing a bad novel instead.

My scholarship included a summer job split between the NAACP LDF and the Shearman & Sterling law firm. There are only twelve summer slots at the LDF, for which hundreds of the nation's top students apply. Jobs at the top ten law firms are equally sought after, so not having to spend my spring semester desperately seeking employment was a blessing. We 1992 S&S scholars (two of whom were my classmates; one was at Stanford) split our summers between them, earning the weekly wages of a first-year associate—$80,000 a year.

I spent the summer of 1993 in Manhattan, living in a overpriced crackerbox room in the NYU Law School dorms. Most of the LDF interns were an interesting and committed bunch. Unfortunately, several were a sad continuation of DNC/HLS faux radicalism and hatefulness masquerading as a belief system. One woman, a Howard Law student, constantly berated us for attending Harvard, charging that we needed to be with whites to feel worthy, and kept insisting (unasked) that Howard was its academic equivalent. Even as we spoke, Howard Law was in danger of losing its accreditation, a situation it struggled with for many years. (That, of course, was mere white trickery.) Worse, this woman was a flat-out racist and thug. She exulted in her memories of terrorizing the white Howard Law students when they agitated for a White Law Students' Association. She and her comrades had circulated details of the whites' meeting and a goon squad of black students showed up to intimidate them. Her eyes glowed as she relived crowding the hallway outside their meeting and following them to their cars, all but yelling "KILL WHITEY!" She made no bones about the fact that they consciously intended to frighten them out of organizing (they were successful). As well, a fellow S&S scholar was treated like a race traitor for being a successful businessman, anti–affirmative action, and a social conservative; he might as well have been an open pedophile. Several claimed to disdain the S&S scholarship program itself as "pimping" for white law firms.

On the other hand, I worked half the time for Steven Hawkins on capital punishment cases. His intense, quiet commitment and abstention from silly leftist posturing were so inspiring I hated to take a lunch break. What if I broke my concentration and missed something? The other half, I worked for Dayna Cunningham, a firebrand voting rights lawyer who made me want to change my plans and practice. I simply avoided the lower level where the lazy, backbiting interns hung out.

The second half of the summer I spent at the law firm. Among the young, misery was palpable in the law firm air. Why they stayed, I still don't understand. What good is money you're never home to spend, a life spent at work you hate? In any event, the firm wasn't stupid; partners knew not to work summer associates as hard as the regular associates, so we enjoyed ourselves, mostly. I knew I was leaving on a particular day at a particular time, and the egghead in me loved researching lots of different issues on topics I knew nothing about. Nearly every day, there were expensive lunch outings that summer associates were all but ordered to attend; I sometimes couldn't get my work done because my partner-adviser Kathleen would order me to an outing. Several days a week, I ate at the best restaurants in New York. I was ferried about by car service. There were box seats at sporting events, disco outings, take-over-an-entire-video-arcade outings. Those of us in the scholarship program (i.e., black associates) were especially feted, since the firm had such a difficult time recruiting and retaining blacks, as do most major firms. The firm had no black partners, four black associates, and eight S&S scholars. I spent weekends in partners' Cape Cod summer houses and New Jersey estates. Ah, but the best-laid plans.

At the capstone event of the summer—a day at a luxurious country club on Long Island—pathetic racial politics almost made a mockery of all the firm's work in wooing blacks. After a day of swimming, tennis, softball, and exquisite food, everyone was drinking, eating the sumptuous banquet food, and dancing. One of two black women summer associates who were always crying racism went ballistic when the DJ told them he'd been ordered not to play the reggae she'd requested. She came over screeching.

"DID YOU HEAR THAT?! NO REGGAE! DID YOU HEAR THAT! CAN YOU BELIEVE THAT! NO BLACK MUSIC!"

Several of us tried to quiet her (screaming was unprofessional, to say the least) but she wouldn't be soothed. She marched back over to the (black) DJ and demanded to know who'd put reggae off-limits. He told her and she stormed back, lynch ropes and branding irons in her eyes. She bore down on the unsuspecting Hallie, the summer associate coordinator. Though Hallie phrased it diplomatically, it was obvious that she'd outlawed reggae because she thought it low class and foreign; easily two thirds of the music blaring for the past few hours was black, downright hip-hop. But the summer associate only became more outraged. Still screeching, still looking to fire us up to join her in taking a stand.

My five fellow S&S scholars (with one exception, who was the other racial hysteric and also the only scholar failing at the firm) happened to be at one table with a few scattered whites (why not? All-white tables aren't suspect). We were a pragmatic bunch, working diligently at the firm and enjoying the perks; perhaps our Ivy League schools, scholarships, guaranteed summer jobs, *and* guaranteed post-graduation jobs—none of which the reggae militant had—made us complacent. Maybe we had been bought off, like Hazel Dukes, with a little stroking. It was easier for us to stay calm, explain away insults. Maybe we really were fat, dumb, and happy. Or perhaps this was just stupid. Most of the music we'd been hearing all night was black; I dislike reggae too and was glad not to be hearing it. In any event, she was looking to us for backup, so sincere in her outrage her shoulders shook. When we tried to mediate, reminding her that Hallie had treated us like nieces and nephews throughout the year, far beyond the call of her job, and that perhaps we should hear her out, she stormed off to handle the situation alone.

I couldn't help it. I cracked up. One by one, we all did.

"Reggae?" we kept sputtering. "Reggae?"

Millions, literally millions invested in an attempt to lure blacks to the firm and it all comes down to reggae at the company picnic. For this Martin died on a filthy balcony? For this, four little girls died at Sunday school? It was so ridiculous, all we could do was smother our snickers and hope not to attract attention. This was one "black thing" I didn't want to have to explain.

Without our support, she marched off in disgust to John Greenblatt, the partner who was the heart and soul of the S&S scholars program (it was his Cape Cod house we summered in). Struggling with his recalcitrant toddler, he looked up long enough to express confusion and mumble, "You want reggae? Tell the guy to play some reggae."

Fired with righteousness, she marched back to the DJ like Fannie Lou Hamer marching into the 1968 Democratic National Convention. Head high, she demanded a reggae song.

Everyone but those of us who'd stood idly by during Shearman & Sterling's own March to the Selma Country Club stumbled, drunken and oblivious, onto the dance floor for reggae songs most were too high to even be aware of.

I started singing just loud enough for our table to hear. "Nobody knows de trouble . . ."

We lost it. Finally, the blacks broke up their segregated group as we scattered so no one would know we were all laughing at the same thing and wonder what it was.

I was finding that the better off some blacks become, the harder we look for reasons to remain discontented. Survivor's guilt and bourgeois self-involvement, I think. Like in the stand at the country club, blacks at Harvard squeal and squeal about less and less from their ivory tower when the gold-plated faucets get the least bit clogged.

My second and third years, I was a resident tutor at Currier House. In exchange for room and board, I lived in an undergraduate dorm and advised prelaw students. That decision was the final element that made my HLS years warm and homey, two descriptions most Harvardians will find incomprehensible. The first element was having invested in a study group that evolved into lifelong friendships. The second was my *Record* column, which was well received enough that HLS admin staff, professors, and fellow students often sought me out to pay compliments (even hugs) or stuffed my Hark box with laudatory notes. (My enemies wrote to the *Record* but they never personally confronted me.) Finally, of course, I had discovered writing itself, a passion so fulfilling that by second year I knew that was my true calling. I may be the only alum in history to have experienced the famously chilly, cutthroat Harvard University as a warm place.

To be sure, HLS's general atmosphere was sullen and neurotic, but the tutorial staff at Currier was composed of grad students and tenured professors from every discipline. I had no choice but to set aside my legal focus and listen to heated discussions about German literature, ethnomusicology, or particle physics because the only other lawyer in the house was my partner law adviser. It was a lively intellectual and social community. Parties were frequent and table conversations ranged from the deadly serious to the latest *Simpsons* or *Star Trek* episode (which we watched en masse). I was amazed to eventually learn how enormously talented and credentialed some of my fellow tutors were because they wore it so lightly. Perhaps they swaggered in their departments but few did at home. Of the twelve houses in the Harvard College system, Currier House was the Brady Bunch House. People came down to Sunday waffle brunch in bunny slippers and fuzzy bathrobes. We stayed at the tables long after dinner was over talking and laughing. Once a month, we held the Senior Common

Room, a cocktail party and dinner for dignitaries, scholars, and professors, with a few invited undergrads. This is where I interacted with Harvard's disgruntled black elite.

At my first Senior Common Room, I made a point of introducing myself to one of the few other blacks there, a middle-aged man who was a university administrator.

I said, "Hi. I'm Debra Dickerson, law student. I just moved here to Currier."

Apropos of nothing more than the color of my skin, he spat out churlishly, "You need to understand what kind of place this is. The racism is unbelievable. UNBELIEVABLE. You have to watch your back constantly."

The heat of his bitterness made me take a reflexive step back. I could feel the smile on my face shrivel up as he shrugged half the weight of four centuries of oppression into an even load between us.

It was like a French movie, strangers saying inexplicable things to each other. Downright pleadingly, so taken aback was I, I said, "Can't we go a minute without invoking white people? Can't we?"

"You think you're *in?* You think you're *Harvard?* That's what they want you to think. They'll get you if you let your guard down. Don't think you've *overcome* or anything like that just because you're at almighty Harvard. This place is awful, just awful." He looked like he might throw up.

He'd been on staff nearly twenty years, however. "*Someone* has to fight these people," he sighed bravely.

I turned away without another word. Oh, the self-pity of the pampered.

HLS quickly taught me two things: my lefty family was no more open-minded than my military one. Second, I wasn't nearly as far to the left as I'd thought, especially when it comes to the nature of activism. In the beginning, I wrote only satiric, often sophomoric *Record* pieces making fun of HLS. I didn't consciously eschew politics, I was just having so much fun being silly. Exploring my newly discovered zany side kept me pretty busy; I was like a baby who'd just discovered her toes. Also, I'd arrived at HLS just after the turmoil of the late eighties—the South Africa divestiture movement and, most contentious of all, the faculty diversity movement—and I was ambivalent about getting involved. Given the state of the nation, I was disgusted by the self-involvement of the privileged and could only care just so much whether a white elite or a black elite got to teach at HLS. I was writing because it was bringing me joy and I didn't want to become a mouthpiece for either side. The *Record* was replete with barely voting-age pseudopundits mouthing off from comfortable chairs and I was determined not to take sides as long as I was unprepared to do the investigative and analytic legwork required to make statements that any reasonable person ought to give weight to. My reverse snobbery notwithstanding, I believe in faculty diversity. Given that Dean Clark and the right-wingers had triumphed, in large part by painting themselves as the beleaguered defenders of impartial tradition, I decided that the best I could do from our position of defeat was to deny him coverage. My main focus in writing, though, was to enjoy myself. I've written a great deal since then, but I doubt that any writing I ever do will make me happier than my goofy *Record* column.

Quickly, I interspersed many political columns among the comic ones, though I continued to refrain from commenting on HLS politics. HLS was already too self-absorbed and preen-prone. Toward the end of the semester, a radical, activist black student paid me a dubious compliment. She told me she'd been afraid I was going to write only funny columns and was glad to see me tackling serious issues. This was about politics—approval and disapproval—not the quality of my writing. The weight of the race was on my shoulders and it was selfish, nay, traitorous, of me to be making the white folks laugh. She came from a thoroughly FBI-filed radical family, took her studies seriously, and was never confused about why she was at HLS (far more students *claimed* they came to work for change than actually did so. The vast majority of both black and white students filed off to big law firms at the end of the day. Why they just couldn't admit to their true motivations, I'll never know). I liked her. Yet she typified leftist thinking: why was I required to tackle serious issues? What's wrong with humor? with mysteries? with westerns? What about the practical fact that a black woman was an important voice at HLS? Why must a black person be political every moment of every day?

Another black leftist friend from the same kind of radical, activist background was just as dismissive of my column when it wasn't serious even though we'd traded life stories and she could see how happy it made me. Further, she was completely dismissive of the blacks who were aiming at law firms—they were ipso facto sellouts. She was one of the women I suffered through BLSA meetings with and we frequently bemoaned BLSA's intolerance of dissenting viewpoints together, yet she was no less intolerant. I must have asked her a thousand times: Why can't the concept of the division of labor apply to black people? Somebody's got to show up for work every day while the rest of us are manning the barricades, don't they? For that matter, why can't the First Amendment apply among black people and leftists? I chose neither humor nor serious commentary from the goodness of my heart but from that which naturally motivated me, yet humor was a choice I wasn't allowed to make and for-profit law a profession no black was allowed to undertake. Had a white person placed such limits on us, we'd have burned HLS down.

I personally believe in the black tax, wherein those of us who have made it should render both attention and dollars to those who haven't, but I don't believe in forcing it on others. While I don't understand that lemming mind-set that drives our best and brightest into a fate they dread, I see the importance of having blacks represented in corporate America. They serve a vital function and I'm glad they're doing it so the rest of us don't have to. I think that any citizen who goes to work every day, obeys the law, pays his taxes, and keeps his dog on a leash is doing his part—everything beyond that is gravy.

Another argument which raged in my lefty feminist circles was the conventional wisdom that Barbara Bush was a closet abortion rights supporter. Instantly, she was denounced as a traitor for not speaking out. Her husband's the politician, I disagreed. She's a wife and mother in a very difficult situation. I think she gets to decide to put her marriage first and keep her thoughts to herself. Oh, the looks I got.

A white lefty made no attempt to disguise her disgust when I told her of my intention to foster black entrepreneurship. "Make sure they actually pay their workers," she sneered. In her defense, she did public interest work defending Hispanic immigrant women doing domestic work who were routinely defrauded, and she offered this by way of explanation when I jumped on her. I didn't buy it, though; her disgust, her disapproval, was too palpable. Nothing is more tiresome than the leftist chestnut that all capitalism is evil. Unchecked, it certainly is, but it's also the only game in town. I believe in subverting the dominant paradigm from within: how revolutionary would it be if tens of millions of the poor and dispossessed got their hands on the means of production? Just thinking about it makes me giddy (although I suspect they would rapidly become everything they used to hate). This Choate, Harvard undergrad, and Harvard Law School–educated, world-traveled woman driving the late-model car her parents gave her while living with every capitalist convenience known to man, however, dismissed my plan out of hand. She also disapproved of bona fide radicals like Duncan Kennedy who were merely intellectuals, or even activists who were not working hands-on. They're sellouts. Multiply that by the goodly chunk of liberals who think this same way, and you see where disaffected liberals like me come from. Again, why no division of labor?

For that matter, why assume that just because you're hands-on you're doing something that matters or that you're doing it well? Once, she tried to volunteer at Greater Boston Legal Services but they blew her off. She concluded that they didn't really care about the poor. Maybe, I said. But maybe the problem is that volunteers eat up resources, especially those precious managerial ones, just like employees do. They can't just give you a key to the office and tune out again. Also, the sought-after, glitzy public interest organizations have their own sources for volunteers and you're trying to circumvent that—maybe they just don't know what to make of you (like Mark's DGA staff). "No. They just don't care," she concluded grimly.

Dwelling among lefties made me understand the extent to which activism is too often about the activist and not those for whom the activist is putatively acting. In that same housing class (a leftist favorite), unbeknownst to me, there were two factions: the student-run, student-staffed Legal Aid Bureau and the Legal Services Center (my faction—staffed by students, run by grown-ups. Jean Charn, one of the coteachers, ran it). Out of the blue one day, the leftist-circular firing squad formed.

A Legal Aid Bureau student attacked Jean and the Legal Services Center for mass-producing our pleadings, a charge which was true. Since we only did certain types of cases, we had computer-based macros which we customized for each case. Also, everyone there specialized. I'd do their housing case, then send them downstairs for another to do their Social Security or welfare case. We aimed at maximum efficiency and representing as many people as possible. At the

Legal Aid Bureau, though, each student handled every facet of a client's case, lack of expertise notwithstanding. Also, each student originated his own pleadings, specific to each case. This was why I'd chosen the LSC, that and because I wanted lawyer supervision. Once I'd chosen, I spent no further time thinking about the Legal Aid Bureau except to assume we were fellow travelers; I certainly had no idea that some there considered us sellouts because of our volume focus. I'd thought this class, famous as a hotbed of populism, would be a haven; instead, it became just another place for liberals to stoke their own egos by disapproving of other liberals.

One bureau student summed up the difference between the two approaches succinctly. He said piously, "When I really take my time to do the pleadings just right, doing the research, talking to professors, I just feel better about it. That way, when Mrs. Jones gets that new sink from the landlord, I know I made that happen." Shouldn't it be Mrs. Jones's happiness that mattered?

I went to the first couple of Coalition for Civil Rights "silent" vigils for diversity outside the faculty meetings. I use sneer quotes because they were the loudest silent vigils imaginable; it is impossible for Harvardians to shut up, so in love are we with the sound of our own voices. One vigil was especially loud because a *Vanity Fair* reporter was there working on a piece about the nastiness of HLS politics. Most of the crowd was throwing bons mots the reporter's way, hoping to get interviewed. No way was politics going to come before publicity.

I laugh at them, but I also had to laugh at myself. I hadn't known that at the culmination of each vigil, as the faculty meeting began, the group would shout en masse, "No justice, no peace," several times before disbanding. I scurried away as the shouting began. Silly, I know, but I was thinking, They're having a *meeting.* It seemed rude and just a little silly to me. Now consciously my father's daughter, I had no trouble tracing this facet of my personality back to its source. I might as well have shook my fist at those "heathens" from a car window. That man is inescapable. It's just that now, I don't fight the weight of him.

On another occasion, I got a call to help read a list of names of professors of color that HLS should consider appointing. Typical students, they called scant hours before the faculty meeting and I had a dental appointment. Also, name-reading? It sounded dubious to me. The next day, the campus was in an uproar. It turns out that the name-reading was a guerrilla tactic. We hadn't been invited or allowed to read; CCR had stormed the meeting and demanded to be allowed to read hundreds of names. The person who'd called had left that little detail out. There was a heated standoff with lots of yelling, scuffling, and the ritual exchange of self-justificatory letters in the *Record*.

That kind of activism just doesn't work for me, especially when CCR's main justification after the fact was that if they'd simply been allowed to read the list (HUNDREDS of names), there'd have been no problem. Unlike my compadres, though I have no personal use for this type of activism, I can see the value of it. Even if I couldn't, I wouldn't consider those who do to be sellouts if their beliefs are otherwise intellectually and morally defensible. I'm not threatened by those who see the world differently than I do; I simply leave this facet of the struggle to others and, as with the law firm drones, am grateful that someone else has that covered.

So ridiculous can the Harvard left be that sometimes blacks and liberals joined together to produce a spectacle so ridiculous, knee-jerk, and insulting, it made you want to join the Federalist Society just to piss them off. The showdown at an obligatory sensitivity training session my second year was one such spectacle.

Surprisingly enough, Harvard students had been known to offend the poor, largely immigrant Hispanic community the Legal Services Center served in Jamaica Plain, Boston. In response, this training had recently been instituted. The facilitators were a white man and a black woman with that special brand of earnestness which can only be found among car salesman, Amway reps, and . . . well . . . diversity training facilitators.

I hate sensitivity training. The USAF had required a healthy dose of it. I have never known it not to bring out the worst in everybody. This time was no exception. We were put through our paces in a series of gooey, goofy exercises like ones where students were culled from the audience to name things which were good and which were bad about whatever facet of their identity they were there to represent. The audience was not allowed to criticize what they said, only to praise it. For instance, there was a "man," a "woman," a "liberal," etc. I knew we were in trouble with the next panel.

Representatives from the different economic classes were called for. Much as I hate that kind of touchy-feeliness, I volunteered to be the working-class representative because, as usual, my classmates were letting things drag on and on by not participating. But no one would admit to being either middle class or upper class. Imagine that. At Harvard. Our earnest facilitators gave up on the latter, but finally a black friend confessed to being middle class and took a seat onstage.

After a little more torture of this type, just before the break, the facilitators had us count off by eights. All the ones would go to this room, the twos to that, and so on. That was all we were told about this exercise. My favorite radical, sitting in the back of the room with the rest of the blacks, said that the blacks wanted to have their own separate group. The room froze. The facilitators, wide-eyed with surprise and muted fear, immediately caved. You could have heard a pin drop.

I was sitting up front with the black radical who had dismissed my nonpolitical columns and considered all law-firm blacks sellouts and the white lefty who hated capitalism and anyone who wasn't working hands-on with poor people of color. We three joined our integrated groups (where we were given crayons to draw our own personal flags) and then all rejoined the beleaguered main group.

Our facilitators led the way in pretending that nothing had happened, though the temperature in the room seemed to have dropped to freezing. One of the HLS Head Negroes, the very personification of the BLSA mentality and a virulent racist to boot, took a fiendish delight in interrupting the resumed session to suggest we discuss what was obviously on everyone's mind, to wit, the black secession from the union. She's the kind of black who likes to terrorize whites.

Because no one else would, my three-woman group criticized the blacks' actions as counterproductive and needlessly divisive. They'd had no idea what the breakout session was about—how could they be sure race would be in any way relevant or helpful? What had they done in their blacks-only group: drawn straws for the red, black, and green crayons? It seemed to me simple masturbation and a pseudo-Marxist sideshow—a great big middle finger to a group of people they knew would be too afraid to answer back.

This division seemed a special betrayal because we'd all just survived six weeks of a boot-camp-like, grueling Trial Advocacy Workshop where we'd had a crash-course, round-the-clock introduction to trial work. We'd all had to act as each other's witnesses, jurors, judges, cocounsels, and opposing counsels while we undertook that special trial by fire. At its end, we'd all felt closer to each other than to anyone else at HLS. We'd seen each other at our best and worst; we'd been forced to work in concert with people we hadn't known, or liked, or respected before. We'd come out of the experience buoyed and warmed by one of the few instances in which HLS was not a cold, impersonal knife fight for primacy. With that request for a separate-but-equal black-only group, all that evaporated. This inexplicable pulling away made our earlier camaraderie, born of shared suffering and teamwork, meaningless.

My white friend was emotional on this point, saying how hurt she felt now that the bond we'd thought transcended race among the group had been severed. She was brave, she was eloquent. But to no avail. She was slaughtered. No white could criticize blacks; the other whites in the room outdid themselves chastising her for her insensitivity and racism. They reduced her to weeping. The way they leapt on her while looking to the black section for approval was appalling. My other friend and I were, of course, immune to criticism—we're black. We were heartsick knowing what was and would be said about us among blacks, but it would have been the height of cowardice to have remained silent in the face of such blatant race-baiting.

Of course, race-baiting is in the eye of the beholder. The woman who had made the original request, bless her radical soul, cried, so overwrought was she as she explained her motivation. As well, several other blacks were very reasonable in their defense of the group's actions. The most often given explanation was that wanting to be in a black-only setting was no reflection on whites or their individual views on integration. It was the *Plessy v. Ferguson* (the turn-of-the-century case which justified Jim Crow) defense: if segregation makes you feel bad, then there's something wrong with you because our purpose is not to make you feel bad but only to be alone with other blacks. Some invoked diversity itself—the blacks-only group boasted mothers, the disabled, foreign-born blacks, etc. How dare we limit the universality of blackness? Several of the blacks invoked the special knowledge that only blacks have. The virulent racist talked about how far beyond whites she was in the area of racial understanding, that there was no way useful dialogue could take place in an integrated setting.

This from the same woman who asked me where I got my hair braided, then grimaced with disgust when I directed her to a ghetto kitchen in Mattapan. "I'm *not* going down there," she nearly spat on the floor. Never mind that Michelle, the lovely child-woman who braided my hair, was a lily floating atop sewage. Never mind that her mother shot her father in the groin; never mind that her crackhead brother had seven neglected kids by a fellow crackhead who, when sober, stalked the family with such intensity they moved constantly; never mind that her sister was an alcoholic who stumbled around their ghetto home like a wraith. Michelle, on the other hand, didn't drink, smoke, or do drugs, had no kids but two jobs plus braiding and nothing bad to say about anyone. Michelle was why I'd come to law school. Why had this silly little woman come? After two years, I knew why: to be the kind of leader the black community can no longer afford and should no longer defer to, two Harvard degrees (and a quicksilver intelligence) be damned.

In their defense, I completely understand the need to escape white scrutiny. I've been the racial Lone Ranger since I was nine. No one knows better than I the weight, the sheer pressure, of doing everything their way than I do. No one knows better the spotlight we exist in for not being white. I'm sick of explaining "ashiness." I'm sick of balding white stockbrokers with swirl-pattern comb-overs saying petulantly, "I just don't get the things you people do to your hair." I'm sick of whites crashing into us while mangling the electric slide and throwing everybody off.

It's bad strategy and ultimately pointless, though, to try to make a statement with that kind of in-your-face separatism. We are a minority. That means, put very simply, that there just aren't very many of us. If we leave the ghetto, we will always be few. Filling up a closet with black people for a half hour at diversity training just won't change that. But we do have a right to a place of our own. That's why I joined BLSA; I knew no whites would come there. Even though I rarely went after first year unless there was an issue I cared about, I kept my dues current because it was important to know that there was a majority-black place I could go if I wanted to. What I didn't know was that no white *could* come there. BLSA wasn't majority-black; it was blacks only. No whites allowed.

Scandal was brewing at HLS; right-wingers were making an issue of the fact that BLSA received law school funding but limited its membership to blacks only. I certainly hadn't known that; most of us hadn't. I had to get out the BLSA bylaws and see it with my own eyes before I could believe it. But it was true. I belonged to a racially exclusive group. I'd never consciously thought about it, but just assumed that whites avoided BLSA because they always avoided large groups of blacks and thought other issues more relevant. Certainly, those things were true, but, ultimately, beside the point. I belonged to a group that excluded by race.

I went off to split my second summer between the firm's New York and San Francisco offices, hoping that the issue would just disappear. That, when we all returned, the rules would just have magically rewritten themselves and rendered the issue moot. On the train to New York, I had hours to consider how different my attitude toward a whites-only group at HLS might have been.

Shearman's New York office is huge—hundreds of lawyers, hundreds of admin staff, from catering to cleaning, to reproduction, to messengers. Hostility was in the air; the legions of secretaries, Xeroxers, and paralegals considered themselves royally mistreated and underpaid and I agreed. Many of the lawyers were rude, dismissive, and thoughtless with the staff, too caught up in their own misery, deadlines, and long hours to consider anyone else's problems. I was caught in the middle of the class struggle. Most of the nonprofessional staff looked at me suspiciously, my guilt presumed and associated with the years of self-absorbed fancy-pants lawyers who'd preceded me.

The secretary assigned to me was so hostile, so lazy, and such a clock watcher, I eventually stopped asking her to do anything but my diaries (lawyers track their time in six-minute increments—we scribble in diaries all day, making sure to account for every billable nanosecond). When I asked her to show me the program that my diary entries had to go into, she had enough pride left to be embarrassed. She snatched it from me: "I'll do it!" It was the only task she performed for me all summer. I once heard her bleat to a caller, "Aw! Take a message? Can't you just call her back?"

Doing my own administrative work was simpler than constantly riding herd on her. What little she did, she did sloppily and usually incorrectly; I couldn't let my name go out on it. The first few weeks, before I gave up, I'd watch her eyes go angrily narrow as I gave her some instruction—she wanted to spit in my eye, it was quite obvious. She was bitter, but she was also scared. She needed the job but she expected to be dissed ("Who the hell is this Little Miss Harvard?" I heard her sniff on the phone to someone my first morning there). She was black; I had thought that might help. Instead, I think it made her dislike me more.

Is this what will happen to that hardworking girl from the DNC cafeteria? I used to wonder.

Eventually, she thawed toward me somewhat—smiling when our paths crossed, asking a few questions about my life—but I never did toward her. I had no respect for her. She only started liking me because I didn't require her to do her job. She was rarely even at her desk. So she gave me a start the day I looked up to see her in my doorway. I had only a few days left.

Blunt and nervous, she demanded to know what sort of evaluation I was going to give her.

She was holding the form clenched in her fist. Her face looked like it had the first few weeks, when she thought I might abuse her or try to make her work, both prospects being equally unpleasant.

I asked her, "Do you realize that this is the only thing you took the initiative to do this entire summer?"

She drew herself up with a hiss.

"Aint nobody begging you for nothing. Say whatever you want," she spat, and left.

I never saw her again. I saw her coat appear and disappear. Noticed that her computer was off when it had been on, and vice versa. I heard her slip into her chair, talk on the phone, disappear again. But I never saw her.

My last day, I left the signed but otherwise blank form on her desk with a Post-it that said, "You fill it in, then you will have accomplished *two* things."

I was dreading a repeat performance of the class struggle at the San

Francisco office. As usual, I had a different problem that I would never have expected.

The San Francisco office was small, fewer than twenty lawyers and perhaps thirty admin staff. There were only four or five summer associates.

My first day, the hall outside my office was dead. But every day the rest of that week, the foot traffic was downright distracting. Eventually, I noticed that I was seeing only black faces. Then I realized that I was seeing the same black faces over and over again. The fifth time I saw a black woman with a head full of wild, unprocessed hair turn away just as I looked up, I called out, "Enough already. Get in here."

One of the admin staff shuffled in, chuckling ruefully.

She spent the next half hour explaining to me how to get my hair like hers. I'd let my hair go natural in 1992 without any idea of what was going to grow out of my scalp. Two years later, I still had not quite mastered its intricacies; she was my black hair consultant.

That day, I had lunch at one of San Francisco's trendiest, most expensive restaurants. The next, I was eating from a plastic tray at a cafeteria with five black women from the word-processing pool.

"We just had to see which kind you were," one teased in response to my jokes about being stalked.

"Hmmm, I'm not sure what you mean. Which kind of what?" I said, wide-eyed with fake innocence. "Oh, which department? Hi, Debra Dickerson, Mergers and Acquisitions," I deadpanned, holding out my hand for a shake.

They laughed. I did too, but I knew this was shaky ground. Whose side was I on? Because I knew no one can possibly be on both. I couldn't bring myself not to associate with them (I *wanted* to associate with them, they were fun and down-to-earth), but I'd worked too hard to deny myself the perks of my newfound position—like ruining some word processor's evening with extra work at the last minute if that's what I decided was required. I listened while they filled me in on office politics, often belittling partners or associates I liked. I was walking a tightrope. I could see it stretching out before me.

As we were coming back from one of these lunches one day, a partner passed our group. He looked so confused, I could almost hear his thoughts: What is a summer associate, a *lawyer,* doing with typists? What's wrong with this picture?

So be it, I thought. If he wants to hold it against me, if my work suddenly seems less competent to him, I'll move on. Nobody tells me with whom I can socialize.

He stopped by my office just a few hours later. He was delighted by "this turn of events." He was happy to see the "rapport" I had with the "staff." Diplomatically, he explained that there'd been a few "misunderstandings" in the past and he thought it was great to have me to run interference.

Warning bells were clanging.

One of the women who was both the funniest and the most militant of the typists had brought a grievance meeting to a halt recently to brandish a *Lawyers Weekly* article trumpeting the firm's unprecedented profits. She'd read aloud the part about the partners' take and demanded to know what percentage of those millions the staff was going to get. Gleefully, the typists had told me about it. Reportedly this partner had been furious, telling her she was out of line for inquiring into things that were none of her business.

I knew what sort of "misunderstandings" he meant and I did not want to be the one sent to "explain things" to the "staff." I had no one to blame but myself for thinking I could straddle the line. What would happen when one of my lunch buddies thought they could slack off on some work for me? What would happen if one of them made a huge mistake? Was I willing to share more of the profit with them? Decision-making?

I was very worried about my future in a world so starkly divided between haves and have-nots because I was pretty sure I would identify with the haves. I'd encourage the have-nots to do the work and join us in the penthouse, but until then . . .

Fortunately for me, there were no barricades to man that summer, no cake to offer the starving instead of bread. I got away with it, that high-wire act I had naively created. I never had to put my money where my mouth was and I knew I had dodged a bullet. I'll respect the nonprofessional staff wherever I am, always, but I will never again pretend to identify with them.

Early one morning, I looked up to find that militant would-be labor organizer standing in my office doorway staring at me.

"Miss Thing? Yes?" I prodded her jokingly, but she just kept staring.

"You look good today," she said with a strange intensity.

"Huh?"

She snapped out of some reverie and blew her nose into a wad of tissues twisted in her hand. She'd been crying.

"I just needed to see you, like this," and she gestured at the pile of treatises on my desk. "Harvard. Everything."

I got her to come in and sit down. Then she told me her story.

The night before, she'd picked her husband up from the country club where he caddied.

(Her husband was a *caddie?* A grown man was a caddie, that still happened?)

The sprinklers had been tossing up rainbows as she waited in the car. The sunset had been so beautiful, the landscape so lush, they'd ended up sitting in their car necking.

Her husband had just called. Security patrols had noted them "casing" the country club and fired him. He'd only just managed to talk them out of calling the police. There were no black marks on his record there.

"So, I just needed to see little Miss M&A today," she laughed between sniffles.

I didn't know what to say, so we just sat there.

"Hey!" I said. "My secretary's white. Want me to call her in and order her around?"

That made her smile. I brought her some coffee, and when she'd collected herself, she made her slow, dignified way back to the word-processing pool.

After a summer spent watching working-class black people struggle with real problems, I returned to Harvard to find that my wish hadn't come true and the BLSA membership issue had not resolved itself. I was torn to pieces. I was militant about our right to a place of our own (though I rarely went there), yet I thought it inexcusable to take law school funds without being open to the whole law school. The reactionary forces demanding an open-door policy at BLSA would rather be expelled than find themselves in a majority-black room, yet they had us dead to rights. Worse, I felt sure BLSA would handle the issue poorly.

I was so committed to my column then, anything that stayed on my mind got written about. So I decided not to attend BLSA meetings on the subject. I was enough of a tribalist not to want to give aid and comfort to the enemy on such a core issue. One way or the other we were going to lose, so I decided we should close ranks and go down united.

The membership consulted Professor Charles Ogletree, our official adviser, former National BLSA president and a criminal law specialist. He gave BLSA the bad news: there was no way to keep the policy, so give in gracefully. BLSA held straw polls and emergency meetings while blowing the *Record* off completely, though the editor, Greg Stohr, pestered the president constantly for an interview. Stohr asked me to try to persuade him, a request which I refused. Personally, though, I had decided that BLSA should remain black-only and stop accepting university funds. Failing that, we had no choice as moral beings but to open the membership to all. If BLSA did neither, I was going to resign, via my *Record* column.

If it meant that much to us, we should be willing to give up what was purportedly the best student-organization office space on campus and go off-campus. HLS's wealthy black alums could help us offset the cost and law firms would still shower us with funds and attention. All we needed was a little determination, a little willingness to look beyond our own creature comforts, a little initiative.

But in the end, BLSA caved. Near as I could tell from all the meetings I'd missed, no one made any bones about the fact that, in the end, it was all about the perks of the HLS letterhead.

We stayed on campus and kept Big Daddy's dollars. Once it was decided and announced, I went to a meeting the point of which was to design the new membership rules. Just as I'd suspected, the talk was only of the huge, law-firm-funded BLSA Job Fair, the BLSA study guides reproduced at HLS expense, the resource base of HLS, and how no one was prepared to give that up. I guess there's something to be said for their bare-bones honesty, but a little bit of shame might not have been misplaced just then. Martin wrote his letter from the Birmingham jail, but the best we could do was write a host of onerous restrictions aimed at dissuading white folk from daring to cross BLSA's threshold. It was grandfather clauses all over again. I heard proposals detailing the ridiculously high amount of committee work new members would have to undertake, the lengthy papers they'd have to write, the high percentage of meetings they'd have to attend. Few BLSA members evinced that level of commitment.

How many bubbles in a bar of Ivory soap, nigger?

What amazed me was how open the discussion about running the white folks off was. When I graduated, new members had to sign a McCarthyite loyalty oath, one which I spoke up against at the last BLSA meeting I attended and which I went on record saying I wouldn't sign. Their matter-of-fact selfishness left me breathless; they had no shame. What they did have, however, was vengefulness. That's what the new killer rules were about.

Lots of blacks went about campus after that dramatically haughty, wearing our unearned suffering and racial superiority like an ermine cape. I thought we should have felt shame. Shame for our greed. Shame for our vindictiveness. Shame because when the moment of truth came, we acted just like them. We'd become what we professed to loathe.

I felt farther removed from the black liberal bourgeoisie in 1995 than I did in 1992. I'd already had several soul-scares, though, a few moments where my own wonderfulness went to my head and I actually believed that I was better off because I was better.

A Shearman partner had been trying to talk me into joining the firm after graduation and I'd avoided the core issue by focusing on New York's crime. This partner packed more pro bono civil rights work into her litigation docket than some LDF staffers, yet she responded to me like the slumlord who had humiliated me and my friend on his porch.

"Not *that* again! Look, safety is about brains. *I* live in a doorman building. *I* take taxis or a car service, not the subway or buses. I stock up so I don't have to go out at night. Jeez, what do they expect?"

"True," I said. Then, "Wait a minute! You're a millionaire."

My head reeled with cognitive dissonance. I'd scared myself so badly I had to sit down and make myself say "People aren't poor and victimized because they're stupid" ten times. Privilege, on the other hand, can make you a moron. It certainly did me a few times.

What I failed to add to the vignette about Mark Gearan giving my job away was the little detail that, back in D.C. just before I left for

Boston, I had respectfully told Mark off. He was nonplussed. That angle (my existence) had not occurred to him. Merely grateful that he'd heard me out, I thanked him for listening and turned to go. He called me back and, without apologizing, asked what he could do to make up for it. Unprepared for this turn of events (all I'd wanted was the dignity of acknowledgment), I thought to ask for a chance to do advance work, which had struck me during the campaign as flight-line-like and adrenaline-fueled. He picked up the phone and I left the next day for a week prepping for a Gore campaign swing through Stockton, California. The people on the advance team, who had presumably struggled up through the ranks, had no choice but to accept Gore's campaign manager's specific "request," this woman from nowhere with no advance-team experience. The team leader watched me like a caged but unfed boa constrictor—not about to piss off someone as important as Mark but furious that I'd been forced on her. I felt like I'd climbed through their windows with a stocking mask on. While I stacked Evian and Gummi Bears in Gore's command-center hotel room, I tried to justify my string-pulling by the work I'd done for Mark and by the fact that I hadn't actually tried to cash in; it had just happened. It almost worked until I began wondering how my "replacement" had justified her own hookup to herself every time I had used my eyes to jab voodoo-doll pins in her.

Just a few months after that, while participating in a BLSA street law clinic in ghetto Boston, the black principal introduced us as students at "the best law school on the planet" and said we'd be making sixty-five thousand dollars a year after graduation. I turned to the person on my left and said, "How gauche." I turned to the one on my right and sniffed, "*Eighty* thousand."

I told a San Francisco doctor treating me that I was sure the diagnosis of a previous condition was correct because it had been made at Harvard.

I used something personal an undergraduate advisee had told me in a *Record* column without a warning bell ever going off in my mind, so focused was I on winning a debate.

I competed for and won the Skadden Arps fellowship, the most prestigious public interest law fellowship, simply because it was the most prestigious. I didn't really want it—by graduation, I knew I wanted to write, that my foundation was on the back burner—I was just an achievement junkie jonesing for another notch in my résumé, just like the classmates I belittled. It should have gone to someone who was serious about the work, not someone who would quit only six months into the two-year term to write.

En route to Erik's posh Palo Alto home while he studied for a Stanford M.B.A. and I worked at S&S's San Francisco office, we passed through the Mission District. The people on the street looked odd to me, their clothes, their pallor. Confused by their appearance and demeanor, I asked Erik, that Princeton-educated son of privilege, "These people . . . they look . . . what's wrong with them?"

He looked at me. Looked at them. Back at me.

"They're poor, Debra."

Oh. Only two years into the upper crust, I had forgotten what reality could look like.

I didn't want to forget. I didn't want to excuse, but I didn't want to forget and, most of all, I didn't want to become *them*. But I was still ambitious, my dreams bigger than ever, my confidence utter. How to avail myself of what I've earned, as well as what I've lucked into, without becoming the enemy?

Having a farewell lunch the day before graduation with my study group, I made a disparaging reference to "the elite." One asked, "How's that work, now that *you're* an elite?"

Me? Elite?

I was furious.

How dare he strip me of the thing I've fought hardest for in my life—a sense of belonging in the black working class. Granted, I'd actually been struggling to rid myself of that connection, but the exact opposite had happened once my emotional maturity caught up to my intellect; I'd learned to accept who and what I am the way I accept being five foot seven and right-handed. It doesn't make me special and it doesn't make me less than. It's just my context and it need have no more control over my life than I choose for it to.

There I was, a humble penitent who'd confessed her sins and begged for absolution. It galled, it burned, to be lumped in with those who can't remain who and what they are without keeping everybody else down. How could my friend wave some magic wand and make me one of those smug toads who'd filled me with the very self-loathing I'd struggled with for thirty years? I'd sacrificed everything to forge an identity for myself in the community of my birth. The more I saw of the black upper class, the less I intended to be part of it: they talked revolution while shopping at Saks.

Me? Elite?

Certainly, I was privileged now, but at least I'd had to earn my perks. Most of the blacks at Harvard were born knowing it's cup and saucer, not cup and table. Sofa, not couch. Red leaf, not iceberg. Dunhill, Marlboro, anything but Kool or Newport. I had to learn all that the hard way with angry blacks and clueless whites looking on. Worse, I'd had so much to unlearn.

Newsweek, not the *Enquirer. The New Republic,* not *Newsweek. Harper's,* not *Ebony. Jet?* Under no circumstances. Diaphragm, not the Pill. The Pill, not withdrawal. Art houses, not cineplexes. Subtitles, not blaxploitation. No air-conditioned summers at home: internships abroad under artificially trying conditions. Foreign, not domestic, white guys.

I hadn't understood then that you can never stop being who you were born being; you can add things but you can never subtract from the baseline. Lord, the pulling, the tearing at my soul as the confused youngster I was tried to split herself in half, be two people in one body. The strain of remembering not to make any slips that might identify me as working class to whites. The feigned ennui of talking skiing and off-Broadway with fancy blacks so no one had to admit to their roots. The painful pleasure of attending a few carefully chosen black events. The stab of self-hatred at my own evil jokes about how wealthy the white guy supplying the kente cloth concessions must be as the wannabe "African" outfits paraded by. Pondering the significance of myself as the only black person my many white friends know. But who was I kidding: I was usually the only black at my own parties then. Most choices caused me no anguish, merely rendering unto Caesar . . . but *Cosmo* over *Essence?* I couldn't do it.

I couldn't wait to tell my friend off. How could that privileged white boy know anything about schizophrenia? About a family, a soul, ripped asunder by the forces of history? About struggle? He would never have the least notion of who I really was and what I'd been through and how hard it was to decide which part of my personality to draw on in a particular situation. I opened my mouth to set him straight with all the ghetto-girl neck-wagging, finger-pointing, infinitive-splitting gusto that I was no longer embarrassed of.

Me? Elite?

Then it hit me.

Yes.

Me. Elite.

No world traveler with a B.A., M.A., and Ivy League J.D. can pretend to be one of the proletariat, no matter her origins. I can understand it. I can commiserate with it. I can suffer, through loved ones, the very real tragedies visited upon those who think they've escaped. I can remain involved, I can fight for its rights, I can tell its stories. What I can't do is claim more than honorary membership. All I can do is stand ready to be of assistance and to take advantage of my unique vantage point.

Me. Elite.

I wandered the Harvard campus, totally at ease, totally at home.

I went to Mattapan, totally at ease, totally at home.

How had that happened? When had that happened?

I didn't want to give up either—I'd worked damned hard for admission to both—but how can they possibly be melded?

As on the beach at Okinawa, I found myself again mourning my dead, the little girl who could now be at peace.

I cried for that little girl who couldn't smile without covering her face so no one would see her nose spread. I cried for the girl who had saved her pennies for bleaching cream and circled the hair-relaxer section till no one was left to see her purchase. I cried for the girl hiding in a closet with a salvaged tape recorder trying to ditch her Southern accent. I laughed through tears to imagine her shock at discovering that it would still be detectable to her more sensitive law school classmates.

In crimson or in a McDonald's uniform, in English or in Korean, I was what I had always been: a daughter of the Great Migration. Though being born in 1959 officially made me a Baby Boomer, I had always shrugged off the moniker; it just feels wrong, as when people call me "Debbie." That just wasn't me. I saw myself as part of my family, not as an individual. My war of personal reference was World War II, not Viet Nam. I valued production, not leisure; I was thirty-four before I was able to put aside my distaste at the lazy decadence of it and nap when given the chance. I endured the nausea and pain of chronic hypertension for years before it occurred to me to see a doctor—I wasn't bleeding, was I?

But at HLS, it became clear to me that I had grafted my Southern Baptist work ethic and hardscrabble determination onto the opportunities for which my progenitors deprived themselves. On their backs, I had transformed myself into that which they could only dream of—a Harvard-trained, world-traveled, neurotic attorney turned writer with a Gold Card who dated interracially but had the home training to be ambivalent about it, who would rather have eaten cornbread and collards than sushi, rather have listened to gospel than hip-hop, and who believed that disrespectful rap artists would burn in hell and was comforted by the thought. But whose favorite food, next to fried chicken and mustard greens, is Vietnamese. Who loves classical music and opera as well as the blues.

I had become a fully realized American. I will not be denied. But then, I no longer expected to be.

JUNE 8, 1995. GRADUATION DAY

There was only one bridge left to burn.

As graduation loomed, BLSA circulated order forms for kente cloth stoles to wear over our graduation robes. My heart sank. What, I wondered, is this piece of cloth, probably produced in Belgium, going to tell the world about me that this face already doesn't? Why distance ourselves from the people we've been through so much with over the last three years? Don't we really have enough in common now to make this gesture merely defensive and self-conscious? Isn't it self-indulgent, cutting off our noses to spite our faces, to dig this one-sided trench? If, as they argued, the cloths didn't mean anything, why wear them? Why wear them on this day and not others? Shouldn't we always be proud of our heritage? What, exactly, was the point?

I graduated without one.

I spent my graduation day alone except for my mother because the rest of my family couldn't afford the trip. My friends' families could, though, so I just wandered in an anticlimactic funk while Mama rested after the ceremony.

I watched my classmates—black, white, other—move about in jovial, mixed-generation groups and speak the common language of upper-middle-class possibility.

Since I had no other choice, I just made my way alone, walking and thinking. On my own.

ACKNOWLEDGMENTS

I've been pregnant since 1995. That's when I began this book. I have been carrying the weight and responsibility of it around with me ever since, wishing I could undo it, fighting for it, planning every decision around it, wondering what it would be like, wondering whether it would survive, how any new endeavor might affect it, would it emerge healthy or fail to thrive, was I working too hard or not hard enough, which lies to tell it and which truths, should I abandon it or just love it more? Whether I was making love or making a left turn, I was thinking about this book. It has been the only constant in my turbulent last few years.

Hard as I worked, however, I realized early on that I while I might succeed as a storyteller, I would fail as a witness undergoing cross-examination. Even with truth serum, how could I possibly (or readably) convey the complexity of the first thirty-five years of my life, four generations of family lore, two parents, five siblings, and the lot of African-Americans in post–civil rights America? When I began quizzing relatives, notebook in hand, a few years ago, I naively thought that that would lead me to "the truth" of what happened in our family, when and why. Shoot, in a family full of ornery cusses like mine, I was wrong to think that would even lead to replies.

Funnily enough, I was the only one who thought our story so emblematic of the Great Migration and post–Jim Crow America that it "just had" to be written down for all the world to see. But I had to see it through, so I did what I had to do. I went commando. I stopped asking direct questions—I'd just keep my ears open. Then, I'd sneak off to the bathroom to scribble on dinner napkins. I'd debrief disgruntled, divorced in-laws and corner unsuspecting old great-aunts from out of town who hadn't been warned. I'd keep wineglasses full and lurk in hallways while unsuspecting loved ones reminisced. Well trained in the ways of disinformation as an Air Force intelligence officer, I'd even toss off history I knew to be so inflammatorily erroneous that no one could let it stand uncorrected. In the end, I learned that no two people ever see the same thing and no one ever changes his or her mind about anything, least of all me. I understand now why the Russians say, "He lies like an eyewitness." All of that to say that no one named either Dickerson or Gooch (my mother's family) wanted me to write this book if only because no two of us can agree on what happened. I focused on succeeding as a principled storyteller.

All I can say is that this is my story and I'm sticking to it. I tried very hard to tell the truth but four years later, I know it's just my truth. I've been over it all so many times, trying to mixmaster my own self-centered memories with the reluctant offerings of not disinterested relatives; I'm well aware that I may just remember remembering some things. Certainly, I re-created dialogue, made calculated assumptions, amalgamated events, and moved things around in time or location for ease of storytelling, but not so as to fundamentally alter their nature. For instance, an incident where my secondhand dress falls off took place at Benton Elementary in the third or fourth grade, not Wade Elementary in the fifth. I say it makes no difference—the point is that it made me resent our poverty—and makes the story flow more smoothly. Names which appear in quotation marks the first time have been changed because I'm uninterested in causing anyone either happiness or sadness with this book. Regardless of what I claim they did, they had no idea how they would figure in my life. I'm long past getting even with them now; I'm simply trying to give my testimony. People who have treated me far worse but don't further my agenda here are not mentioned at all; I'll get to them in fiction. Those given appellations like "Spineless Worm" simply don't deserve to have decent people say their names.

Several years into this process, I realized that the real distortion will derive from my omissions—the things I was told but don't believe, the things I believe but chose not to tell, and most insidious of all, the things I don't remember. A sister recently told me that I'd worn my father's oversized house slippers to tatters in the years after my mother left him and took us with her. I remember those years as the height of my hatred of him; I cannot believe that I did such a heartbreakingly transparent thing, but my mother corroborates this revelation. Conversely, I remember things that no one else does. I have to acknowledge that I most likely blocked things out, made them up, or substantially altered them in my mind (but I don't really believe it: I know I'm right!). Four years of trying to get a straight story out of myself and a thousand other headstrong Negroes just like me has taught me something crucial to understanding humans: each of us is the star of our own personal soap opera with its own plot, its own logic, its own villains, and its own heroes. Regardless of the proof offered, those story lines are unshakeable. I had many opportunities to listen to outrageous lies about an event the liar knew I witnessed, or which defied the laws of time and space (one would have had to be in Indiana and Mississippi at the same time given the previous story). But then, I still can't accept that I cherished my "hated" father's raggedy shoes. It contradicts all the other things I "know" as an eyewitness.

I tried hardest of all to tell the truth on myself. You know by now, of course, that I believe that there is no such thing. For decency's sake, I must state that my oldest sister sees our father entirely positive and will be devastated by my depiction of him. We might as well have known completely different men, so differently do we remember him. In the early years of his marriage, he quite probably was a different person. By the time I came along, though, our home was a different place. We will never agree on whose fault that was or how it came to be. I simply did not know the man she describes (how could I? I didn't exist). We know pieces of the same story from different vantage points to which each of our worldviews is inextricably wedded. The real difference between us? I envy her.

My father, my mother, and my brother are the only family members I discuss in detail in this book. Their stories are simply too fascinating and too bound up with my own to resist. I'm prouder of my mother and brother than of any other people I know, so I hounded them and gave them no option but to cooperate. All I will say in my own defense is that I feel compelled to tell the world about them and all the other working-class, ghetto-trapped tool-users just like them whose leaders aren't fit to shine their shoes. I'll just wait till they forgive me. My brother, in particular, laid himself bare to me in a most heroic and humble way once I had him cornered. His story is much braver than mine, his fortitude much greater. My mother is a saint who should immediately be made galactic president. She is wise and strong and the most difficult thing a human can be: kind. As for my father, I still don't understand him fully because he's too difficult for us to talk about, but the picture I paint of him is one I can understand and is true, I think, as far as it goes. Without a doubt, however, it is incomplete.

Difficult as this process has been, I feel neither good nor bad, happy nor sad about it now. Merely finished. Done. Task completed. It was simply something I needed to do—like acquire a graduate degree or have a painful medical procedure—so I did it. Now I can let it go. Some people work out their issues in therapy. Some over glasses of wine with friends. Some take hostages and climb up bell towers with high-powered rifles. I wrestle with things on paper until they make sense to me. That makes me ruthless with the lives of both myself and others; be interesting around me at your own peril.

My heart is in my family and in the black working class. I write about them to honor them, something people like us have long deserved and seldom receive. Even so, I am going to try very, very hard never to write about my family again. In nonfiction.

Caterwauling completed, let me now acknowledge that I have been befriended by so many people in so many places at so many different times in my life, I'll never know what I did to deserve it. I just pray I leave no one out.

There would be no book and no acknowledgments had not Erroll McDonald and the amazing Pantheon team rescued me and my erstwhile manuscript when they did. Had they not, I might just have climbed that bell tower with that high-powered rifle. Erroll's calm maturity, sure eye, and finely tuned bullshit detector—what a relief. Ron Goldfarb, my agent, was an oasis of sanity as well in the neurotic-rich environment that is big-time publishing. By allowing me to write about him and his incredible courage, my nephew Johnny Townson made my writing career. It was because of him that editors became interested in me in the first place; I'd still be writing $200 book reviews if he hadn't allowed me to invade his privacy. As your grandfather used to say, one day I'll dance at your wedding, Johnny. And without my accountants, Nelson Costa and Stephanie Meilman, I would have gone under long ago. I never cease to be amazed at how seriously they take their work and how much concern they showed me, far beyond the call of duty. Granted, they never gave me anything but bad news (never, ever be self-employed; the IRS hates us) but they always took it as hard as I did. My everlasting gratitude to all of you. Finally, without Ted Halstead and the New America Foundation, I would have had to make lattes at Starbucks to finish this book. Instead, NAF gave me a warm, lively, and challenging intellectual home and all the support any writer could ever fantasize about. You screwed up, Ted—I may never leave. My lasting gratitude.

Some of the folks that follow may be very surprised to see themselves listed here. But their love, support, and failure to panic every time I did gave me the confidence to strike out on my own in the first place and, later, to believe I could write. I've made a lot of bold, fairly desperate lurches upward in my life and it has only been recently that I have done so with any confidence. Many people along the way have dismissed me as merely indecisive and unrealistic, which only fed my self-doubt. These people, though, embraced me as special and helped me dream. More often than not, all I needed was to be taken seriously and listened to, which these kind souls always did. All of these people are overcommitted and stretched every which way at once, but still found the time to give me whatever I was needing at the moment—in some cases, all the way back to elementary school. Some are here because they threw me the work that kept me alive all this time. Some because they cared enough about me and the craft of writing itself to read my many, many drafts. Some are here because I shafted them in my ruthless determination to finish this book and they forgave me. I can't blame the ones who didn't forgive me but I'm eternally grateful to the ones who did. This book would not have seen the light of day without: Jabari Asim, Pete Ballenger, Alex Beam, Jonah Blank, Matthew Considine, Jim Fallows, Jonathan Foreman, Steve Fraser, Henry Louis Gates, Paul Glastris, Bill and Barbara Graham, Jon and Linda Greenblatt, Penda Hair, Duncan Kennedy, Randy Kennedy, Sue and John Leonard, Glen Loury, Erik Markeset, Charles Ogletree, Susan Butler Plum, Ameek Ponda, Samantha Power, Katherine Russell Rich, Diane Salvatore, Ilena Silverman, Darrell Slack, Dave Stilwell, David Talbot, Margaret Talbot, Lenora Todaro, Chris Turpin, Katrina vanden Heuvel, Mike Vazquez, Steve Waldman, Joan Walsh, David Weir. Thank you all.

Finally and always, of course, Scott, the missing puzzle piece. It all makes sense now.

Washington, D.C.
March 2000